FUNDAMENTAL THEOLOGY

Gerald O'Collins, S.J.

D0029666

PAULIST PRESS   New York/Ramsey

Library of Congress
Catalog Card Number: 80-82809

ISBN: 0-8091-2347-9

Published by Paulist Press
545 Island Road, Ramsey, N.J. 07446

Printed and bound in the
United States of America

CONTENTS

for
Peter
and
Ann
Carnley

PREFACE

> *Theology ... is the conscious and methodical explanation and explication of the divine revelation received and grasped in faith.*
>
> Karl Rahner

> *What I like about experience is that it is such an honest thing. ... You may have deceived yourself, but experience is not trying to deceive you. The universe rings true wherever you fairly test it.*
>
> C. S. Lewis

For a long time I have dreamed of attempting to write a coherent and substantial study in Christian fundamental theology. The pattern which has come to define for me the right approach emerges from reflection on the human experience of the divine self-communication.

Far from being a matter of "mere" feeling and unreliable subjectivity, human experience is what happens when reality intersects with a self-conscious being. Any reductionist, "nothing-but" analysis sells short the richness of experience, the place of encounter with the real world and the real God. Hence this book will begin by developing a modest theory of experience before taking up certain basic themes: revelation, tradition and the inspiration of Scripture. But why these themes?

In the course of Jewish-Christian history men and women have experienced and continue to experience God's self-communication. Then through their manifold traditions they have interpreted and transmitted accounts both of this encounter with God and their response to it. As with other book-religions, inspired Scriptures have a special role to play in recording the original experiences of the divine self-communication and in enabling later generations to re-enact those experiences. Thus any adequate discussion of the human experience of God's self-communication will bring into focus at least three themes: revelation, tradition and inspiration.

1

The question of helpful ways to approach fundamental theology has fascinated me for a decade. *Revelation and Theology*[1] examined the divine self-revelation predominantly, but not exclusively, on the basis of the biblical evidence. In *Foundations of Theology*[2] I gave a good deal of attention both to the teaching on revelation developed by the two Vatican Councils and to theologies of revelation coming from the German world. *The Case Against Dogma*[3] took up the complex relationship between God's self-revelation and Church doctrines and "dogmas." Without rehashing those earlier works, I want now to draw matters together more systematically.

In fundamental theology it seems more than normally unhelpful to fling out flurries of questions and doubts and yet not pause to argue anything out in detail. It is, of course, tempting to do so, and there is perhaps no other "area" of theology which can so encourage us to spin out questions endlessly. But I will try to dwell on and explore in depth those three basic topics: revelation, tradition and inspiration. For each of them, three things need to be done. First, we should clarify the conceptuality (*Begrifflichkeit*). How should we use the concepts of revelation, tradition and inspiration? What do these basic notions mean? Then the range of questions (*Fragestellung*) calls for clarification. What are the key questions to be posed regarding revelation, tradition and inspiration? Finally, the way toward answers should be indicated. This is not to lapse back into those misguided attempts to churn out hard and fast replies which were supposed to persuade the reader through some "logical necessity." Today those replies often seem neither logical nor necessary. Many of the conclusions were reached by arguments which even then did not command ready acceptance outside the circle of those who agreed to do theology in a particular way. Nevertheless, we need not go to the other extreme and indulge the taste for unwarranted skepticism. We can and should point the way toward answers, however provisional and imperfect they may appear to be.

In reaching our positions we will need some criteria which are more than just a set of reassuring commonplaces. This is not to commit ourselves then to establish metacriteria for our criteria and so on *ad infinitum*. Such an insatiable desire for metacriteria would lead only to an endless regress. At the same time, however, a proper distrust of the quest for metacriteria would not justify the failure to state any criteria whatsoever.

Such then is the way I intend to tackle fundamental theology. But before holding forth on revelation, tradition and inspiration, I should say something about the presuppositions, object and nature both of theology in general and of fundamental theology in particular. Further, if the human experience of the divine self-communication is to work as the leitmotiv when this book investigates revelation, tradition and inspiration, I should examine what I believe to be true about human experience and, in particular, its religious dimension. Against the background of those two opening chapters (on theology and experience), I can then take up the three major themes selected for this study in fundamental theology.

To any who feel uneasy about the book's leitmotiv and wonder whether the theme of human experience will suppress the *id quod revelatum est,* which is ultimately the mystery revealed in Christ (Eph 1:9f.), I would say this: Please do not ignore the attempt to reconcile the personal *and* propositional models of revelation (Chapter III), the role of apostolic witness (almost *passim*), the theme of faith's confession (Chapter V), the distinction between foundational and dependent revelation (Chapter III, etc.), the descriptive and confessional functions of faith statements (Chapter VI), the quest for the Tradition (upper case) within the traditions (lower case) in Chapter VIII, and much else besides. In a word the book will center on the human experience *of the (historical and transcendental) divine self-communication in Christ.* As a Christian theologian I would find it pointless to discuss the conditions and nature of human experience by itself, as it were.

Obviously, given the traditions which have been decisive in shaping my life and thought, official documents from the Roman Catholic Church—and especially from the Second Vatican Council—will have a significant role in this study. However, I do not wish to confine myself to specifically Catholic sources and circles, but will attempt to launch a fundamental theology which can enter into a wider Christian context. Hence through some major footnotes and in other ways I will place my own presentation in relation to the work of Barth, Bultmann, Macquarrie, Tillich and other non-Roman Catholic theologians.

Finally, the title of this work could wrongly suggest that it aims to cover *the whole* of fundamental theology. In fact it will hardly touch the signs of revelation and the general problems of verification and credibility. But in covering the experience of revelation, tradition and inspiration, I am *not* pretending to offer a comprehensive fundamental theology.

Before closing this preface I wish to thank many people who in different ways contributed to the making of this work: Angel Antón, Peter Carnley, Jack Carroll, Mauro Ferrari, Roseleen Glennon, Karl Holzbauer, René Latourelle, Edward Malatesta, Alfred Singer, Nico Sprokel, Frank Sullivan, Leslie Wearne, Jared Wicks, various groups at the Gregorian University, and my last class at St. Michael's College, Winooski (Vermont). I am deeply grateful for all their help, although I would not want to saddle them in any way with the responsibility for what I have written.

In a different (sometimes a very different) form several sections of this book have appeared in *Gregorianum* (1976), J. Henley (ed.), *Imagination and the Future,* a *Festschrift* for J. D. McCaughey (Melbourne, 1980), *Irish Theological Quarterly* (1977 and 1979), *Problemi e Prospettive di Teologia Fondamentale* (Brescia, 1980), *Rassegna di Teologia* (1978 and

1979), *Science et Esprit* (1978), and *The Way* (1979). These sections are reprinted with permission.

Gerald O'Collins, S.J.
The Gregorian University, Rome
May 23, 1980

I. FROM THEOLOGY TO FUNDAMENTAL THEOLOGY

Intellege ut credas. Crede ut intellegas.
St. Augustine

Sola experientia facit theologum.
Martin Luther

What are we doing when we "do" theology?[1] What is the proper "object" of this discipline which is commonly described as "faith seeking understanding"? What method does it follow? What sources and criteria does it use? What presuppositions may be brought to theological reflection? Should we, for instance, necessarily suppose that the theologian has faith and belongs to the community of the Church?

We could face such questions head on, choose the question which promises to lead us to the point of departure for theology, arrange the other questions in some supposedly logical order and then progress in linear fashion from one item to another. However, it may prove enlightening to try another tack and reply by indicating five pairs of factors which are held in tension and characterize the work of theology. Then we might happily find that "light dawns gradually over the whole."[2] Such a version of theology in general will allow us to complete this introductory chapter by "placing" the work of fundamental theology in particular.

I
THEOLOGY

1. Spiritual Practice and Critical Theory

To speak of "faith seeking understanding" (*fides quaerens intellectum*) obviously implies that faith is a condition for the possibility of theology. We begin theology from a standpoint of faith. However, this suggests to some that theology will fail to meet respectable "scientific" requirements and cannot take its place alongside properly intellectual disciplines. Would matters be improved by reversing the classical slogan to make it read "understanding seeking faith" (*intellectus quaerens fidem*)?[3] In this case theologians would adopt the kind of honest, "unprejudiced" approach that open inquiry in an academic setting calls for. Nevertheless, many reject such an approach: it wrongly calls into question the certainty of the theologian's own faith and threatens the faith of others.

All in all, the theologian appears to face an awkward dilemma: either faith seeking understanding or understanding (possibly) seeking faith. His choice seems to lie between intellectual respectability and pastoral irresponsibility. One can opt for certainty without understanding and join the fundamentalists. Or one can choose understanding without certainty and line up with the skeptics. In their professional activity must theologians *either* respect divine faith but fail in rational consistency *or* respect human reason but regard religious commitments lightly?

We can, however, break this dilemma by recognizing that theology entails holding in a fruitful tension *both* religious faith and scientific understanding or—to put this another way—both spiritual practice *and* critical theory. Apropos of the quality of authority which theologians enjoy, the International Theological Commission made the same point:

> Theologians derive their specifically theological authority from their scientific qualifications; but these cannot be separated from the proper character of this discipline as the science of faith which cannot be carried through without a living experience and practice of the faith.[4]

Theologians, while developing their discipline critically and systematically, should do so starting from faith, guided by faith and aiming to enhance faith. In short, theology needs to be "faithful" as well as rational. To speak of God the theologian must have experienced God and been taught by God. To put this another way: What we can expect of the theologian is an intelligent and self-conscious faith that combines the sympathetic understanding of an insider with the detachment of an outsider. Let me pursue in detail what such sympathy and detachment involve.

First of all, spiritual practice. A Christian believer should not begin theology by methodically putting aside the faith attested by Scripture and tradition and then attempting to establish critically the existence of God and the validity of claims about Jesus Christ. No one in his right mind would expect a literary critic to start his work by doubting the validity of literature. Likewise the firm decision to abstain from any personal judgments and merely chronicle what others have said about novels, poetry and drama would effectively block anyone from ever becoming a literary critic. Few university committees would be impressed if a candidate for a chair in the visual arts offered the assurance, "I promise to begin courses by calling into question systematically the value of all painting and sculpture. In fact I have come to doubt the existence of objective aesthetic values." On the contrary, it is precisely an insider's commitment to literature and art that motivates and enables critics to do their proper work. They can resonate with the experience of artists and writers because they enjoy a knowledge from the inside. This sympathetic faith of an insider guides and illuminates their critical investigations. We might describe this work as a faith in literature and art which "seeks understanding" and interprets itself. Of course, we should regard an uncritical enthusiasm with dismay and distrust. But a controlled enthusiasm that seeks understanding would qualify and not disqualify candidates for chairs in literature and the visual arts. Likewise participation from the inside or personal involvement in the subject matter helps rather than hinders theological description and explanation. Here, as elsewhere, commitment (even total commitment) and critical reflection can and should be mutually supportive, not mutually exclusive.

One might, however, deny the parallel with theology. After all, the world is filled with works of literature, painting and sculpture. They are visibly *there*, whether we like it or not. But the Father, Son and Holy Spirit are not in that sense simply there—to the delight of believers and the distress of unbelievers. Does the alleged analogy between the theologian and the literary or art critic prove anything?

Nevertheless, we can urge the parallel in two ways. Critics, if they venture beyond the university campus and sometimes if they stay on the campus, must sooner or later meet philistines who simply brush aside any talk of the meaning and truth to be found in literature and the arts. Such philistines must admit the obvious fact that books, paintings and statues exist as physical objects in our world. But they may cheerfully reject most or even all literary and artistic values as no more than arbitrary conventions. This state of affairs will distress the art and literary critics, but it should not plunge them into an orgy of methodical doubt about the existence of the truths and values to which they have dedicated their lives.

Second, Hans-Georg Gadamer among others has convincingly challenged what he calls "the prejudice against prejudice."[5] He rightly argues against continuing any Cartesian-style efforts in theology, history, aesthetics and similar disciplines to wipe out presuppositions and begin from some allegedly neutral grounds. What is needed rather is a proper awareness of these presuppositions or "pre-judices" and the willingness to let them be modified as reflection takes place. In the case of Christian theology this means being aware of—and not setting aside—the major presupposition: theologians know the triune God and do so primarily in the light of Jesus' life, death and resurrection and the events closely linked with that story. Theologians will probe, test and check the various fundamental convictions entailed in the spiritual practice of their faith. They will examine what they believe to be true, analyze the conditions for the truth of these beliefs and so forth. But all such critical reflection does not as such involve even a temporary suspension of the judgments and commitments that make up that faith. To be properly "scientific" theologians do not have to call into question, doubt and then set aside their basic principles and beliefs. But they do need to be self-consciously and critically aware of their positions, attentive to evidence, and coherent in elaborating their discipline. In brief, there *is* a genuine analogy between the right functioning of theological faith and literary or artistic faith.

Three further points press themselves on our attention before we turn from spiritual practice to look more fully at its dialectical partner, critical theory. In my experience non-believers rightly spot the *artificiality* implied when Christian theologians attempt to begin their work with a methodical doubt. From the outset the non-believers properly suspect that the theologians who adopt that procedure will finish up with all the "right" answers. They step outside the circle of believers to scrutinize the evidence for their commitments, or—to vary the image—they dive off the ship of faith to see how convincing and attractive it looks from the surrounding water. There is a whiff of excitement about it all. Yet how many theologians who follow this procedure fail to make it back to the boat or decide not to step inside the circle again? The pretense of methodical neutrality serves to make such theologians mistrusted—at least by the sincere non-believer. One knows that they *will* successfully justify their faith after all.

What is called for is not artificiality but a certain *critical realism*. Theologians should gratefully and realistically acknowledge what they believe rather than indulge in little doubting games out of a mistaken respect for some demon of pseudo-honesty within them. Realism requires the *recognition* of what they actually are and what they hold. Honesty demands that they reflect *critically* on what their Christian existence and beliefs entail.

Honesty also prevents theologians from alleging that their faith produces perfect spiritual practice. For theologians, as for anyone else, there is no such thing as being a believer. There is only becoming a believer or becoming an unbeliever. The tug of war between high beliefs and low performance—or, if you like, between orthodoxy and orthopraxis—will continue for a lifetime. Like other Christians, theologians will be relentlessly pursued by the need for ongoing conversion.[6] If theology is the exercise of faith seeking understanding, that faith will often trail along struggling with doubt and feeble commitment. Theology is not perfect faith seeking (comprehensive) understanding.

Nevertheless, we should recognize the substantial difference between those who profess Christian faith and those who profess agnosticism and atheism. Is then all access to the world of theology closed to the non-believer? Is the subject matter available only through faith to the extent that none but believers with their "spiritual" knowledge can make any sense of theology? Here two considerations (one an everyday fact and the other a matter of faith) should moderate any feverish attempts to restrict all theological reflection absolutely to the world of believers. First, there is the everyday fact that believers and non-believers discuss theological matters. Communication does take place. Non-believers can collect reasonably adequate information about a possible alternative to their positions. Second, as I will argue later, God's saving and revealing action touches everyone. No man or woman is utterly alien to that divine self-communication and the call to faith.[7] Just as there is no such person as a total believer, so there is no such person as a total non-believer. The faith and spiritual practice which give rise to theological reflection may be only minimally present but it is never totally absent. If we insist that one cannot think and speak intelligently of God without the experience of faith, we need to add that this experience is never totally foreign to anyone. Those non-believers who inform themselves about theology, dialogue with believers, reflect on the information provided and try to understand the positions of Christian faith are not doing theology in the proper sense. But if they do come to believe and then engage in theology, that activity will be substantially, but not totally, new to them.

These considerations should be supplemented. First, the distinction between questions of meaning and questions of truth can be applied helpfully here. Questions of meaning are logically prior to questions of truth, as it is necessary to know (roughly) what a proposition means before deciding whether it is true or not. In exchanges between believers and non-believers questions of truth can be bracketed and questions of meaning discussed without raising (or before raising) the issue of truth. Different presuppositions, experiences and interests will doubtless affect the way either side interprets the meaning of the various propositions discussed. Nevertheless, information can be imparted, meanings can be clarified, and both believers and unbelievers can appreciate something of what the alternatives to their positions involve. In short, the non-believer can share in theological reflection—at least at the level of clarifying meaning. We return to this point later when discussing apologetics.

Second, I should try to dispel possible misunderstanding about what I have called "a matter of faith"—namely, that "there is no such person as a total non-believer." This statement could easily look like a kind of religious imperialism which claims sovereignty over the world of unfaith. What of such non-believers and anti-Christians as Hitler and Stalin who look like personifications of evil if ever anyone did? Or—to leave pathological cases behind—what about passionate but rational non-believers like Bertrand Russell? Surely he was a total non-believer, if ever there was one?

There is obviously no point here in arguing everything out in detail. That would entail indulging an enormous parenthesis on themes like Rahner's "supernatural existential" and "anonymous Christian." Let me press only one point which seems more a matter of common observation than of Christian faith. The basic stance of non-believers bears comparison with that of believers. Faith involves three things: believing *that* such and such is the case about the world and human destiny (= confession), believing *in* the God revealed in Jesus Christ (= commitment), and having a certain trust *for* the future (= confidence). (We will return in detail to this analysis of faith in a later chapter.) Now we find something just a little like all that in the fundamental attitude of non-believers, especially passionate non-believers who at times will speak of "the faith of an agnostic" or "an atheist's creed." They hold that such and such is the case about the world and human destiny, and on that basis they elaborate particular beliefs and value systems which are by no means totally different from those of their believing neighbors. They can share too with these neighbors the conviction that the confession both of faith and unfaith must respond to such questions as: What is the meaning and purpose of life? How can we interpret and cope with physical suffering and other evil? Then both parties can rightly expect from each other some commitment in the light of their different confessions. Finally, all action becomes absurd unless one has at least a minimal confidence that it makes some sense to move forward into the future, even if only into the immediate future of tomorrow and the next day. Hence, if non-believers come to accept faith, their second state is by no means utterly new, as if they carried with them nothing of their previous situation. Embracing belief and salvation does not mean accepting something totally alien.

These then, in a highly condensed fashion, are some reasons for recognizing that the world of theology is not totally closed to the non-believer.

Thus far I have attended mainly to the first element in the pair "spiritual practice and critical theory." "Faith and reason" would serve as a roughly equivalent pair. Reason or critical theory—I use them here as interchangeable—has the task of checking, scrutinizing and systematically reflecting on the practice of faith. It does this not to indulge mere sterile criticism but to support faith and save it from lapsing into mindless piety, bizarre enthusiasm, sick superstition or blind dogmatism. Fundamentalists of all kinds are prone to dispense with rational reflection and take the reality of religious experience to be enough. Of course, nothing can substitute for the personal experience of God. Nevertheless, theology can help believers to describe, explain, interpret and account for their faith. They know *that* they believe in the God revealed in Jesus Christ. Theology makes it easier or even possible to say just *what* it is they believe. With this help they can state their faith to themselves and others.

Emil Brunner somewhere offers a useful comparison. Chemists can take some food and analyze it for its nourishing value. The food they analyze is no longer fit to be eaten, but their work aims at preventing malnutrition and encouraging healthy eating habits. The same is true of theology. If it is concerned to know and express truth, this knowing and expressing should lead (a) at the personal level to acknowledging and addressing God in the prayerful practice of faith, and (b) at the public level to clearer testimony and more effective preaching.

Beyond question, theology moves away from the simple directness of faith. At Caesarea Philippi Peter says to Jesus "You are the Christ." In this direct encounter we have the spontaneous response of personal faith. After Pentecost Peter and the other apostles preach the good news: "He is both Lord and Christ." Such testimony is one step removed from the immediacy of personal encounter. Peter uses "he" instead of "you." We see here the beginning of the movement toward the precise Christological doctrines of Church councils and all the theological efforts to study the mystery of Christ. A shift takes place from confession to testimony, from testimony to teaching, from teaching to a theological reflection which moves beyond the immediacy of a conscious personal relationship with the Son of God. Nevertheless, theology brings a gain in clarity and precision. Such reflection serves faith and was never meant to set itself up as a coldly analytical, independent study which divorces itself from, and even threatens to damage, real practice.

Few of us need reminding of that academic theology which can get lost in abstract concepts and hair-splitting analysis—far from the simple directness of the Gospel message. It can lapse into a mass of intellectual distinctions and definitions that neglect active love and faithful obedience. Such theology seems to call on Christians to accept a list of certified doctrines rather than live out a personal faith. It builds a barrier of words against the God revealed in Jesus Christ.

It is this danger which Dorothy Sayers appears to envisage when in her *Whose Body?* she has Lord Peter reprimand his brother-in-law, Inspector Parker: "I don't think you ought to read so much theology; it has a brutalizing influence."[8] No one has reckoned with this possibility more poignantly than Franz Overbeck. In scientific theology he saw an element that could destroy religion: "Every theological activity, insofar as it brings faith into contact with knowledge, is irreligious." Hence it is hardly surprising that Overbeck took theologians to be the grave-diggers rather than the representatives of Christianity.[9]

Nevertheless, "scientific" theology need not and should not war against "orthodox" belief and genuinely faithful practice. Some valid roles for critical reason can be indicated as follows. Theology draws on philosophical reason for theories about such decisively important topics as knowledge, symbolism, the imagination, meaning and truth.[10] What, for instance, happens when we *know, symbolize* and *imagine?* General theories of knowledge will obviously affect ways of describing and explaining what we mean when we claim to *know* God revealed in Jesus Christ. If theology at every level means "faith seeking understanding," what is it to know and understand? What are the conditions for the possibility of coming to such understanding? Theories of symbols and the human drive to symbolize will shape reflection on the sacraments and further areas of theology. Then do we agree with David Hume's cautionary remarks about the imagination and extend them beyond philosophy to theology: "Nothing is more dangerous to reason than flights of the imagination and nothing has been the occasion of more mistakes among philosophers"? Or was John Keats right in maintaining that "what the imagination seizes as beauty must be Truth"?[11] Our choice between Hume and Keats will go hand in hand with the role we assign the imagination in theology.

Furthermore, the faith that seeks understanding is a faith that seeks meaning and truth. Philosophers have devised ways of interpreting the meaning of statements. Any such skilled advice will aid the theologian who wishes to understand what the faith expressed in biblical, theological and credal statements means to say. And then how do we go about elucidating and establishing the truth of what is stated? Once again philosophy can suggest some criteria for sorting out truth and falsity. It is neither human nor Christian to appeal simply to some special guidance of the Holy Spirit and reject the readily available means for clarifying meaning and truth.[12]

There should be little need to labor the point further. Philosophical reason can make massive contributions to theological reflection. Ultimately for a theologian it is not a question of having or not having a philosophy but of having an examined or an unexamined philosophy. In fact Christian theology has proved the greatest employment agency for philosophers the world has ever seen: from Aristotle and Plato down to Hegel, Heidegger, Wittgenstein and Bloch. Success in the application of these or other philosophies can be evaluated by the degree of clarity and self-consistency attained. The only proviso is that our theological reflection is being helped, and not rigidly controlled, by outside categories.

Theologians should not presuppose that they will always be able to adopt unchanged philosophical notions and theories. They cannot expect to pass simply and without difficulty from the language of philosophy to that of revelation. They may have to modify significantly what the philosophers have to tell them about knowledge, symbolism, imagination, meaning and truth. For instance, any philosophical theory of knowledge will need to reckon with the truth of faith that knowing God is a knowledge communicated by grace. The doctrine of grace will likewise modify what a philosopher might have to say about human and divine free will. In general, the Jewish-Christian belief in God's spontaneous initiatives may at times have to temper ideas of necessity which underlie much philosophy. As we will see in the section on inspiration, the biblical approach must qualify reflections on truth drawn from Western philosophy. Otherwise, we will get into a mess about the truth or inerrancy of the Bible. All in all, theologians should not allow any philosophy to engage their affections so completely that they neglect the need to choose and modify what that philosophy offers them.

It would, of course, be a mistake to contrast philosophy and theology as if they were two *strictly different* disciplines which within limits could mutually contribute to each other. At the deepest level the use of philosophical notions does not represent the intrusion of alien matter into theology. To the extent that philosophy deals with ultimate reality, it does not come to theology from the outside. Hence it is incorrect to speak of philosophical structures on which we can build a (separate) theological superstructure. It is also ultimately misleading to talk of the philosophical prolegomena to theology, as if philosophy were totally pre-theological.

Finally, the Christian faith that seeks understanding should look beyond philosophy to confront the findings of and seek help from other academic disciplines. Many disciplines obviously interpret that human existence which can respond in faith to God's revelation in Christ. Take history, for instance. Inasmuch as Christianity's spiritual practice derives from and points back to certain persons and events in history, theological reflection should take note of critical theories concerning historical knowledge and interpretation. Christian faith, precisely because it is mediated historically, must consciously make the best use it can of historical reason.[13]

In fact, as Karl Rahner points out, *all* academic disciplines or "sciences" (in the widest sense of that word) interact with each other: "Because of the unity of human consciousness all sciences depend on one another, whether consciously or not."[14] Theology cannot choose to be either influenced or not influenced by other disciplines. The choice lies rather between being unconsciously affected by such influences or critically aware of them. Rahner's remarks concern not only the theoretical sciences but also technology and the practical sciences. An Apollo space flight, the development of the neutron bomb, techniques to eradicate leprosy and new breeds of "miracle" rice all modify the ways human beings *understand themselves*. The faith that *seeks understanding* may not close its eyes to fresh forms of human self-understanding today. The link between theology and the sciences, both theoretical and practical, is not adventitious but necessary and positive.

In varying degrees this book will make use of several "sciences."

Some hints from philosophy can partly shape the chapter on experience, which in turn will help to interpret later material. As always, historical considerations must play a role in the reflections on revelation. At points cultural anthropology touches themes dealt with under the headings of revelation and tradition. Then certain approaches to literary criticism can contribute to the final section on the inspiration and interpretation of Christian Scriptures. In all these and other ways critical reason has its valid roles to play for the work of theology.

2. The One and the Many

Thus far we have reflected on one pair of factors which should be held together in fruitful tension and not allowed to go their separate ways: spiritual practice and critical theory. The individual and the community form a second pair to be recalled when we examine the work of theologians.

Individual theologians draw on their own religious experience. They are endowed with their personal vision and special charisms. Nevertheless, theology is more than a statement of faith from an individual theologian. In theology it is the faith of the community which seeks to clarify and express itself. Christian theology is an activity and function of the Church. It does not exist apart from a social context. The community is vested with a mysterious authority to guide and decide in the search for theological clarity.

We can press this point in two ways. First, *any* quest for understanding, meaning and truth takes place in a human community bound together by language, culture and tradition. We understand things, interpret the meaning of texts or events, and find truth in a highly complex web of social fellowship. Our intellectual quest, whether theological or otherwise, takes place in an environment of human inter-subjectivity. Such a quest is impossible without *some* kind of group support and interaction. The point is as old as Plato's dialogues. Socrates needed both the sophists and his own disciples if he was to track down the nature of courage, justice, inspiration and the rest.

The *very language* theologians speak and write is that of the community. It is linguistically impossible to use words meaningfully without paying attention to the conventional rules of one's community. This condition is even more basic than having others as sounding boards or opponents with whom to interact. Of course, individual theologians will rightly extend, modify and change meanings so that the community's usage will shift over the centuries. Nevertheless, the quest for theological understanding essentially presupposes a community bound together by its conventional rules of language.

Second, Christian theology seeks to understand and interpret what

God has done in the story of the Old Testament, the New Testament, the Church and all mankind. At every level the theologian should check his reflections against the religious experiences of that vast community. It is the community which produces the raw material for analysis and criticism. Theology's subject matter gives the lie to any attempt to theologize on a solitary basis outside the community of faith. As the International Theological Commission put it, "theology can only be done in living community with the Church."[15]

What has just been stated, however, should not encourage us to play down or even ignore the fact that inevitably there will be some tension between the individual and the community. On the one hand, theologians should not become lonely armadillos, encased in the narrow shell of their own ponderings. They need to listen to the community (both past and present)—especially to other theologians and to those who are called to teach authoritatively in the Church. Theologians who do not know the history of theology and the Church may be condemned to repeat the mistakes of that history. Those who fail to listen to councils, popes and other official teachers and proclaimers of the Christian message will miss privileged and divinely endorsed instances of that message being interpreted and applied to the changing situations of the past and present. On the other hand, however, theologians would not genuinely serve the Church community if in a mechanical way they merely repeated the classic creeds, declarations of councils, the teachings of popes, and traditional pieces of doctrine drawn from their predecessors in the Church. Their task is to reflect on behalf of the community. That entails clarifying obscurities, renewing dead language, offering fresh insights and scrutinizing current developments in Christian theory and practice. By simply acting as mouthpieces for common traditions, theologians would deprive the Church of a needed and creative challenge.[16]

We can describe an important feature of the service which the community should expect from theologians as "faith seeking *a new language.*" Christians express their faith through worship, preaching, teaching, pastoral care and social action. Theologians, more than other groups, have the task of testing, criticizing and revising the language which—in all these activities—the community uses about God and the divine revelation communicated through Jesus Christ. This testing is necessary because language can become clumsy and ineffective. Or else Christians may lapse into an idolatry of words by assuming that a given verbal definition not only refers to some divine reality but in a thoroughly satisfactory manner describes and even "contains" that reality. Then too a gap can open up between the words the community continues to use and the experiences they actually undergo. Whatever their particular needs, theologians are in the business of checking what theological language actually does express, purifying old language and creating new language. Their products should both express the theory and encourage the healthy practice of the community's faith. Their new language needs to awaken, light up and interpret the experiences they share with other members of the Church.

Finally, if theologians have a job to do in critically reflecting on developments in the language, theory and practice of the community, proper self-criticism is also required of them. What lies behind their "new language"? How does their practice of Christianity affect their theological theories? In what ways are hidden or not so hidden purposes shaping their answers to questions of faith? The kind of Christian (or un-Christian) life they lead will partly determine the way they think, the issues they consider important and their openness to wider human concerns. A socio-economic analysis will also press the need for further self-examination. For whom are the theologians working? Who is paying their salary and how does that affect their theology? How does the social environment supply and guide what they believe themselves to know as theologians? As theology is never a private affair nor even "merely" a Church activity, theologians need to ponder not only the public relevance of what they say or fail to say, but also the social influences shaping their teaching and writing.

3. Old and New

Part of the healthy tension between the individual theologian and the community concerns what Jesus called acting "like a householder who can produce from his store both the old and the new" (Mt 13:52). Theologians share in the general Christian responsibility of preserving the good news about the life, death and resurrection of Jesus. But they may be so intent on preserving this message intact that they fail to elucidate and share it. A wooden insistence on maintaining the purity of the Gospel can lead to their becoming downright unintelligible and unhelpful to their contemporaries. Hence theologians ought to be in contact with the changing questions, changing language and changing interests of their age. The Second Vatican Council recalled this task: "Recent research and discoveries in the sciences, in history and philosophy bring up new problems which have an important bearing on life itself and demand new scrutiny by theologians."[17] This is to encourage theologians to be innovative but without losing continuity with the essential pattern of the past. Their task is to produce *both* the new *and* the old.

A comparison with art might help here. One could say that doing theology is like doing painting. There are different styles, various materials and new methods. To try to do theology *exactly* as our predecessors did it would be as inappropriate as attempting to paint just like Rembrandt— not to mention lesser artists. Goya, Titian, Rembrandt and others remain our masters, but they cannot paint our pictures nor can we paint theirs.

Likewise Augustine, Aquinas, Barth and Rahner may remain our theological masters, but we cannot do theology as they did it nor can they
do our theology. In painting we need curiosity, imagination and a proper
"irreverence" which allows us to break through apparent limits to something new. No less than the painter, the theologian needs such a curiosity,
imagination and "irreverence" which would allow new insights and fresh
approaches to emerge.

Under this heading of "the old and the new" we should, of course,
do more than merely note how new questions are coming up in a rapidly
changing world to encourage theologians to seek properly innovative styles
of theologizing. "The old and the new" catch hold of a basic tension
in Christian theology: between the memory of the past and the hope for
the future. Theologians both look back to a once-and-for-all set of events
in the life, death and resurrection of Jesus and look forward, trusting
in the promise, "Behold, I make all things new" (Rev 21:5). They remember in order to hope. The "no longer" of memory is the basis for
the "not yet" of hope. In their own way theologians are proclaiming the
death of the Lord until his future coming (1 Cor 11:26). Kant concluded
his *Critique of Pure Reason* with his classic set of questions: "What can
I know? What ought I to do? What may I hope for?" Both for themselves
and the whole community theologians *ought* to *know* what they can of
the past in order to catch hold of the future in *hope*.

In the pull between the historical past and the eschatological future
the tide runs more strongly toward the future promise. Theologians can
learn from that warning with which Ernst Bloch begins his *The Principle
Hope:* "Philosophy will have a conscience for tomorrow, a bias for the
future, a knowledge of hope, or it will no longer have any knowledge
at all." Theologians, we can add, will have a conscience for tomorrow,
a bias for the future and a theology of hope. Or else they will have no
theology at all. The prospective rather than the retrospective mood should
dominate their work. To parody an observation of Léon Bloy: "We find
the only excuse for theologizing in waiting for the resurrection from the
dead." Ernst Cassirer remarked: "We live much more in our . . . anxieties
and hopes about the future than in our recollections or in our present
experience."[18] Is it too much to say that we do our theology much more
in our hopes about the future than in our recollections or in our present
experience? A joyful hope for the future should shape the house style
of theology. The new takes its precedence over the old because he who
is and was presents himself also as the one "who is to come" (Rev 1:8).

4. Dialogue and Identity

We come to a further pair of factors which characterize the work
of theologians. Christian theology should cherish dialogue with other re-

ligions,[19] contemporary scientific disciplines and such ideologies as Marxism and secular humanism. Here it picks its way between the extremes of (a) losing contact with the environment and (b) being so relevant to this environment that it has lost its self-identity. Nowadays the latter may be the more serious danger. A theology which tries too hard to be relevant may lose its specific character and simply merge with the surrounding culture. It can forget to ask: *What* must be relevant? Theology should do more than respect contemporary experience and engage in dialogue with contemporary disciplines like sociology and cultural anthropology. It has its own contribution to make as it reflects on what is to be coherently believed and systematically said about God and the world in the light of Jesus' life, death, resurrection and future coming.

Ultimately, I believe, theology establishes and preserves its self-identity through the death and resurrection of Jesus rather than through other Christological mysteries like the incarnation. Still less can that self-identity be finally structured around the teaching of the Church. This teaching has, of course, to grow as it reckons with new questions and faces the challenges of fresh situations. But it is always anchored in the traditional memory and inspired record that focuses on the founder of Christianity himself. No Church doctrine, even the most solemnly defined dogmas, can ever be as ultimate as the person of Jesus Christ. For his "story," Good Friday and Easter Sunday—rather than Christmas, for example— are decisive. Christians from the beginning have known that baptism draws them into the crucifixion and gives them the promise of resurrection (Rom 6:3–5). They do not understand themselves to be baptized "into the incarnation." Their Eucharist proclaims the death of the risen Lord until he comes in glory (1 Cor 11:26). They do not celebrate the Eucharist to proclaim the birth of Christ until he grows to manhood.

The doctrine of the Trinity offers another way of illustrating how Good Friday and Easter Sunday give Christian faith and theology their specific character. That doctrine, elaborated by the early Church councils, summarizes the story of the crucifixion and the resurrection. The Father, as St. Paul repeatedly puts it, raised the dead Son. Both sent the Holy Spirit into the world. What we know of Father, Son and Holy Spirit essentially centers around the paschal mystery. There the two great and distinctive features of Christian belief are found together: the sign of the cross and the doctrine of the Trinity.[20]

All of this touches theology's dialogue with contemporary reason and culture. The dialogue takes place between human culture and a theology focused on the crucified and risen Christ. It is in that way that theology ultimately identifies itself when it presents itself to contemporary culture.

The Second Vatican Council's Constitution on the Church in the Modern World, *Gaudium et Spes,* represents as well as any text the right balance between dialogue and identity. In the entire history of the Church no other conciliar document has ever attempted to describe at length and enter into the whole situation of mankind. *Gaudium et Spes* recalls and examines the hope and anguish, the profoundly changed conditions, the broader desires and deeper questionings, the forms of atheism, the lines of cultural development, the socio-economic issues, and the shape of national and international politics which characterize human life as we move through the second half of the twentieth century. In this document of dialogue addressed to all the world, the bishops at the Second Vatican Council did not weaken or waver in maintaining the proper identity of their faith. Nothing less than Christ's dying and rising discloses the ultimate meaning and hope of human life. It takes, they insisted, "the paschal mystery" to throw the needed light on "the mystery of man" (n. 22).

Theologians who take their cue from *Gaudium et Spes* will work at a double task—both upholding the Christian Church's identity and addressing the broader community of men and women. They will be enabled to engage in such dialogue without loss of identity by centering their reflections on Good Friday and Easter Sunday.

Dialogue and identity suggest a thrust which is both *horizontal* and *vertical,* both immanent and transcendent. Christian theologians talk about and talk with other human beings, but they do so in the light of the God who raised Jesus from the dead. They seek coherently and profoundly to understand the world. Yet any such ultimate interpretation must include the God who creates, redeems and promises to fashion a new heaven and a new earth. To speak in depth of men, women and their world is to speak of God and vice versa. Finally, anthropology and theology intersect and merge. A deep dialogue with humanity brings theologians to their final point of self-identification: the divine creation and the new creation in Jesus Christ.

5. Mystery and Intelligibility

Lastly, how far should we expect theology to take us in our search for understanding? Any answer here must nominate some middle ground between two extremes: rationalism and fideism.

First, Christian rationalists demand too much intelligibility. They forget the truth that the First Vatican Council insisted on: "The divine mysteries by their very nature so transcend the created intellect that, even when they have been communicated in revelation and received by faith, they remain covered by the veil of faith itself and shrouded as it were in darkness" (DS 3016). So far from making everything clear, revelation confronts the believer with God as the primordial mystery. The classical "negative way" (*via negativa*) dwelt on the fact that theological knowledge is to a large extent knowledge "not of what God is but of what God is not."[21] Before the divine mystery St. Paul cries out in wonder: "O the depth of the riches and wisdom and knowledge of God! How unsearchable are his judgments and how inscrutable his ways" (Rom 11:33). A rationalizing strain in theology not only forgets all this but also reaches for the language of necessity. It leaves behind the mystery and moves easily from (a) the way things *are* with God or between God and the human race to (b) the way those things *must* be.

Rationalist theologians of all kinds are simply too "knowing" about God and the world. They can readily ignore the fact that all reality is always greater than any "scientific" analysis or the results of all "objective" observations.

In any case theological work is always unfinished. Previous generations of theologians often paid lip service to the fact that their search for truth could never yield definitive insights or final statements. An intellectual optimism slipped over the second word in the traditional account of theology as "faith *seeking* understanding." "Seeking" should have alerted them to the fact that theological work does not yield definitive, final answers. Theology always demands fresh questioning and a continual search for meaning. It is not just that new data becomes available—for instance, from history and archaeology—and forces the reopening of issues. From the very nature of their subject theologians can never dare say: "Now, we *know* God and have the final answers." Questions must be constantly put again. In each new generation theologians need to give an account of the faith with which they continue to struggle.

On the other hand, a kind of mindless fideism that disdains the search for clarity and understanding may be tediously familiar but is no real option. Oppressed by the burden of rational argument, we might feel the temptation to make a liberating leap from the ambiguities of debate to the moral purity of generous self-engagement. But it should be clear that fundamental problems will not be solved that way. Reason will assert itself to ask: What can we coherently say about the God revealed in Jesus Christ?

In short, the demands of divine mystery and human understanding must be honored. This last pair of factors, "mystery and intelligibility," hearken back to the first pair we discussed, spiritual practice and critical theory. From start to finish theology entails holding together *both* a deep spiritual respect for the mystery of God *and* a serious desire to let intelligent reflection play its role.

This chapter might have tackled Christian theology in a traditional way. I could have listed and analyzed the object, method, sources, criteria and presuppositions of theology. Or else it might have been helpful to name and examine outstanding practitioners of theology—both past and present. By sampling their writings we would find that rich variety of procedures at work which makes theology no simple, easily grasped phenomenon. Instead I have talked about doing theology in terms of five pairs of factors which continue to be persistently characteristic: spiritual practice and critical theory, the individual and the community, the old and the new, dialogue and identity, and mystery and intelligibility. Theology prospers not by suppressing any of these factors but by keeping them all in fruitful tension.

The chapter has mixed together description and prescription. It has moved back and forth between the way many theologians have in fact practiced their profession to set up guidelines for going about the theological business. Not everyone will agree with the five pairs of factors and the manner of describing and explaining them. But what has been said about one person's version of theology will, I hope, have let light gradually dawn over at least this whole. However, before closing this introductory chapter some indications should be given about the place of fundamental theology within the general practice of theology.

II
FUNDAMENTAL THEOLOGY

1. The Presuppositions of Fundamental Theology

All the questions about Christian fundamental theology[22] cannot be raised, let alone answered, together. But there is one initial question which we should not slide around and which promises a helpful way in: *What does fundamental theology presuppose?* Is this activity, despite its name, really a *pre*-theology, in that it assumes the significance of various human experiences and powers of reason but *not* a believing stance toward the fact and data of divine revelation? By defending this line we would demand a willing suspension of belief and turn fundamental theology into an extrinsic, pre-theological basis on which theology could subsequently build.

However, fundamental theology should not begin with some artificial doubting game but with a critical realism—just as has been argued for theology in general. To be genuinely "scientific," fundamental theology does not have to set aside basic beliefs and principles. But it does need to be self-consciously aware of its presuppositions and to elaborate critically its positions. This means being alert to three kinds of presuppositions: the reality of faith, the nature of human experience and the role of reason.

Fundamental theologians do their work in the light of Christian faith, realistically acknowledging that they belong to a community of believers and share in the experience of faith. This explicit recognition of their faith in the God who raised Jesus from the dead separates fundamental theologians from philosophers of religion and, as we shall see, from apologists. The divine revelation which reached its climax in the life, death and resurrection of Jesus Christ and has been transmitted through the Church tradition and Scriptures provides the premise, impulse and material for fundamental theology, as for all theological argument. Accepting his personal faith, the fundamental theologian proceeds to reflect on the basic conditions that make the experience of faith possible.

Here we reach the second presupposition for fundamental theology: the human experiences of oneself and of the world in which and through which the divine revelation occurs. If fundamental theology presumes the human faith which responds to divine revelation, logically it presupposes also the existence of those *conditions* in human experience which make men and women *open to receive revelation*, whatever form it takes and whenever it comes.

The third major presumption that fundamental theology makes is that critical reason can effectively function to clarify systematically faith, human experience and their inter-relationship. Fundamental theology presupposes the powers of reason and agrees that, without destroying or excluding faith, they can provide a "scientific" understanding that truly illuminates and expresses faith.

On the basis of these three presuppositions fundamental theology tackles a *twofold task* by (a) methodically reflecting on the source of theological knowledge in the divine revelation recorded in tradition and Scripture, and (b) calling attention to the way human experience is open to receive that revelation.

Where the various branches use the data of revelation (communicated through tradition and Scripture) to reflect on particular themes like the nature of the Church and the sacraments, fundamental theology deals with *revelation as such:* its nature, the criteria for identifying it, its expression in tradition and Scripture, its interpretation and so forth. If particular sections of theology draw on various parts of Scripture to support specific conclusions, fundamental theology asks: What *as such* does the interpretation of Scripture involve?

Such systematic reflection on the source of theological knowledge in divine revelation (and the human faith which responds to it) obviously entails the need to examine and clarify such fundamental concepts and terms as revelation itself, faith, tradition, inspiration and interpretation before moving on to identify and examine the basic questions suggested by and associated with these terms.

Fundamental theology ponders also the human experience of contingency and finitude in which one can see how men and women are open to see, hear and accept revelation. More than previously, fundamental theology scrutinizes the human possibilities for receiving the divine self-communication. The next chapter takes up this theme of experience.

2. Apologetics and Fundamental Theology

This account of the presuppositions and task of fundamental theology can be further clarified if we put our finger on the differences between apologetics and fundamental theology.[23] In their presuppositions and scope these two activities are sharply distinct from each other. Precisely because the task of apologetics is to present, defend and justify rationally the Christian faith for unbelievers, its discussions with various kinds of "unbelievers" will presuppose human experience and reason but *not* faith—or at least not full Christian and Roman Catholic faith. Where both sides share fully in the Catholic faith, we could still have a discussion or even a debate between fundamental theologians, but we would have left behind the conditions required for apologetics.

The agreed presuppositions and themes for apologetics can vary enormously from place to place and from decade to decade. As it faces the shifting questions and presuppositions of today, apologetics will need to adapt and change more than any other theological discipline. It will also vary from person to person. An "apologetic" dialogue with an agnostic philosopher in Cambridge, with an anticlerical in Rome and with a Moslem in Djakarta must respect the actual state of the other person. The philosopher will not allow the Christian apologist to assume truths drawn from revelation but will engage in discussion on the basis of rational, philosophical and historical evidence. The anticlerical Italian may very well agree to let the Christian faith in the God revealed in Jesus Christ form a presupposition for dialogue but will not assume that the official Catholic witness to this revelation is substantially and necessarily sound. Belief in God but not in Jesus as the incarnate Son of God will shape the premises for the exchange with the Indonesian Moslem. In short, the Christian apologist can assume only what the dialogue partners, be they strict unbelievers and "outsiders' or doubting "insiders," agree to presuppose. Thus the believing apologist will begin with points which already have meaning and validity for *the given* dialogue partners, and this will always entail setting aside at least some affirmations of faith.

With one person the apologist will begin from the cultural phenomena of religious experience to establish that the ground and object of such phenomena lie in God; with another person this can be presupposed and the task will be to legitimate the belief that God "was in Christ" (2 Cor 5:19)—and so forth. In all cases the ideological, religious and philosophical positions of the given partners in dialogue will determine the range of the presuppositions. At the same time, a proper awareness of the presuppositions will help make the Christian apologist sensible to the valid elements in opposing positions and to the difficulties in his or her own faith.

Here I should hasten to stress that apologetics can be addressed not only to various classes of non-believers but also to believers (including the Christian apologists themselves), inasmuch as challenges and doubts arise about such matters as the fact of revelation, the inspired nature of the Scriptures or the divine endorsement of the Church. In facing such basic issues and justifying these fundamental beliefs, apologetics will speak also to believers.

At all times apologetics should aim to be effective—not only in negatively defending the Christian case against the tide of objections which may surge in, but also in positively clarifying and justifying faith for those who doubt or reject it. If the apologist (like the fundamental theologian) can describe and use with some logical consistency basic concepts like revelation and tradition, this should render more understandable the realities to which these concepts are attached, as well as throw light on related ideas and realities. Any genuine clarification inevitably helps to justify what is believed. The apologists can also press reasons which substantiate their claims and encourage others to share their experience of faith. Divine revelation, for instance, meets and addresses human beings in their inner selves and in a profound way corresponds to the ultimate potentialities of men and women. Yet apologists, even if they are in the business of justifying their case intellectually and urging the moral obligation of recognizing and accepting God's self-communication, cannot and should not, of course, hope to provide arguments that are—psychologically or logically—truly compelling. And at all times Christian apologists should show integrity in giving an "account of the hope" that is in them (1 Pet 3:15) through what is a genuine dialogue and not an exercise in soft compromise. If they aim to banish false problems, they will let those who do not share their faith see where the real "scandal" lies: in the "foolishness" of the cross and the stunning challenge of the resurrection.

These then are some differences (and similarities) between the *presuppositions* and *tasks* of fundamental theology and apologetics. On the basis of the differences, we can only agree to keep these two activities firmly apart. It would confuse everything to attempt once again to merge fundamental theology and apologetics.

Excursus:
Philosophy and Theology

Philosophy[24] forms a special part of the human culture with which theology must dialogue. The relationship between philosophy and theology, as we have noted, coincides to a considerable extent with the relationship between speculative reason and faith. Right from fundamental theology on through the other sections of theology, philosophical reason functions to clarify, elaborate and systematize the content of faith. Hence we need to look at and describe somewhat the links between philosophy and theology.

We can try on various theories here, but we may finish up wanting a clarity we cannot get, unless we pay some attention to the *history* of Western philosophy and its complex relationship to theology. Some people accept without much fuss A. N. Whitehead's view of philosophy as a series of footnotes to Plato. Others would insist more on the differences between Platonic and Aristotelian modes of thought. But everyone will recognize how Greek philosophy, both directly or more often in a diluted form, helped theological musings and at times even held them together. Some theologians may have refused to espouse Aristotle's four causes, his teaching about "prime matter" and his reflections on "substance and accidents." Nevertheless, to a degree all shared in the one perennial philosophy deriving ultimately from the Greeks. Not only was philosophy, in the traditional phraseology, the handmaid of theology, but also there was only one such handmaid. But from the sixteenth century the two disciplines have pulled apart, pluralism in theology has expanded, and philosophical thought has split up into different and new systems, even if much debris from the perennial philosophy still lies around. From Descartes to Heidegger and Wittgenstein, philosophers have stood back from their culture, surveyed centuries of intellectual history, and quite consciously tried to take philosophy and human thought in new directions. There have been these attempts at revolutionary change, almost as if no one before the particular revolution in question had "really" been doing philosophy. Earlier thinkers and writers may have called themselves philosophers, but—in the eyes of this or that latter-day philosophical revolutionary—they do not now truly count as such.

After all these shifts, whether they took place dramatically or more subtly, the result is clear. Philosophers today endorse so many different starting points, terminologies, methods and systems that it can only be more questionable now to risk generalizations about the connection between philosophy and theology. Not only has the handmaid come of age and asserted her independence but she has turned into many "ladies of philosophy": transcendental Thomism, neo-Thomism, existentialism and Marxism in various forms, personalism, branches of phenomenology, latter-day survivals of idealism, linguistic analysis and the rest. These philosophies, so far from behaving toward each other as tolerant sisters, can readily dismiss rivals as preposterous and absurd. Each of them may have set out to produce something valid for all thinking persons but—notoriously—have failed to do just that. Irreconcilable schools of philosophy continue to exist. In such a contentious situation it looks possible to do no more than discuss the relationship of some particular philosophy to theology. Yet some general observations can still be risked.

In a broad sense theology and much philosophy seem to be after the same "object." Both deal with *ultimates,* offering some organized body of knowledge about what is ultimate in reality. Yet one should hasten to add that they differ in their sources. Theology draws on the divine revelation which was specially communicated through the history of Israel and of Jesus Christ and which will reach its goal in the final coming of the Lord. Theology deals with historical ultimates which center on Jesus as *the* Savior and *the* Revealer. Philosophy, however, takes shape by exercising autonomous reason and not by accepting mystery and interpreting the data of divine revelation. By the light of logic and reason alone it investigates what is ultimately "there." It seeks the basis and ground of things that happen repeatedly and everywhere. Philosophers, if they decide to take up the God-question, can only reach some statements about the Creator and the divine goodness but not about a saving God who is disclosed in history. There is still a point to Pascal's distinction between the God of Abraham, Isaac and Jacob and the God of the philosophers. Philosophy, generally speaking, tends to circle around human existence and its ultimate condition, whereas theology must give priority to the God who acted and spoke in Jesus Christ. In short, although philosophy and theology both concern themselves with ultimates, their matter and method of attack look quite different.

So too do their results. Clearly the two disciplines have undergone changes, sometimes drastic changes, over the centuries. "Outside" factors like the burning questions of a particular age can work for change in both philosophy and theology. Or else philosophical shifts may trigger theological change. For instance, the struggle with the problem of knowledge from Descartes, through Kant and down to the present time obviously encouraged theologians to elaborate views on revelation and the nature of revealed knowledge. However, cumulative and progressive results do not occur in both disciplines. Philosophers can build on the work of their predecessors to develop what is genuinely new. Modern epistemology, hermeneutics and language analysis were not already there in the work of Plato and Aristotle. We know more than the Greeks. Philosophy has been enriched by progressive work. Theology, however, in its essential "given" does not tolerate an increase, even through the reflections of the most brilliant thinkers. As it seeks to understand the divine revelation accepted in faith, theology does not experience in any essential way cumulative and progressive gains in the human interpretation and expression of the truth about God. The wisest and holiest theologians, even if supported by the full range of the Church's teachings, the latest findings of scriptural studies and the best work of historians, can hope to do no more than lose as gracefully as possible in their efforts to understand and speak of God. At the end even Thomas Aquinas looked back at his achievements as so much straw and not as labors which had helped theology to progress intrinsically and essentially.

Yet some considerations cushion any attempt to make too much of the differences we have been recalling. In both philosophy and theology human knowing and understanding can only be basically the same. Theologians will apply reasoning powers cultivated in philosophy to reflect, argue coherently and systematically, and induce and deduce conclusions in the light of the data. In both disciplines truth can be tested by success or failure in maintaining inner coherence and external correspondence to one's sources.

A further point mitigates any excessive insistence on the differences. On the one hand, the final authority in *philosophy* is reckoned to be autonomous human reason. Yet philosophers—at least great ones like Plato—seem to break (or be led) through to special insights and spiritual intuitions. What we can call the imagination of faith qualifies the "mere" use of reason. Plato and others do not finally confine their philosophy "within the limits of reason alone." In this century some thinkers, following Jaspers' terminology, if not necessarily his precise view, speak of a "philosophical *faith*"—an initial feeling and/or insight which predisposes the shape of their philosophy. On the other hand, *theology* may be guided by the instinct of faith to enjoy spontaneous and privileged insights. Nevertheless, if the insights produced by that instinct are to be publicly available, they must be clearly and cogently expressed. The claim that "I have an insight or feeling about this issue" should carry no theological weight unless the matter can also be stated rationally. To sum up: Any hard and fast separation between mere philosophical reason and the instinct of faith does not fit these facts.

Philosophical thinking comes across as *free* from traditional, biblical and communitarian authority. It is not tied down, as theology is, to the data of revelation found in tradition and Scripture. Philosophers appear to possess enviable freedom to shake off conventional constraints, change direction, fashion fresh terminology, and strike out on their own to put forward whole new systems. However, if we review the past and present scene in philosophy, such freedom does not appear to be uniformly present. Philosophical traditions have exercised their subtle or not so subtle pressures. Descartes thought that he was making a clean break with the past, but in fact he continued to be affected by the philosophical tradition of decadent Scholasticism. In most contemporary departments and faculties some schools of philosophy are in and others are out. The existing community of philosophers in various centers controls to a large extent the thinking of new recruits. From Aristotle down to Wittgenstein the writings of certain philosophers have enjoyed the force of holy writ for many of their disciples. Then too the sheer necessity of finding and holding an academic post may make a decisive impact on one's philosophical choices and reflections. What the head of the department wants taught can affect a philosopher in much the same way as the Church community and its faith influence the work of a theologian.

If philosophers often fail to appear much "freer" than theologians in the *content* of what they say, what of the *language* used by the two professions? From time to time Church doctrines fix linguistic boundaries for theologians. For pastoral reasons some expressions are excluded and others encouraged. This official regulation of speech affects theologians, although we must admit that the impact remains pretty minimal compared with the massive control exercised by the traditional jargon of various theological schools. But do the philosophers look more liberated in the matter of speech? Often they take over language from their predecessors and contemporaries as readily as theologians do. Every now and then a Heidegger or a Wittgenstein introduces fresh terminology. But for the most part philosophers, like theologians, repeat the common jargon. In short, it would be debatable to maintain that philosophy is strikingly "freer" than theology from their respective forms of traditional and "biblical" authority—in the matter either of content or of language.[25]

Could *personal commitment* and *public responsibility* serve to differentiate between theologians and philosophers? It would be easy to say that philosophers can be content to deal with ideas, terminologies and systems of thought, whereas Christian theologians must deal with the person of Jesus Christ. Or we might also urge that philosophy as such trains us to think, but not necessarily to live and commit ourselves. Theology, however, supposes a personal relationship with the Subject (rather than to some object or objects) and entails religious practice. There is not such a pressure on the philosopher to be a good and committed person as there is on the theologian. We will know philosophers more by the way they talk than by the way they act.

Yet I wonder whether this picture quite matches the facts. One could perhaps "do" philosophy as a mere hobby and with a minimum of personal commitment. But normally we would expect the activity of philosophers to shape and express their lives, although not necessarily in the manner we would expect from Christian theologians. We might even hope that philosophers would be ready to die for the truth their philosophy aims at, if their essential integrity as human and philosophical beings were truly bound up with some issue. Admittedly it is hard to nominate any important figures other than Socrates and Boethius who have actually done so. But for that matter few theologians of stature suffered martyrdom before Bonhoeffer.

In their somewhat different ways both philosophers and theologians have need of conversion. A theological conversion may be associated with some traumatic experience of evil (for instance, an encounter with some horrible war) or with an intellectual crisis of faith. Analogous things can happen to the philosopher. Just as theologians should turn constantly toward the God revealed in Jesus Christ, so philosophers must pursue with passion their reflections on ultimate reality and live out in practice the results of their ponderings.

Yet we should temper this expectation of conversion. The high beliefs of a valuable theologian may be accompanied by low Christian performance. A lofty and helpful philosophy could come from someone whose life fails to match his thought. Conversely, of course, high religious experience and practice will not turn anyone into a top theologian unless the person possesses the necessary intellectual equipment. Nor does a superbly coherent human life necessarily carry with it a well-articulated philosophy.

All things considered, not much weight could be placed upon a theory that too sharply differentiates between philosophers and theologians over their *personal* commitment. What of their *public* responsibility? Earlier in this chapter we touched on the social role of theologians who should serve the community by clarifying the common faith, curbing superstitions, fashioning fresh language and so forth. Theologians must not shun their pastoral responsibilities toward their audience. What of philosophers? Many may be obscure academic figures, but some at least like Camus seem called to articulate the voice of their contemporaries and to speak *for* society. A few like Kierkegaard may be called to speak prophetically *to* their society. All philosophers, engaged as they are in the rational search for what is ultimate, bear some public responsibility for the truth. Their profession makes all the more serious any charge of corrupting the youth or corrupting the community in general.

Thus far we have been chewing over differences between philosophy and theology and tending to minimalize possible points of contrast. Some formidable figures in human history have, of course, taken another line. On the one hand, Pascal held that faith should humiliate reason, and he took the order of the heart to be above the order of reason. Kierkegaard interpreted faith as overcoming reason. On the other hand, Kant declared in the preface to his second edition of *The Critique of Pure Reason:* "I must, therefore, put aside knowledge, to make room for belief."

However, neither an open conflict between philosophical reason and theological faith is properly acceptable, nor a cold war in which philosophy threatens faith (or vice versa), nor even a simple divorce between the disciplines of theology and philosophy. Truth cannot contradict truth. Faith should not be seen as denying philosophical reason nor vice versa. There may be tension. For its part, theology cannot demand that *all* philosophical thought must have a theological aim and so prove serviceable. Philosophy is after all "free" thought and does not as such presuppose the data of revelation. In their turn philosophers need to accept that theologians will find some philosophical models or even entire systems more suitable for expounding and clarifying faith than others. Ultimately the history of philosophical reason and theological faith suggests this healthy ideal: a certain interdependence alongside a separate identity.

Can we pin down more specifically this interdependence? Philosophers who are highly committed believers like Augustine and Kierkegaard make it more difficult to distinguish contributions which theology receives from philosophy and vice versa. It is not just that they do philosophy in the light of their theological convictions. Belief is woven right into their study of philosophy. In these and other cases we may not be totally clear where philosophy ends and theology begins, or how the dependence of one discipline on the other is to be defined.

Nevertheless, there is still much truth in the conventional observation that theology depends on philosophy for two things: *concepts* and *questions.* "Concepts" should be understood here broadly—to cover not only individual notions but also terminology and even entire philosophical schemes. Thus a particular philosophy can/could offer sacramental theology not only an account of "symbol" as an isolated concept but also an elaborate terminology and entire philosophical theory about symbolism. Another example: For Rudolf Bultmann and others Heidegger's philosophy yielded a satisfactory analysis of human existence—and not just some scattered concepts and terms.

Then come the questions. From the time of the pre-Socratics on, philosophy has been asking, reflecting on and refining ultimate questions about the world and human life and their origin, nature and destiny. Faith and theology offer replies. Thus revelation answers the questioning about God and the final meaning of life. Doctrines of sin and grace throw light on personal insufficiency, the struggle with the absurd, and that general sense of human disorder and frustration which has drawn the attention of many modern philosophers.

These two items call for some qualification. First of all, philosophers may contribute ideas, terms and schemes of understanding and can rightly expect that theology will use clearly and consistently what they have provided. At the same time, as we have indicated earlier, theologians will modify the material—at the very least in the sense of clarifying it further. For instance, what the Jewish-Christian revelation indicates about the origin, nature and destiny of human life must modify any versions of human existence drawn from Platonism, Aristotelianism, this or that form of existentialism or some other philosophy. It is not that any true or worthwhile philosophical ideas about humanity can ever be genuinely "alien" to the good news revealed in Jesus Christ, but the incarnation, life, death and resurrection of the Son of God will fire and fuse these ideas into a new framework. In short, philosophical concepts should not be expected to move simply unchanged straight into theology. There will be an analogy, not an identity, between the "same" concept in philosophy and theology.

Second, I shrink from giving the impression either that philosophy is just in the business of raising questions to be answered in theology or that theology does not generate some of its own questions. It would be extremely odd to think of one discipline (philosophy) being limited to asking questions for which another discipline (theology) provided the replies. About the processes of human knowledge and imagination, for instance, philosophers ask their own questions to be answered within their own discipline. Further, some of the questions facing theologians will come "from within" (either from themselves or from other members of the believing community), and will not necessarily come "from outside"— from philosophy, the natural sciences or the contemporary culture generally. For example, no mound of official words can shut off the question which many believers spontaneously raise today: What is the relationship between the risen Christ and the institutional Church?

Theologians should hear the full and varied range of questions coming today from many sources. Distortion would occur *only* if the questions of philosophy alone—and that means in practice the questions of one particular philosophy—were allowed a hearing. In such a case the contribution of that philosophy would become a takeover. Its particular questions and interests would lead to congenial theological elements being emphasized and others being neglected.

In this excursus I have tried as far as possible to avoid technicalities like the various distinctions which concern the role of understanding and reason: for instance, the distinction to be drawn between *Verstand* and *Vernunft,* between the intellect which seeks to *know* the truth and reason which searches for and *thinks* about meaning. It may have been a mistake not to have taken up technicalities. But I hope the excursus goes some way toward satisfying the need for an interpretation of the complex interrelationship between philosophy and theology.

More generally, it seemed necessary to begin by placing the activities of theology, fundamental theology and philosophy. Against that background the book can now begin to take its specific shape around its central theme, the experience of God's saving and revealing self-communication.

II. HUMAN EXPERIENCE

We had the experience but missed the meaning.
T. S. Eliot, *Dry Salvages*

Religious doctrines will have to be discarded. You know why: in the long run nothing can withstand reason and experience, and the contradiction which religion offers to both is all too palpable.
Sigmund Freud, *Future of an Illusion*

If anything can be said for the validity of religious statements, it must come from the discrimination and analysis of experience itself.
John Macquarrie, *The Scope of Demythologizing*

The central theme of this book—the experience of the divine self-communication recorded and transmitted through tradition and Scripture—lets loose a swarm of questions with its first word: experience.[1] Does all human experience enjoy a religious dimension? Or do only some (privileged?) experiences deserve to be called "religious"? Then possible and probable differences between classes of religious experience call for examination. Does Christian experience, for instance, differ from the mystical experience of Buddhists and other types of religious experience?

These and further questions press themselves on the attention of anyone attempting to reflect theologically on experience. Obviously the *Fragestellung* or range of questions needs to be clarified. But so too does the conceptuality (*Begrifflichkeit*). This chapter will first elaborate a general account of experience and, from time to time, suggest how the account could apply to various persons, episodes, and themes in Jewish-Christian history, faith and theology. After developing this working account, we can then attend to the religious dimension present in *all* human experience.

Many thinkers have contributed to our appreciation of what "experience"—religious or otherwise—might mean and entail. I think here of writers like John Dewey, Wilhelm Dilthey, Hans-Georg Gadamer, Edmund Husserl, William James (*The Varieties of Religious Experience*), Karl Jaspers ("boundary-situations"), Jacques Merleau-Ponty (the symbolic character of "primordial experience"), Abraham Maslow ("peak experiences"), Friedrich Schleiermacher (religion as "the feeling of absolute dependence") and Paul Tillich. In the hands of these and other writers the term "experience" has differing meanings and shades of meaning. However, I do not wish either to follow the version of experience developed by *one* of these thinkers or to attempt a critical survey of *all* the major contributors in this field. None of them has in any case ever managed to describe fully, let alone explain exhaustively, what human experience is really made of. My main purpose is to reflect on ordinary speech, take up everyday meanings and thus work out a reasonably tight and tidy answer to the question: What is happening when we are experiencing? This approach promises to be more immediately helpful for theology than elaboratedly technical accounts.

On any showing "experience" is a very complex notion. To guide our exploration it seems useful to examine various aspects of experience under three headings: (I) the subject, (II) the experience itself, and (III) the consequences.

I
THE SUBJECT

(1) *Immediacy* is an obvious aspect of any experience. Experience implies a direct contact with someone or something. We do not experience persons or things by hearing about them from a distance, but by coming into living contact with them. We may actively reach out to touch some reality. Or we may experience ourselves more as receiving something. Whether our role appears more active or more passive in a given experience, in either case we directly encounter some object or person. We shift, for instance, from merely reading the books of some author to meeting that man or woman for ourselves. It is the move from knowing about this person to knowing him by acquaintance.

Our contact with what is experienced may display various degrees of *intensity.* People like prophets, poets, and artists are often credited with enjoying more intense experiences than other people. This need not, of course, be so. One poet, for instance, may express an intense experience, while only feeble sentiments and a faint experience may lie behind what another poet says. At times, however, people's awareness of their experiences can be so heightened that they need sedatives.

But my point here is this. No matter whether it is (a) more or less intense or (b) more or less passive, experience involves direct and immediate contact.

(2) This means that there *cannot literally be second-hand experiences.* What we experience we must experience for ourselves. Others can talk to us at length about swimming, being married, surviving a street riot, and working as a parish priest or a rabbi. But we have not experienced these realities until we step into the water for ourselves, contract a marriage, get hit by a rock or blinded by tear-gas, and take over a parish or a synagogue. Likewise, we may learn about Chinese ceramics from some authority in the field, or without demur accept from our community a traditional belief about the good old days under some king. But we cannot talk about our experience in these matters until we have a first-hand contact with some ceramics or a monarchy. Other people can encourage us to face a new experience. Experts may instruct us how to begin and provide us with some tantalizing glimpses of their specialty. But, *as such,* experience can never be literally taken over from others. Personal involvement is required. In that sense no one else can learn to swim, fall in love, get married, visit Rome or receive the Holy Spirit "for us."

(3) Furthermore, even where no one else intervenes, we do not talk about experiencing something which forms the conclusion of our rational argument. For instance, archeological discoveries may allow us to conclude that Roman galleys visited the east coast of India, but we do not directly experience for ourselves the arrival of those sailors and traders from the west. Pieces of historical evidence can fall into place and allow us to trace the events leading up to the death of Edward V and his brother, but we do not experience the murder of the two boys in the Tower of London—no matter how vivid our historical imagination is. Experience may not properly be identified with the process and results of such argumentation.

Nevertheless, experience and abstract reason should not be viewed in isolation. They are distinct but not genuinely separable. Reflection will render explicit what is given and implicit in experience. Thus, even as we view the archeological finds or peruse the historical documents, we can begin to deduce our conclusions.

(4) As Gadamer[2] and others remark, *the life of the subject reveals itself in experience.* One way of interpreting the "original" sense of the German verb *erleben* ("to experience") puts this point nicely. "Er-leben" is to be alive when something happens—to be alive to what is happening to us. This catches up the active ("to be alive") and passive ("to what is happening to us") moments of experience.

Our life expresses itself in experience. Experiences disclose what our life is and is to be. We are and will be what we experience. We identify ourselves and the course of our life through deeply lived experiences of fear, love, joy and guilt, as well as through the realities which confront us in day-to-day experience.

(5) A genuine experience affects *the entire existence* of a human being. In one way or another the experiences of being profoundly depressed, migrating to another country, or being seriously ill—as well as the daily flux of less striking experiences—touch all aspects of our personal existence: the imagination, the emotions, the mind, the will, the memory and our other (spiritual and bodily) powers. There is a multi-leveled structure to human experience.

This observation about experience may look innocent and obvious. Its importance lies in the area of human knowledge. Is all experience somehow conscious? Without taking time off here to prove this assertion in detail, I want to maintain that there is *no experience truly prior to knowledge.* We can experience innumerable things, without being either fully aware of them and their implications or capable of properly verbalizing their significance. The experiences of childhood are typically like that. Recollected in tranquillity or non-tranquillity, years later they may betray their meaning for the first time. However, for such a process to occur, these experiences must have been once known. There is always at least a minimal cognitive dimension to experience.

St. John's Gospel offers some striking examples of experiences which the evangelist presents as *both* known by the disciples during Jesus' ministry *and* later interpreted by them in the "tranquillity" of the post-Easter period. As John tells the story, Jesus spoke of his coming passion under the image of a temple which would be destroyed and resurrected. The Gospel writer adds: "When therefore he was raised from the dead, his disciples remembered that he had said this; and they believed the Scripture and the word which Jesus had spoken" (2:22). Something similar occurs when Jesus entered Jesusalem riding upon a young ass—in fulfillment of some prophetic words (Zech 9:9). John remarks: "His disciples did not understand that at first; but when Jesus was glorified, then they remembered that this had been written of him and had been done to him" (12:16). For the disciples to recall and understand the significance of Jesus' words and actions, they had first to know him.

All of this insistence on the cognitive dimension of experience might seem a pointless exercise like exhuming and beating a thoroughly dead horse. However, there is a hardy philosophical tradition that reduces experience to something which makes its appearance prior to real cognition—as a stage in which the data is gathered on which the proper processes of human knowing can then work. "Experience" is understood as *sense* experience and not as *human* experience in its rich fullness. John Dewey—at least in the way he phrased his definition—went even further in downplaying the cognitive dimension of experience. He wrote:

> The organism *acts* in accordance with its own structure, simple or complex, upon its surroundings. As a consequence, the changes produced in the environment *react upon the organism* and its activities. The living creature undergoes, suffers the consequence of its own behavior. This close connection between *doing* and *suffering or undergoing* forms what we call experience.[3]

Here experience was taken to be the action and reaction of an organism. Explicitly nothing at all was said about knowledge as such. Over against any approach that regards knowledge lightly, Dilthey and Husserl took experience to be primarily cognitive.

Ultimately, two reductionist moves should be avoided here. On the one hand, experience is not to be reduced to "mere sense" experience. On the other hand, experience is not to be simply identified with knowledge, as if it were "merely cognitive."

(6) Thus far the subject of experience has been taken as the individual person. But we can also speak of the *collective experience* of some community: that is to say, an experience not only *of* others but also *with* others. In this case the community in question is the subject which shares historical experiences, expresses them (through rituals, monuments, books, art, and other means), and may, in fact, cling to one deep experience as the very raison d'être for its present existence. A nation can shape its life by recalling the common struggle and triumph of some war of independence. The Roman Catholic Church has found itself committed to a new and profound search for religious identity through the Second Vatican Council. The Jewish community around the world participated in and continues to participate in the experience of the holocaust.

For Israel the call of Abraham initiated a collective history. Several times in the Old Testament (Deut 6:20–25; 26:5–9; Jos 24:2–13) we find formulas which in common acts of worship described this history and may have been the source of the Pentateuch in its basic outline. What these ancient confessions expressed vividly was the community's sense that it shared in the whole set of experiences following Abraham's call. Deuteronomy 26:5–9 reads:

A wandering Aramean was my father; and he went down into Egypt and sojourned there, few in number; and there he became a nation, great, mighty, and populous. And the Egyptians treated us harshly, and afflicted us, and laid upon us hard bondage. Then we cried to the Lord, the God of our fathers, and the Lord heard our voice, and saw our affliction, our toil, and our oppression; and the Lord brought us out of Egypt with a mighty hand and an outstretched arm, with great terror, with signs and wonders; and he brought us into this place and gave us this land, a land flowing with milk and honey.

Gerhard von Rad remarked on the solidarity manifested by this confession: "There is no divinely addressed Thou; the whole thing is completely and strikingly divested of every personal note. The speaker recapitulates the great, sacred facts that constitute the community. He abstains from all individual concerns and in this moment identifies himself completely with the community."[4] In brief, the text of Deuteronomy reflects a collective experience founding and supporting a common hope.

Through the Old Testament period into the time of Jesus the community was looked upon as *the* natural subject of experience. The group experienced a Babylonian captivity, a return from exile, the ministry of Jesus, his resurrection, the gift of the Holy Spirit, and so forth. The individual emerged only secondarily as the subject of such experiences. In his letter to the Galatians St. Paul remained true to his religious and cultural world when he interpreted justification as a social happening which establishes a solidarity between alienated groups and creates one people, "the Israel of God" (3:26–28; 6:16).

Today, however, things are reversed. We talk primarily of the individual person as the subject of experience and only secondarily of the community. Indeed, for some people, talk about "collective experience" creates difficulties and may even seem an improbable piece of mythology. Even in such simple affairs like a small committee meeting the participants can experience the proceedings in quite different ways. One is bored. Another is delighted to have rammed through his proposal to modify the curriculum. Taking the minutes may preoccupy the third—"and so forth and so fifth," as P. G. Wodehouse has one of his characters remark. Matters become more complicated when we come to an event like the Second Vatican Council which touched the lives of several hundred million Catholics—not to mention its impact on people who were not members of the Roman Catholic Church. Laymen, laywomen, bishops, priests and religious participated in the council in an almost endless variety of ways. Was it possible for them to find some common element(s) in their commitments, hopes, fears, and reactions so that they might truly say as a collective subject: "We had the same experience"? If they did not have the same experience, how could they do other than miss some (possible) common meaning? Still less could they find the right language to express this meaning.

Difficulties thicken when we apply the notion of collective experience not just to millions of *contemporaries* but to *successive generations* stretching over hundreds and even thousands of years. What is "the" collective experience for later Russians vis-à-vis the occupation of the Winter Palace (October 25, 1917), for later Americans vis-à-vis the Declaration of Independence (July 4, 1776), for later Irishmen vis-à-vis the battle of the Boyne (July 11, 1690), or for centuries of Christians vis-à-vis the events of the first Good Friday and Easter Sunday (A.D. 30)?

The obvious mobilizing power of such foundational events should, however, soften any prejudice against recognizing them as collective experiences. Many Russians, Americans and Irishmen may not value one or other of the events just mentioned. Only some Christians may find the *entire* basis for their existence in the event of Jesus' death and resurrection. Nevertheless, the impact of all these events is undeniable. In generation after generation, groups of people have recalled and re-enacted them, appropriating them again and again as their own experience. The members of these different communities wish to align themselves somehow with the same foundational events. To that end they come together to worship in the same church service or to be involved in the same parade. They read the common texts, hear the same address, or sing the same hymns and national anthems.

All in all, whether dealing with groups of contemporaries or with succeeding generations, we can legitimately speak of collective experiences. Of course, the individual responses of people in any given community will vary in quantity and intensity. Influenced by inherited assumptions, past experiences, personal attitudes, and degrees of self-awareness, individuals will participate in some common experience in differing ways. Nevertheless, the points made above about the individual subject of experience apply, *mutatis mutandis,* to the collective subject. By enacting or re-enacting an event, the community stands in a direct contact with it, knows it at first-hand, and does not simply accept its existence as the mere conclusion of some process of reasoning. The community reveals its life in the common experience—be it a committee meeting, a Church council or a service of worship—and lets that experience affect in major or minor ways its whole existence.

II
THE EXPERIENCE ITSELF

"The experience itself" is a second heading which allows us to classify some further aspects of the complex notion under study. We might prefer other headings and rearrange our observations accordingly. But "the experience itself" can cover the following five items:

(1) All experience has *meaning*. The meaning or meanings may be difficult to identify. It can take years before the significance of some baffling episode dawns on an individual or a community. Experience and meaning, if not simply synonymous, are closely interrelated. W. H. Auden somewhere remarked about the pessimistic wing of the existentialists: "The existentialists declare they are in complete despair, yet go on writing." Individual experiences, no less than the whole of life itself, can be trusted to carry meaning and make sense. The thesis of total and definitive absurdity finally proves impossible to sustain. Some ten years ago I saw a German film in which the tragic-comic hero experienced a bewildering variety of improbable and seemingly absurd adventures. Throughout he kept up his refrain: "Alles hat seinen tiefsten Sinn" (Everything has its deepest meaning). The truth lies there rather than with the doomed Macbeth who soliloquizes:

> Life's but a walking shadow, a poor player
> That struts and frets his hour upon the stage
> And then is heard no more: it is a tale
> Told by an idiot, full of sound and fury,
> Signifying nothing.

We can expect the world, and our experiences to make sense, provided we do not insist on a simple and immediate sense. We may bump up against what looks like meaningless disorder in human affairs or be appalled by pointless atrocities. Such episodes do not yield up their meaning easily. But there is meaning to be found and not missed. Any developed notion of experience needs to recall the theme of meaning.

(2) All experience bears with it a certain purposefulness or finality. It takes us in some direction. The experience of genuine love turns out to be other-enriching and personally liberating. Some common struggle for justice brings a group together and creates a surprising bond of friendship. Admittedly there is no great difficulty in recognizing the point and purpose in such positive experiences, be they great or small. It is the frustrating, sad, and tragic occasions that can leave us puzzled as to their possible finality. Let me at least state my conviction here, even if I do

not develop it in detail. All experiences, whether "positive" or "negative," enjoy a certain directedness. They all lead us somewhere, no matter whether their impact is enormous or—as with most things and persons we experience—it almost thins to nothing.

(3) Third, experience is nothing if not *concrete.* Experiences do not exist "in general." A nation cannot be liberated in general. It is delivered from this or that oppressing power. A girl does not fall in love in general but with this boy. Catholics witness and live through particular Church councils. It may prove difficult to make a precise diagnosis and find a remedy, but no one can be sick "in general." The experience of God in prayer occurs only at particular times, in particular places and to particular persons.

(4) Both ordinary and academic use of language suggests a fourth aspect about experience. We tend to look for the *newness* it entails. Maslow's talk about "peak experiences," Jaspers' "boundary situations" and David Tracy's terminology of "limit-experiences" get accepted easily. Theoretically we may admit that quite ordinary things and the utterly uneventful actions we repeat each day count as experiences. However, when someone remarks, "That was an experience," we expect to hear about something strikingly new, at least in degree if not in kind, which the speaker has been through. "Experience" readily suggests something new and unexpected which leaves its mark on the subject and opens him for other new experiences in the future. We normally take a person of "wide experience" to be one who can easily face the new and cope with the unexpected. Such persons are not hermetically sealed, as it were, against novelty and unwilling to accept anything more than numerically different instances of what they already know. Rather what they have hitherto experienced has left them with an openness for the unforeseen, if not totally unexpected, events of the future.

In short, language suggests how we may be reluctant to apply "experience" to what is utterly expected. In one way or another genuine experience surpasses our anticipations.

Nevertheless, the scheme proposed in the first section of this chapter and the points already made in this section apply to routine things and quite predictable episodes. We are, after all, in immediate contact with our breakfast, we do catch the commuter train first-hand, our life expresses itself in the daily program and so forth. In all these cases new and unexpected elements normally remain at a minimum. Some readers might like to distinguish "Experiences" from "experiences" on the basis that novelty bulks larger in the first class than in the second. It is the difference between what is uncommon and what is common. Taking advantage of the fact that German offers two words here, we can speak of *Erlebnis* (uncommon and moving Experience) and *Erfahrung* (common and repeated experience).

This distinction, of course, should not lead us to ignore or even deny the mystery in what regularly happens. G. K. Chesterton's *Manalive* celebrates the wonder and the mystery of a man's home, wife and country. In that novel a man elopes with his wife, travels around the world, returns to his own country and breaks into his own house. Chesterton seems to be saying something like this to us: The mystery of what is always there constantly provokes—or should provoke—fresh experience.

Finally, a respect for newness should not make us overlook the proper role of repetition. An experienced pilot has repeatedly made "normal" take-offs and landings and has not been constantly coping with extraordinary storms and other unusual situations. An experienced conductor or liturgist will use successfully a well-known text without modifying it at all. In the hands of experienced persons, the flight, the symphony and the Eucharist will be literally repetitious but never dull. Such persons have not only learned *from* experience, but have also learned both *how* to experience and *how* to communicate experiences to others. What is different comes in on top of what is the same. The new blends into the old.

(5) Fifth, experiences can be described as *positive, negative,* or *seemingly ambiguous*. In *Gaudium et Spes* the Second Vatican Council spoke of "the call to grandeur and the depths of misery" as "both part of human experience" (n. 13). Our major problem here concerns our standards for judging the differences and making the classifications. Taking pleasure and pain as criteria, we would list things like a nation's defeat in war, episodes of personal sorrow, poverty, terrifying physical danger and a painful death as "negative."

But should we simply adopt such criteria? What one person reckons to be a peak experience another will dismiss as a "trough" or nadir experience. Pleasurable experiences can turn out to be destructive. Painful experiences can be fruitful sources of meaning and have obviously positive consequences. The Bible repeatedly makes that point. To cite just one passage, the Letter to the Hebrews speaks of Jesus in these terms: "Although he was a Son, he learned obedience through what he suffered; and being made perfect he became the source of eternal salvation to all who obey him" (5:8f). In this view the crucifixion gets classified as a positive experience—at least as positive in its results.

In general, it is obvious that sickness and death assault our personalities, erode our bodies and threaten us with annihilation. Yet it may be only the experience of sickness that will convince us of our limits and only the threat of death that will bring home to us our contingency and state of radical dependence.

III
THE CONSEQUENCES

Four words gather together much of what can be called the aftermath or consequences of experience, especially experiences of a striking kind: discernment, interpretation, expression and memory. There is nothing more personal than experience, but there may be nothing more difficult than rightly discerning, interpreting, expressing and remembering one's experience. Here I should hasten to add that the words "aftermath" and "consequences" are *not* meant to suggest optional extras. Discernment, interpretation, expression and memory belong essentially to human experience. They are there from the outset—giving color and shape to any experience. Let us take them up in turn.

(1) This chapter began by noting the immediacy of experience. In experience we stand in direct contact with some reality. The experience takes place. With undeniable certainty we know that we have experienced something. But what is/was it that is/was experienced? We may feel like Jacob wrestling in the dark with we know not what. An exact or even some provisional identification of the experience may elude us. What is the reality that we experience? In short, the issue of *discernment* is crucial—whether for the individual person or for the group who are the subject of the experience.

Experiences are self-imposing but not self-authenticating. How can we discern and "demonstrate" that what we or others experience genuinely derives from the reality we take to be its origin? Moral criteria are often invoked here to establish the authenticity of experiences which are held to come reliably "from God." This or that experience develops my sense of responsibility, helps me to cope with the complexity and finitude of human existence, and in general modifies my life in what are agreed to be good ways. Hence I can know that such experiences truly originate in God. Thus in Matthew's Gospel Jesus invokes obedience to the divine will and doing good as criteria that the community should use to discern who are the genuine prophets they experience in their midst.

> Not everyone who says to me, "Lord, Lord," shall enter the kingdom of heaven, but he who does the will of my Father who is in heaven. On that day many will say to me, "Lord, Lord, did we not prophesy in your name, and cast out demons in your name, and do many mighty works in your name?" And then will I declare to them, "I never knew you; depart from me, you evildoers" (7:21–23).

In his Corinthian correspondence, St. Paul appeals to a range of criteria in support of his position as apostle. For various reasons the church at Corinth can be sure it experiences in him an apostle authentically sent by God. There are moral criteria such as his obvious "anxiety for all the churches" (2 Cor 11:28). Paul appeals also to that *historical* episode which swung his life onto a new course: "Am I not an apostle? Have I not seen Jesus our Lord?" (1 Cor 9:1). Further, the very existence and life of the communities created by this apostle also establish his authenticity. Thus he writes to the Corinthians: "You yourselves are our letter of recommendation" (2 Cor 3:2).

The lesson comes through loud and clear from Matthew's Gospel, Paul's letters and a thousand other sources. Some range of criteria must be pressed into service. The process of discernment will normally need to invoke some signs establishing authenticity.

The criteria can help or hinder the process. On the one hand, discerning a fresh experience calls for some criteria which have a certain priority vis-à-vis this new case. On the other hand, experiences which do not properly conform to pre-existing expectations are not necessarily and always inauthentic. We need to allow for criteria that have a certain freedom over and against our clear presuppositions.

(2) Essentially discernment concerns identifying authentic experiences—that is to say, experiences which are reliable and trustworthy in the sense of deriving from the reality we take to be their origin. But we need also to *interpret* fully and correctly these authentic experiences. To echo T. S. Eliot, we may have an authentic experience but miss much of its meaning, truth and value.

It would be a dangerous mistake to drive a wedge between an experience and its interpretation, as if we were dealing with successive and quite separable events. Instinctively and unconsciously we choose and interpret what will be encountered in the experience itself. Right at the outset large parts of reality may be blocked off or modified in ways that decisively affect the quality and range of the experience. From the start a selective and interpretative process will be at work to determine the data which we later interpret consciously.

Cultural, religious and sociological influences of all kinds shape the way our interpretations will go. The history and language of our society are always there to influence any experience and its interpretation. Our own personal mind-set, *Weltanschauung,* memories, ideas and sensibility will affect both the experience itself and any subsequent reflections. There is no such thing as unpremised experience. Presuppositions, settled beliefs and pre-conditioning of all kinds will determine—at least partially—how we receive and interpret our experiences. We meet the new reality within an "horizon" of questions, expectations and prior experiences. The horizon (which could just as well have been considered in the first section under the "subject" of experience) limits our field of vision and shapes the conditions for any possible experiences. There is both a *collective* horizon (which we share with our group, our culture or our religious community) and the *personal* horizon proper to us as individuals. At both levels our attitudes, systems of value and the rest will heavily predetermine the range and quality of possible experiences, as well as tugging, in generally predictable directions, the interpretations to which our experiences give rise. Elements will always enter into the experience which derive from ourselves and which will modify the way we decipher, spell out and interpret what happens.

Sometimes those interpretative elements will be drawn very much "from outside"—for instance, in scientific experiments or when new experiences in Church and society are manipulated and "explained" through existing structures and systems of value. At other times the major interpretative elements will be clearly given *with* and *in* the experience itself, as with profound experiences of love, fear, guilt, joy and so forth. Yet even then both the collective horizon of society and the personal horizon of the individual will *always* to some degree shape and color the experiences. They are never totally and simply *given* to us. There is no such thing as a purely "objective," neutral and non-interpreted experience.

Two examples could help here: the Old Testament prophets and Roman Catholic reactions to the Second Vatican Council. In his *Prophecy and Tradition* R. E. Clements points out how traditional elements shaped the way individual prophets accepted and understood their call and subsequent experiences.[5] These inherited elements shifted the course of both the experiences themselves and their later interpretations. In the last decade or so Catholics (and others) have interpreted the Second Vatican Council as being everything from a total success to an unmitigated disaster. The differences between the presuppositions, perspectives and expectations of the various groups help to account for this "conflict of interpretations" (Paul Ricoeur). They all "had the experience" of the Council but could not agree on its meaning. The (often widely) divergent ways in which Catholics structured their world affected both the experience itself and their interpretations of it.

A Zen story given to me by Alan Webster, the Dean of St. Paul's Cathedral, highlights the dangerous role which presuppositions may play. A Zen master invited a visitor to tea. The guest arrived, bowed, crossed his legs and sat in silence. The Zen master then took the teapot and started to fill the cup. He filled it to the brim and still continued to pour until the floor was covered with tea. The guest was horrified and inquired why the Zen master was so careless. "Because," the master replied, "I feel that your head is like this teacup—so overflowing with ideas that it would be impossible for me to add anything to what you already know. You cannot hear what I say." One can add: Often we fail to hear what an experience, especially a strikingly new experience, is saying to us. It may be impossible for us to let our pre-conditioning be called into question by what we experience. The mind-set we bring into play simply excludes that possibility. To vary the image—a new experience may knock forever on a deaf man's door.

However, a powerful conversion can deal with and drastically modify that horizon of settled presuppositions, questions and expectations we bring to some experience. Such a conversion can bring about what Bernard Lonergan and others have called an horizon shift.[6] Powerful and memorable experiences can provoke transforming decisions that reshape the course of our lives or dramatically unify an unintegrated existence. The new experience cannot be assimilated without a radical accommodation. It "converts" us by shifting our horizon and making a drastic claim on us to live in new ways.

To offer an example, in his fascinating study on St. Paul, "Call Rather Than Conversion," Krister Stendahl rightly stresses that the apostle describes his experience on the Damascus road "in terms of a prophetic call similar to that of Isaiah and Jeremiah." It is not that Paul "gives up his former faith to become a Christian. . . . Rather, his call brings him to a new understanding of his mission, a new understanding of the law which is otherwise an obstacle to the Gentiles." As Stendahl insists, "Paul remains a Jew as he fulfills his role as an apostle to the Gentiles." For these and other reasons Stendahl argues against speaking of the apostle's "conversion."[7] What is missing here, however, is the recognition that precisely Paul's "new understanding of his mission" and "new understanding of the law" brings an horizon shift which deserves the name of conversion. After the experience on the Damascus road, he takes in the world and faces further experiences in a new way.

Before leaving the theme of interpretation, one further item should be recalled: the dialogue between *tradition* and experience. *Tradition* offers socially available ways of evaluating experiences and recognizing their significance. Through its prevailing traditions the community helps individuals to interpret their experiences. We face here ambiguous phenomena which will claim our attention later in this book. If tradition offers us the means to interpret new experiences, it may also limit what we allow to happen or even misinterpret in advance experiences which do occur. Certain individuals like poets, prophets or playwrights from time to time will have to dissociate themselves from some traditional approaches and reinterpret for others the experiences in which a whole generation has shared. They will cry out against some traditions for misinterpreting these experiences.

(3) Besides discernment and interpretation, we need to recall also *the spoken or written expression* of experience. It would be unnerving to find ourselves in the situation of having to admit: "We had the experience,

thought we had interpreted correctly the meaning but could not find the right language to express that meaning." What happens when we describe and explain our experiences? We use our common language to express what has happened. There is a shift from the immediate and particular level of experience to the mediate and generalized level of language. The verbal account makes experiences and their meaning public. The flesh of personal experience becomes a word to others. Our language thus makes the experiences amenable to being passed on and inherited. This sharing can evoke and even control such experiences for others.

When we articulate and formulate our experiences, we lose a certain vibrant dynamism. Nevertheless, such articulation helps us and others to appreciate these experiences more profoundly and enjoy certain aspects that could otherwise be missed.

The goal of our language can vary a great deal. Some language will attempt to say all that can be said about an experience. Other languages will say almost nothing of what might be said: for instance, the language of intimacy where innuendo predominates and the presuppositions enable some given expression to communicate much more than it literally states. The language of intimacy points to experienced realities which lie beyond any possibility of verbalizing them satisfactorily. To a degree such experiences always remain ineffable.

Language is, of course, not the only medium for expressing experience. It is perilously easy for theologians to overemphasize the spoken or printed word. Sculpture, painting and Church liturgy with its rituals and symbols and, indeed, a person's whole style of life are among the many ways, apart from writing, in which experience finds expression. Often non-verbal symbols and the ritualized formulations of experience can communicate better than a mere verbal exposition. The "objectifying" of experience takes place at many different levels and through many different channels.

Such objectifying of experience—one must add—is not a secondary item. The self cannot live through an experience without in some way conceptualizing, exteriorizing or expressing—whether in language or otherwise—that experience. Without such expression experience has no meaning and is essentially incomplete. In fact, unless some such objectifying takes place, the self cannot be conscious of experience and can hardly be said to have the experience. All of this objectifying happens, of course, with varying degrees of consciousness, deliberateness and success. Experience, especially any deep experience, will never be adequately expressed. Nevertheless, some measure of expression always belongs to experience. We seriously blur this point whenever we slip into that frequent phraseology about "having an experience and then attempting to clothe it in words."[8] Language does not simply express some experience *after* it has happened. Language organizes and shapes the experience, the body under the clothes.

Finally, a word about the formulation of *shared* experiences. The first part of this chapter indicated the hesitations we might have in agreeing to speak of genuinely common experience. Even when we are satisfied to put aside these hesitations, we might suspect the success of, let us say, a common document that interprets and expresses some collective experience: "We all had the experience but missed *the* meaning" (italics mine). Eliot's line might lead us astray. "*The* meaning" all too easily suggests that one experience = one meaning. However, if the most perceptive reflections of a gifted individual will not exhaust the range of meanings carried by some important experience, all the more so is this true of collective experiences. A group cannot fully and finally interpret some shared experience in the hope that all will agree, "*That* was *the* meaning." At both the individual and the collective level a pluralism of meaning is built into experience itself.

(4) Further, Eliot's "we *had* the experience" (italics mine) could sound as if the whole business were over and done with. However, experiences—particularly profound experiences—lodge themselves in the *memory* both of individual persons and of groups to live on powerfully and productively. The Jewish community could not say of the exodus, "We *had* the experience of the exodus," as if that were a completed matter belonging simply to the past. The *Mishna Pesachim* remarks: "In every generation a man is obliged to consider himself as if he had moved out of Egypt" (X, 50). Even more so the Christian community could not refer to Jesus and say, "We *had* the experience of his death and resurrection." As crucified and risen, Jesus remains uniquely active and present. The experiences of the exodus and the paschal mystery endure. No individual or community has or ever will interpret once and for all what such events meant or mean, as if we could be finished with and forget them. They continue to be remembered ritually re-enacted, reinterpreted and re-expressed.

This observation about memory, and the "after-life" of experience is far from a dubious assertion fueled by a pressing religious need. Eric Berne and other psychologists argue convincingly that something deeply experienced never disappears from the memory. Our lives are more than a series of discrete episodes. Experiences live on in the memory. Constantly we need to take time out to ponder and reinterpret the experiences that make up our personal and collective past.

Gabriel Marcel observes: "The more we grasp the notion of experience in its proper complexity ... the better we shall understand how experience cannot fail to transform itself into reflection, and we shall even have the right to say that the more richly it is experience, the more, also, it is reflection."[9] We can properly extend the point of these remarks. The richer the experience itself, the richer will be the continuing reflection sustained by memory.

IV
RELIGIOUS EXPERIENCE

So far this chapter—largely on the basis of everyday speech and meanings—has set out to elucidate the notion of experience. This discussion moved from the subject of experience to the experience itself and its aftermath. From time to time the examples chosen to illustrate some point have been explicitly religious ones. The overall aim was to provide a usable scheme for reflecting theologically on revelation, tradition and Scripture. Before this chapter ends it seems advisable to tackle the religious dimension implicitly present in all human experience, and to distinguish this from the conscious religious experiences which belong to historical revelation and salvation.

In every experience there is an ultimate (and hence a religious) element. In all experience there is this ultimacy which relates the human person to God. Either God is somehow there in *every* experience or God is not there at all. Always and everywhere human life realizes and enacts a saving dialogue with God. The religious dimension is a plus-factor in our entire experience, a primordial given in all acting, reacting, knowing, willing, feeling and symbolizing. There is an absolute and ultimate (as distinct from a relative and proximate) ground, horizon and concern found in all human activities.

Large assertions fill the previous paragraph. Let us focus on three things in turn: (1) "transcendental" experience which constitutes *transcendental revelation,* (2) "depth" or "religious" experience which constitutes *historical revelation,* and (3) the human response to both transcendental and historical revelation.

(1) In every particular experience of someone or something we concurrently experience not only ourselves but also our openness to an unlimited horizon of being. In any specific experience of knowing, willing and acting there is also involved a universal aspect and an absolute, spiritual horizon, which is God. Hence every concrete experience also means experiencing ourselves and God. In all our activity God is revealed and we are revealed to ourselves. If Augustine prayed, "Lord, that I might know myself, that I might know thee," a primordial knowing of both oneself and God is *already* there in every act of knowledge.

But can we substantiate or at least clarify somewhat these claims?

Here it seems advisable to take up the theme of "transcendental" experience, as developed by Karl Rahner.[10] What this theme entails can be indicated under ten headings.

(a) The human subject displays an openness and tendency toward an ultimate horizon of unconditioned being, that furthest limit which circles and encloses all our experiences. Against such an horizon we experience some particular being, grasp some specific meaning, know this particular truth and desire some specific good thing. Within such an horizon we also know—albeit in an unthematized and unreflective way—ourselves as subject with our finitude and relativity.

(b) The ultimate horizon is not one determined object among others. Knowing it is not just one more instance of knowledge in general. It is there as an unthematized and unreflective element. Even when through subsequent reflection it becomes the object of explicit attention, it can never be totally and adequately thought through and objectivized.

(c) The human subject enjoys a "transcendental" experience of his horizon, in the sense that the experience goes beyond any particular acts of knowing and willing. This horizon not only transcends all specific acts as acts, but also does not depend upon this or that particular content. Hence the experience of his horizon can be called transcendental.

(d) The ultimate horizon is always affirmed, even in the explicit act of denying it.

(e) This ultimate horizon is the *a priori* condition for the possibility of any human experience. When, for instance, some specific act of knowledge occurs, that is because there already exists a knowing subject oriented toward this horizon.

(f) As the absolute fullness of being, meaning, truth and goodness, this absolute horizon is to be identified with God.

(g) Hence we can speak of transcendental experience as transcendental *revelation*. This is the primordial form of God's self-communication. In every transcendental experience (which means in fact the transcendental aspect of every particular experience), we encounter the divine mystery and God's saving presence, even if this dimension of the experience is not explicitly reflected upon. Hence the so-called proofs for God's existence are not ways that lead us to know and experience God for the first time but are secondary reflections on our basic, transcendental experience of God.

(h) The divine self-communication involved in transcendental experience is a gratuitous, supernatural gift from God. If it is there in the actual order of things, this self-communication is not something owed to us. Rahner brings together these two elements in his notion of the "supernatural existential."[11] On the one hand, transcendental experience is a reality of human existence as we know it (an "existential"). On the other hand, the divine self-communication is a ("supernatural") grace which does not belong to the "natural" human condition.

(i) As the ultimate horizon needed to create the possibility for any experience, God is known to every human person. Whether or not they realize this consciously and accept it willingly, all human beings receive the transcendental experience of God's primordial self-communication. This self-communication sets up the conditions for men and women to decide consciously for or against God. Through the transcendental experience God is "closer to me than I am to myself"—the "Deus interior intimo meo" of Augustine.

(j) Finally, transcendental experience/revelation establishes the presupposition and condition for receiving divine revelation and salvation in the specific forms of historical existence—above all through the historical experience of Israel and the life, death and resurrection of Jesus Christ. Transcendental revelation assumes the shape of historical revelation in and through the concrete experiences and free decisions of communities and individual persons. These specific experiences and their interpretation will, of course, differ widely through the influence of cultural forms, inherited religious traditions and so forth. This distinction between *transcendental* (*a priori*) and *historical* (*a posteriori*) experience revelation will concern us later.

(2) In the sense indicated by Rahner and other transcendental Thomists, one sees how experience always carries with it a primordial religious dimension. Rahner's transcendental experience concerns the *a priori* conditions for the possibility of any experience.

In the first part of this chapter we took an *a posteriori* approach and for the most part reflected on everyday experiences. Within the total flux of such experiences we can sometimes spot certain profound episodes. Through situations of extreme danger, seeming absurdity, solitude and pain we can be confronted with two things: on the one hand, our own weakness, finitude and contingency, and, on the other hand, a power, meaningfulness and benevolent love that supports us. We sense then in a deeper way than usual how limited we are and how we live in dependence upon what is graciously given to us. Or else we are confronted with surprising experiences which we did not predict, program and decide on. Things do not depend upon our will and wisdom. Whatever form they take, such profound experiences can change the course of our lives. If human existence constantly enacts a saving dialogue with God, this holds true all the more for such deeper experiences. There more than elsewhere we sense the ultimate dimension of our life and change (or rather are changed) accordingly.

We can apply the term "religious" to all those experiences of depth which consciously concern our ultimate purposes and relationship with the holy God.[12] Such profound limit-experiences characterize human life, even if they are not always and necessarily identified as religious.

Three points should be noted here. First, those who confine experience to the domain of the senses will obviously have difficulty in understanding what is meant by religious *experience*. Like human beings, animals are bombarded with sense data. Those who reduce experience to sense knowledge should logically speak of animals as experiencing. However, they would probably draw back from attributing religious experience even to dogs, not to mention less favored animals. In brief, talking about "religious" experience entails a non-reductionist view of what experience in general entails.

Second, "religious" experience pushes beyond the minimal, unthematized awareness of God and ourselves involved in every act of knowing and willing—that is, in transcendental experience. We might decide, of course, to speak of that universal horizon in every experience as religious (lower case) experience and give the name of Religious (upper case) experience to a properly conscious concern with God and our ultimate destiny. However, it seems less confusing to avoid this lower-case/upper-case distinction and reserve "religious" for those particular, "historical" experiences when we *consciously* experience the depth and ultimacy in life.

Third, religious experience can obviously take the shape of explicitly experiencing God as *holy*—as the " fearful and fascinating mystery" (the *mysterium tremendum et fascinans* of Rudolf Otto). In that case we experience God as the ultimate mystery which infinitely transcends us, inspires reverent awe (because of the divine majesty and our sinful weakness) and yet draws human beings toward peace and fulfillment. The numinous, overpowering and "awe-full" otherness and attraction of the holy God evokes our creature-feeling.

(3) Finally, what claims do transcendental experience/revelation and consciously religious experiences make on us? In all knowing, willing and acting we experience the reality of God and ourselves. A primordial divine self-communication takes place. This self-communication summons us to "obey" and hear with a primordial faith the reality, truth and goodness we encounter. We can call this dimension of every experience the pri-

mordial revelation which invites our primordial faith.[13] This revelatory/ believing aspect, found in every human experience, need not be expressly identified as such. It is otherwise with consciously religious experiences where the divine revelation comes through some historical word and event to summon us to a self-conscious faith. To this we turn in our next chapter.

III. THE DIVINE SELF-COMMUNICATION

Omne verum, a quocumque dicatur, a Spiritu Sancto est.

Ambrosiaster

The lion has roared; who will not fear?
The Lord God has spoken; who can but prophesy?

Amos

The previous chapters have been but a prelude to what lies ahead. The first chapter argued that from the very outset the theologian must share as an insider in the living experience and practice of Christian faith (which is recorded and evoked by the Scriptures and tradition). Thus theology can be called "religious experience seeking understanding." Then the second chapter's account of experience (both concrete, "historical" experience and "transcendental" experience) aimed to provide a base for reflecting on the fundamental notions of revelation, tradition and inspiration.

This chapter on God's saving revelation would begin in chaos if we fail to ask at the start: (1) *What* is "revelation"? How should we use this term? What meaning should we attach to it? Then other questions can follow. (2) How does revelation enter human experience (=the *means* and *mediators* of revelation)? (3) Can one effectively *discern* that alleged experiences of revelation and salvation are genuinely authentic? How sound are our interpretations of religious experiences? (4) *When* and *where* did or does the experience of revelation occur? Was the divine self-communication confined to certain times and places in Old and New Testament history? What about those who came later? Is revelation closed for them? That should be enough questions to keep us busy for a while. The next chapter can raise such further questions as: Should Christian theology maintain that all experience of God's saving revelation relates

53

to Christ, so that one should hold that "outside Christ there is no revelation" (*extra Christum nulla revelatio*)? What position should one then take up as regards the experience of revelation among non-Christians and in non-Christian religions?

1. Revelation

What is revelation?[1] Christians believe that through the history of the Old and the New Testament the Father, Son and Holy Spirit are disclosed as a God who cares for us with an infinitely merciful love. Christianity is a revealed religion. Revelation is constantly presupposed by every discussion about particular events and specific details of the Christian religion. One's understanding of revelation encloses and affects the whole of theology. Revelation is among the most general terms available to designate comprehensively the object of faith (the self-revealed God) and the content of theology (what God has manifested to us). The study of revelation is not only an initial and fundamental task but also is in a real sense co-extensive with the whole of theology.

As regards revelation it has become commonplace to note the way theology—and, specifically, Roman Catholic theology—has shifted its ground. In "the bad old days" this theology treated revelation as if it were identical with (a) the *communication* of a set of divinely authenticated facts (otherwise inaccessible to human reason and now accepted on God's authority), and (b) the *body* of information thus communicated. This "propositional" view primarily presented revelation as the supernatural disclosure of new truths which significantly enriched our knowledge about God. Although it also spoke of God being "pleased *to reveal* himself and his eternal decrees" (DS 3004; italics mine), the First Vatican Council favored the propositional approach. The upshot was that revelation came to be closely associated with notions of doctrine and creed. The assent of faith was explained as an assent to truths. It was believing "the things" to be true which God had revealed (DS 3008). From here it was only half a step to allowing "correctness" of verbal expression to predominate over the lived experience of God's self-communication. Faith often turned into barren orthodoxy. It was supposed that language could encapsulate the collection of revealed truths and that these could be handed on like a parcel dispatched intact from one century to another.

This propositional version of divine revelation has its partial counterpart in ordinary language. Every now and then we are confronted with such newspaper headlines as: "Startling Revelations; Russian Scientist Defects," or "Minister Resigns; Government Reveals All." In such cases the public suddenly receives some unexpected and important pieces of information which may significantly change its attitude toward East-West relations or the national government. We are asked to accept the word of the scientist or the prime minister for the facts which we would not have known unless these people had communicated them to us.

A squad of Catholic theologians both before and after the Second Vatican Council, not to mention many Anglican, Orthodox and Protestant theologians, moved away from a propositional view of revelation to develop the model of revelation as interpersonal encounter or—in a word—dialogue. Instead of being interpreted primarily as God revealing truths, revelation was now understood to be God's self-revelation. It was expounded first and foremost as the gratuitous and saving self-disclosure of God who calls and enables us to enter by faith into a new personal relationship. Revelation is a person-to-person, subject-to-subject, I-Thou encounter. The appropriate primary question is "*Who* is revealed?" rather than "*What* is revealed?"

Roughly parallel with this change in the theology of *revelation* came also a change in the theology of *grace.*[2] Instead of asking "*What* is received?" when God justifies and sanctifies human beings, theologians recognized that they should have been asking "*Who* is received?" What should have been obvious came as a grand discovery. "Uncreated" grace or the indwelling of the Trinity takes precedence over "created" grace in its different forms. The divine Giver comes with the gifts. Much more than being a matter of receiving "things," grace means a new personal relationship with God.

But, to return to revelation, undoubtedly a massive shift has taken place from a propositional to a personal model of revelation. Nevertheless, the two models are not mutually exclusive, even if the second now proves more helpful and popular. In fact the models imply one another. The revealing and saving dialogue between God and human beings is not so wholly private and incommunicable that it remains locked within an inarticulate subjectivity. Talk of "personal encounter" is not a way of vaporizing the essence of revelation into a set of indescribable experiences. The faith which arises in this encounter with the self-revealing God talks about itself and what it now knows of God. St. Paul put it this way: "Since we have the same spirit of faith as he had who wrote, 'I believed, and so I spoke,' we too believe, and so we speak" (2 Cor 4:13). A once popular German expression for personal revelation put matters this way: "Gott redet uns an" (God addresses us). In addressing us, however, God says something which we can formulate and pass on. Provided that the formulations of faith give some genuine account of and insight into the divine-human dialogue, they may be described as expressing revelation. In this sense we can call revelation *propositionable.* It can find expression in true propositions about the divine dialogue with human beings.

Moreover, revelation as an interpersonal encounter between God and human beings does not merely give rise to true propositions, as if the role of language were merely to put into words what had already taken place in some wordless state. Revelation comes about when human beings are addressed: through the Scriptures, sermons, doctrinal statements, the sacraments, sacred art and other accounts drawn from previous revelatory encounters with God. Thus the formulations of faith not only issue from such encounters but also provoke them. An account of the "things" which God has revealed can bring about fresh revelatory situations and initiate the faith of later believers. To sum up: Even if the personal question ("*Who* is revealed?") is the primary one, the propositional content of revelation (the answer to the question "*What* is revealed?") continues to enjoy its proper place. The personal model highlights the *knowledge* of God which revelation brings. But this implies that the believer enjoys a *knowledge that* God is such and such. The communication of the truth *about* God remains an essential part of revelation, albeit always at the service of the personal encounter *with* God.

Granted that the propositional and personal models complement rather than exclude one another, should we leave matters there in dealing with the "*What?*" of revelation? Not altogether. Both models have their limitations, precisely inasmuch as they are both strongly *cognitive*. The personal model attends primarily to our "knowledge of" God rather than our "knowledge about" God. Nevertheless, it continues to speak of knowledge. Those who have developed the personal approach will describe revelation as God's self-disclosure or a divine-human dialogue. All the same, such a "disclosure" involves emerging from concealment to make oneself "known." Dia-*logue* (dia-*logos*) implies a "word" that is communicated or some "meaning" that is understood All the adjustments in our theology of revelation still have to make allowance for the fact that both in its denotations and in its connotations the language of "revelation" retains its firmly cognitive sense. Theology and Church teaching have shifted from speaking about the manifestation of meaning, truths and mysteries (in the plural) to speaking about God's revelation in Jesus Christ who is *the* Meaning, *the* Truth and *the* Mystery.[3] But the old cognitive aura still hangs around this updated language. There is a meaning to be "understood," a truth to be "known" and a mystery to be "disclosed."

Yet what is wrong with the strongly cognitive tendency that we find in all language of revelation? What hangs upon this observation? Does it aim at supporting a voluntarist line that would purge theology and Christian discourse generally of "intellectualist" terminology? What all this calls for is rather an awareness of the inevitably cognitive concerns in the term "revelation" and its normal synonyms.

The Christian Scriptures and faith should be recalled at this point. Gerald Downing rightly notes how "saving activity" words enjoy an overwhelming priority in the New Testament over such "communication" words as "revealing" and "making known."[4] It is more faithful to the

New Testament to confess "I accept Jesus as my personal Savior" than to confess "I accept Jesus as my personal Revealer." In both the Old and the New Testament salvation words predominate over terms for revelation. Furthermore, Christians acknowledge the whole reality of evil and sin from which God saves them. Salvation language extends more widely than revelation language to indicate the range of problems which affect our entire existence and for which we seek a solution. The Apostles' Creed and the Nicene Creed respect this reality, as well as the general thrust of the Scriptures, by confessing the motive of the incarnation to be "for our salvation" (*propter nostram salutem*). It would be less satisfactory to have declared Christ's motive to be "for the sake of revealing himself to us" (*propter revelationem sui ipsius nobis*). Almost inevitably the terminology of revelation fails to cover the full human condition and the scope of what God does for us. It narrows things down to our quest for meaning and the answer to our mental bewilderment—in brief, salvation for our intellect and reason.

Edward Schillebeeckx, for example, writes: "Revelation . . . is God's saving activity in history experienced and expressed by believers in answer to the question about the *meaning* of life."[5] What bothers me here is the word "meaning." Schillebeeckx does not talk about "problems," "evils," "sufferings," "felt needs," "sin," or "our whole predicament." His choice of language belongs to the theology of revelation and inescapably turns us toward the human reason which searches for and thinks about meaning and then receives from God the answer to its questioning about life.

Once it is recognized that "salvation" expresses better than "revelation" God's work in Christ and has a firmer basis in Scripture, where do these reflections lead? I see solid arguments against following Downing who wants simply to phase out the language of revelation in favour of salvation talk.[6]

We could perhaps agree to let "revelation" designate the "cognitive" aspect of salvation—that is to say, make our theology of revelation a section in a wider theology of salvation. Revelation would then be salvation for our mind, the solution of our intellectual bewilderments. Or we could reserve revelation for the initial encounter with God and the first call to faith. Salvation would be the whole subsequent working out of this initial experience, the transformation that follows when we accept God's word and allow it to change our lives.

Or else we might counter-attack in defense of revelation terminology. After all revelation is both informative *and* effective. The very fact that God speaks to us is a saving and transforming gift. Revelation is no presupposition *prior* to salvation. In and through the divine self-manifestation God saves us. The word of God shows itself to be dynamic, "living and active" (Heb 4:12), as well as noetic. If it signifies and communicates something, it also effects what it signifies and brings about a saving communion between God and human beings. Thus St Paul understands his apostolic preaching to communicate the realities it proclaims. As the word of God this preaching creates the faith and reconciliation it announces (2 Cor 5:18–20). The apostle's proclamation is no mere "disinterested" narration of past events. This word brings the revealing and saving action of God to bear on its hearers (Rom 10:14ff.). Such a dynamic understanding of revelation finds its Old Testament roots in passages like this classic one from Isaiah:

> For as the rain and snow come down from heaven, and return not thither but water the earth, making it bring forth and sprout, giving seed to the sower and bread to the eater, so shall my word be that goes forth from my mouth; it shall not return to me empty, but it shall accomplish that which I purpose, and prosper in the thing for which I sent it (55:10f.).

This appreciation of the word draws support from much twentieth-century speech-theory which notices and incorporates the effective and dynamic dimension of truly human dialogue. Genuine sharing and self-disclosure affects the partners in dialogue. They do much more than reveal facts about themselves. Through self-revelation and mutual acceptance they change each other.

To sum up: Two possible moves present themselves. We could make the theology of *salvation* dominant, but hasten to acknowledge that essentially there must be a revelatory side to salvation. God's mystery is manifested definitively in Christ our Savior, and we find there livable answers to our questions and bewilderments about suffering, sin, death and the rest. Or else we could let *revelation* play a primary role, while insisting that God's self-revelation is ever so much more than the mere communication of information. Salvation and grace form the other side of the coin. God's word always bears with it healing and saving grace. When it calls its hearers to faith, it powerfully enables them to respond in just that way. If it is a word, it is "the word of life" (1 Jn 1:1). It is the truth which transforms.

Two feasible versions of the divine self-presentation in Exodus 3:14 indicate the way revelation and salvation lie very close together. We could paraphrase the passage to read: "I reveal myself as the one who reveals himself" or "I am (active as) the one who is at work."[7] The first rendering highlights revelation, the second suggests salvation.

The Second Vatican Council did not choose between "revelation" and "salvation" but employed the terms almost interchangeably. In *Dei Verbum,* for instance, articles 2, 3 and 4 shuttle back and forth between the two terms. Take this passage from article 2:

> This economy of *revelation* is realized by deeds and words, which are intrinsically bound up with each other. As a result, the works performed by God in the history of *salvation* show forth and bear out the doctrine and realities signified by the words; the words, for their part, proclaim the works, and bring to light the mystery they contain. The most intimate truth which this *revelation* gives us about God and the *salvation* of man shines forth in Christ, who is himself both the mediator and sum total of *revelation* [italics mine].

As far as the council was concerned, the history of revelation is the history of salvation and vice versa.

However, instead of either using the terms as practically synonymous or fretting over the choice between "salvation" and "revelation," we could use a "higher" terminology that embraces both and speak of the divine "self-communication." This involves both a revealing and a saving activity from God. Salvation and revelation constitute the history of the divine self-communication.

That revealing and saving history takes place within human experience, if it is to take place at all. Revelation entails the divine Revealer, the act of revelation and those who receive the revelation. Likewise salvation entails the Savior, the act of salvation and the saved. Revelation and salvation cannot, as it were, hang in the air without reaching their "object" and being accepted by their addressees. If God is revealed and salvation takes place, that revelation *comes to* the community (and individuals) and people *experience* salvation. In this sense revelation and salvation simply cannot happen *outside* the experience of human beings. Experience (understood in terms of the full analysis given in Chapter II) is the place where God's revelation and salvation have occurred and will continue to occur.

Hence I propose to speak of revelation as part of the total process of *experiencing the divine self-communication.* "Experience" recalls the place where the individual subject and the community meet God. "Self-communication" reminds us that revelation always entails grace, that active *presence* of the triune God who delivers us from our evils and comes to share with us the divine life.

No other writers have more beautifully expressed the human experience of the divine self-communication than John and Augustine. (Both here and later, for the sake of convenience I speak of "John" without thereby intending to take a position on the authorship of the Gospel, the letters and the Book of Revelation. For the purposes of this work it is enough that the Johannine corpus comes from Christians of the apostolic Church.) The first letter of John begins by testifying to that revelation which was *heard, seen* and *touched* in Jesus Christ. It proclaims the apostolic experience of the Father's self-manifestation in his Son:

> That which was from the beginning,
> which we have heard,
> which we have seen with our eyes,
> which we have looked upon and touched with our hands,
> concerning the word of life—
> the life was made manifest,
> and we saw it, and testify to it,
> and proclaim to you the eternal life
> which was with the Father and was made manifest to us—
> that which we have seen and heard
> we proclaim also to you,
> so that you may have fellowship with us;
> and our fellowship is with the Father
> and with his Son Jesus Christ (1 Jn 1:1–3).

In his turn Augustine fastens upon the five senses to describe his conversion. He heard, saw, smelled, tasted and touched God. Or rather God took the initiative and spoke to him, shone upon him, shed fragrance about him, touched him and let him taste the divine goodness.

> You called to me; you cried aloud to me; you broke my barrier of deafness. You shone upon me; your radiance enveloped me; you put my blindness to flight. You shed your fragrance about me; I drew breath and I gasp for your sweet odor. I tasted you, and now I hunger and thirst for you. You touched me, and I am inflamed with love of your peace (*Confessions* X, 27).

All of this is nothing else than a powerful and poetic way of expressing Augustine's total experience of God—that is to say, the saving revelation which broke in and changed Augustine's life.

Both John and Augustine invoke the immediacy of their experience. John's statement gives considerable space to the active aspect of the apostolic experience: "What we have heard, seen, looked upon and touched we testify to and proclaim." Augustine's language highlights his own initial receptivity in the face of the divine activity: God called to him, cried aloud to him and so forth. Then comes Augustine's response which puts matters much more intensely than John: "I gasp, I hunger and thirst, I am inflamed with love of your peace." The degree of intensity and activity/passivity can vary, and—as I will later draw the distinction—John deals with the experience of "foundational" and Augustine with that of "dependent" revelation. Nevertheless, in both cases human beings contact God directly and not from a distance.

Furthermore, both John and Augustine speak of events in which they are personally and deeply involved, not pieces of information they have picked up second-hand from some authority nor conclusions they have reached through argumentation. They are very much alive when the experiences happen to them. These experiences disclose what their life is and is to be. Their entire existence is affected; we can spot a multi-leveled structure in what they go through. Their accounts show us how—in different degrees—the human senses, intellect, feelings, will, memory and other powers are involved. A further point: If in Augustine's case the subject of the experience is the individual person, John proclaims the collective experience of the apostolic community. What "we have seen and heard" has called that community into existence and shaped its destiny. Where Augustine's individual concerns come through strongly, John's proclamation summarizes a collective experience which founds and supports a common life and mission.

What I have just been doing, of course, is to apply to the passages from John and Augustine the first part of the analysis of experience provided in Chapter II. What was said there about "the subject" of experience fits nicely the classic testimonies both of John and Augustine. One might doggedly go through in detail the items listed under "the experience itself" and its "consequences" and match them with our two passages. For instance, the First Letter of John conveys the *concrete* nature of the apostolic experience ("what we have heard, seen, looked upon and touched"). The Fourth Gospel also suggests this theme of particularity by testifying that "the Word became flesh" (1:14). "Flesh" does not exist in general. "There" in the bodily person of Jesus the Word of God could be experienced concretely. Likewise the experiences of John and Augustine have meaning and purpose, reveal novelty, and can be classified as positive. Both writers discern, interpret, express and remember what they have undergone.

The account given of experience in general offers a means of reflecting systematically on the religious experiences which John and Augustine record and which are nothing if not experiences of God's revealing and saving self-communication to human beings. If then we want a brief answer to the question "*What* is revelation?" we can hardly do better than point to the experiences which—in their different ways—these two writers describe.

2. Means and Mediators

How was/is revelation experienced? Some years ago at a wedding luncheon in Oxford the guest next to me inquired what I was doing. "At the moment," I replied, "I'm writing a book on revelation." Excitedly he asked: "Have you had any revelations yourself?" Obviously he supposed that revelation always implied special, intense experiences in which one sees a vision or in an ecstasy hears some heavenly voice. This was to forget "the many and various ways" God has spoken and continues to speak (Heb 1:1). As *all* human experience entails an ultimate, religious element, it bears a primordial, transcendental revelation and can become a consciously religious experience to constitute an historical self-communication of God. Every experience has then the potential to convey in a particular way God's revealing and saving grace.

Hence the means of revelation encompass both common and uncommon experiences, all manner of positive *and* negative experiences, "what is past, or passing, or to come" (W. B. Yeats), and experiences of nature as well as those of history. Likewise the mediators of revelation can be indefinitely various: they stretch from the prophets, by whom "God spoke of old to our fathers" (Heb 1:1), through Christ and his apostles to some tired and sweating preacher in the Australian outback.

(a) First, the *common* and *uncommon* experiences. The Old Testament records an almost endless variety of experiences which have left their mark as means for the divine self-communication. An extraordinary vision mediates Isaiah's prophetic vocation (6:1ff.). But God also speaks to the prophets through ordinary inner states of anxiety or joy, through the current events of the external world and through everyday sights. Jeremiah sees an almond branch (1:11f.), a boiling pot (1:13ff.) and a potter at work (18:1ff.), and these sights all bring him God's word. Ezekiel's ecstasies, the patriarch Joseph's dreams and the theophanies experienced by Moses convey God's revealing and saving purposes. But these purposes manifest themselves also through ordinary episodes like the fall of Jerusalem in 587, a minor political catastrophe which has happened over and over again in secular history. The psalms of individual lamentation and thanksgiving repeatedly speak of such all-pervasive human troubles as sickness, false accusation, loneliness and persecution. The anonymous sufferers recall those situations and their experience of God's activity on their behalf. An example:

The cords of death encompassed me,
   the torrents of perdition assailed me;
The cords of Sheol entangled me,
   the snares of death confronted me.

In my distress I called upon the Lord;
   to my God I cried for help. . . .
He reached from on high, he took me,
   he drew me out of many waters.
He delivered me from my strong enemy,
   and from those who hated me (Ps 18:4–6, 16f.).

The Israelites come to appreciate God and the purpose of life both through exceptional moments and highly dramatic events like the exodus from Egypt and, as in the case of Qoheleth, through facing and quietly pondering the everyday experience of death which says so much about the vanity of human wishes.

The psalms testify to one way the Israelites experienced God's presence and power in situations that regularly recurred or through activities in which they repeatedly engaged—like pilgrimages to Jerusalem and worship in the temple. Yet the same people were invited by the prophets to await and accept God's intervention in what was not common and ordinary but new and extraordinary. Once upon a time the prophets were mistakenly credited with foreseeing and foretelling in a precise way the experiences that lay ahead. Such detailed foreknowledge concerned above all the coming Messiah, as most (though not all) of the passages about the Messiah are found in the prophetic writings. This much, nevertheless, remains true: in the name of the God who brings the future, the prophets called for an openness to new experiences and unexpected situations.

Amos expected Israel's present existence to end through some new divine action (8:1f.; 9:1–4). Hosea proclaimed a renewal which would let the people experience a fresh start: "The children of Israel shall return and seek the Lord their God, and David their king; and they shall come in fear to the Lord and to his goodness in the latter days" (3:4f.; see 2:6f., 14f.). Isaiah announced a new David (9:1–6; 11:1–10), Jeremiah a new covenant (31:31ff.), Ezekiel a new life for the people (37:1–14) and Second Isaiah a new exodus (40:1ff.). Nothing expressed more strongly the need to reckon with new, surprising experiences than the divine command in Second Isaiah: "Remember not the former things, nor consider the things of old. Behold, I am doing a new thing" (43:18f.). H. W. Wolff sums up the way in which the prophets called the people to face new events in which God's saving and revealing activity would be experienced:

The breakthrough to what lies in the future is the heart of their mission and the essential element in their prophetic office. To be sure, they are concerned with Israel's traditions and history, and even more with its present, but the accounts of their calls and of the missions entrusted to them make it clear that the absolutely decisive factor is the announcing and bringing in of what is radically new.[8]

It seems incontestable. The experiences which carry divine revelation into human history can stretch from what is utterly common to what is stunningly new and unique. This conclusion emerges easily from reflection on the Old Testament with its rich variety of historical, sapiential and prophetic writings. This record of Israel's experience is four times as long as the New Testament and took something like a thousand (as opposed to a hundred) years to come into existence. One gets the sense that in their human and religious experience the Israelites noticed everything and forgot nothing.

At the same time, however, the briefer New Testament record substantiates the same thesis: all manner of ordinary and extraordinary experiences mediate God's saving revelation. In his preaching Jesus introduced a wide range of everyday events which point to God's mercy, presence and power: a woman hunting through her house for some mislaid money, a boy who leaves home to see the world, the growth of crops, straying sheep and many other items which belonged to daily life in ancient Galilee. Jesus' ministry took place in the violent setting of a divided country occupied by a foreign power—a tragic situation that turns up repeatedly in human history. In such a context the killing of a religious reformer like John the Baptist and the slaughter of those Galileans "whose blood Pilate mingled with their sacrifices" (Lk 13:1) came easily. At the end Jesus himself was executed in a way which had become, as Zeffirelli's *Jesus of Nazareth* powerfully portrayed, a "normal" enough affair under the Roman administration. In that sense the crucifixion also belonged among "ordinary" experiences which convey God's saving revelation. Nevertheless, one must also remember the miracles of the ministry and the other extraordinary experiences—above all the resurrection—which belonged to the means by which revelation reached us. Nothing could be more "extraordinary" and "uncommon" than Christ's victory over death, the beginning of the new creation.

All in all, few would disagree with the assertion that in the Old Testament, in the New Testament and, for that matter, in our situation today God's saving revelation is communicated through an indefinitely wide range of experiences: from the most dramatic to the most ordinary and from the most unusual to the most commonplace. God's purposes can here be served by events and activities of all kinds—from the remarkable language of Second Isaiah to the dull words of some twentieth-century preacher. Family life, political episodes, religious worship, aesthetic experience, economic movements and other human realities can all provide the raw material through which God's saving word comes to us. In a few pages I want to insist on and clarify the distinction and difference between revelation in the biblical or foundational period and revelation in the post-biblical or dependent period. Here I wish simply to note that in *both* periods an endless variety of experiences could or can transmit the divine revelation. That looks beyond contention.

Resistance, however, might occur if we reflect on "primitive" means for conveying revelation. In the Old Testament did God really communicate through the dreams of the patriarch Joseph (Gen 37–41) and the casting of lots (1 Sam 14:37)? Embarrassingly enough, we find the dreams of St. Joseph and Pilate's wife in Matthew's Gospel and—perhaps worse still—the vision which came to Paul by night and led him to evangelize Macedonia (Acts 16:9f.). Of course, Jung and others encourage us to assign more importance to our dream-life and agree that it might not be a concession to some "primitive" instinct of human beings if God were to use dreams as means of revelation and salvation. A magical (?) practice like the casting of lots to determine Judas' successor in the apostolic college (Acts 1:15–26) might still make us wince. Would God genuinely indicate the divine choice that way?

(b) More serious doubts will flare up once we start talking about positive *and negative* experiences as means that mediate divine revelation. It provokes little argument to nominate among those means the deliverance, the prayer, the visions, the conversion and other positive and "peak" religious experiences of individuals and groups. "Neutral" means like dreams and the drawing of lots might be fairly readily accepted. But what of suffering, evil and sin? Yet we must not blot out the role of such negative experiences when we respond to the question: How is God's saving revelation communicated to us?

Some examples serve to establish the function of negative experiences. If the Israelites knew their God through the peak experience of their deliverance from Egypt, God also spoke to them through the trough experience of their subsequent deportation to Babylon. The passage we examined above from the First Letter of John builds itself around "the word of life" which has been "heard," "seen," "looked upon" and "touched." But the same Johannine literature witnesses as well to the experience of Christ's death and invites us to "look on him whom they have pierced" (Jn 20:35–37). St. Paul recalls the dramatic meeting on the Damascus road which turned his life around (1 Cor 15:8; Gal 1:11ff.). Yet he also sees the divine power of salvation manifested in the "weakness" or utter vulnerability he continually experiences (2 Cor 4:8ff.; 6:4ff.; 11:23ff.; 12:10). Pope John and the Second Vatican Council belong among the latter-day signs of the times, but so too do Auschwitz and the holocaust.

In theory and even more in practice, many people show a real reluctance to admit that episodes of ugliness rather than beauty, of hatred rather than love, and of sin rather than virtue can become the channels of God's saving revelation. Such experiences seem destructive rather than redemptive, confusing and threatening rather than illuminating. Nevertheless Christian Scriptures and human experience agree: evil, including sin, can form the means by which the divine revelation takes place. When King David committed adultery and murder, his sin occasioned some profound moments of truth about his state before God (2 Sam 11–12).

In this case the courageous intervention of the prophet Nathan helped David to discern and interpret the situation very quickly. Frequently, however, episodes of evil and sin do not reveal their meaning and finality so readily. It might take years, a lifetime or even more before some disorders or seemingly pointless atrocities can be appreciated for what they genuinely say about revelation and salvation. Sinful and tragic experiences can leave us endlessly puzzled. If the first Christians rapidly appreciated and interpreted the positive experience of the resurrection, their master's shameful death did not quickly yield up its meaning and purpose. Initially little sense seems to have penetrated their reflection on the experience of Good Friday. At first they could only say that the crucifixion happened "according to the definite plan and foreknowledge of God" (Acts 2:23), which is about as minimal an interpretation as one might offer.

On the basis of innumerable examples from the Bible and Christian (not to mention non-Christian) religious experience, the conclusion stands. Negative episodes of suffering, evil and sin, as well as happier "moments of glad grace" (Yeats), can convey the divine self-manifestation.

(c) As regards *time* we should also admit a large view. Experiences past, present and to come can all communicate the saving revelation of God. In the Old Testament the theme of God's "glory" (*kabod*) illustrates this helpfully. The liberation from Egypt lived on powerfully in the Israelite memory; in that *past* event God had manifested his glory. The ancient song of Moses began by declaring: "I will sing to the Lord, for he has triumphed gloriously" (Ex 15:1; see 14:18; 15:7; 16:6f.). Second Isaiah associates the divine glory with the experience of a deliverance *yet to come:*

> Every valley shall be lifted up;
> and every mountain and hill be made low;
> the uneven ground shall become level,
> and the rough places a plain.
> And the glory of the Lord shall be revealed,
> and all flesh shall see it together (Is 40:4f.).

Finally, the notion of glory is extended to the *ever-present* sights of nature. Psalm 19 begins thus:

> The heavens are telling the glory of God;
> and the firmament proclaims his handiwork.

What can be experienced day by day manifests God's glory.[9]

The Book of Revelation presents the Lord God as "the Alpha and the Omega," the almighty Savior and Revealer, "who is and who was and who is to come" (1:8). In present experiences, remembered experiences from the past and hopes for the future, human beings know that revealing and saving activity of God which aims at creating "a new heaven and a new earth" (Rev 21:1–4). "What is past, or passing, or to come" serves the divine self-communication to human beings and their world. This theme will recur when we discuss the "when" of revelation and its definitive climax in Christ and the apostolic experience.

(d) Like the means and times of the divine self-communication, the *mediators* and messengers of that saving revelation have been and remain indefinitely various. It is not that those mediators always and necessarily enjoy a personal head start for themselves in the business of salvation. But a constant characteristic breaks through the whole history of God's self-communication, both inside and outside the Jewish-Christian story: certain individuals enjoy uncommon (religious) experiences or else they display an uncommon capacity to discern, interpret and express the experiences which their community shares in common. Either way they play a special role in communicating the divine revelation and salvation. Whether institutionalized (for example, as bishops and priests) or non-institutionalized (like prophets), these individuals prove themselves to be chosen channels through which people at large experience God's self-communication. In this sense there is no absolute democracy in the human experience of God. Hence part of our answer to the question "*How* does the divine self-communication occur?" must consist in pointing to the role and variety of mediators and messengers.

Such mediators people the pages of both the Old and the New Testament: Abraham, Moses, the prophets, Mary of Nazareth, the apostles and—the supreme case—Jesus himself. The history of Christianity (and non-Christian religions) shows a constant line of men and women whose special gifts helped to convey God's saving word to others: saints, founders of religious movements and families, great artists, outstanding Church leaders, prophetic figures and the rest. Nor should we pass over in silence the innumerable lesser mediators: from Christian parents in Mexico to catechists in Africa, from parish priests in California to Sisters of Mercy in London slums. We will examine later the roles of some of these mediators, in particular Christ and his apostles. Here let us dwell on one group, the *Old Testament prophets*.[10]

Even a cursory glance at the phenomenon of Old Testament prophecy reveals its rich variety: from the early prophets like Deborah, Elisha and Elijah, through such classic prophets as Amos, Hosea and Isaiah, finally down to the post-exilic prophets like Haggai, Zechariah and Malachi. In a wider sense Moses (Deut 18:15ff.) and David (Acts 2:29f.) were called prophets. The name belonged also to the non-Israelite Balaam (Num 22–24) and to those bands of ecstatic Yahwistic prophets who used music and dancing to enter a state of frenzied exaltation and induce divine utterances (1 Sam 10:5ff.; 19:23f.; 1Kgs 22:10, 12). These court prophets were hardly distinguishable from their Canaanite counterparts among the prophets of Baal (1 Kgs 18:17–40). Prophetic elements also showed up in the life and work of Nazarites like Samson. The Old Testament record of prophets and prophetic experiences exhibits a remarkable diversity.

One way or another, all prophets were called to interpret and make known the divine mind and will. God was specially present to the point of identifying with what they said (or did). Their personal judgments and human words became endowed with divine authority. In the Old Testament the expression "the word of God" occurs 247 times, and in 225 of these cases we are dealing with a prophetic word.[10a]

The story of the prophets matches point after point from the account of experience given in Chapter II. Let us first take up some of the items listed under "the subject of experience" which can help us to reflect systematically on the prophetic experience. Amos records the *intense immediacy* of his call; it was something which suddenly and directly came to him, even though he lacked apparent preparation and training. God abruptly intervened and swept Amos into a new existence. The shepherd-turned-prophet explained to the priest of Bethel: "I am no prophet nor a prophet's son; but I am a herdsman, and a dresser of sycamore trees, and the Lord took me from following the flock and the Lord said to me, 'Go, prophesy to my people Israel' " (Am 7:14f.; see 3:8). Amos and other classical prophets did not take the initiative in actively seeking a prophetic career. They experienced a call coming to them from the outside. God unexpectedly overwhelmed them and, as Jeremiah's complaints vividly illustrated, prophets might accept and follow that call with deep reluctance (see, for instance, Jer 20:7–9). Hence, if the prophetic experiences exemplified the immediacy of a direct and deep encounter with God, the role of the prophets—at least initially—was passive rather than active. They reacted only after God had acted upon them.

Further, the life of the prophets got revealed in their experience. It disclosed what their life was and was to be. If God's call took Amos' life in new directions, this was even more startlingly true of Jeremiah. His life coincided with his prophetic vocation and experience.

Then again, the prophetic experience comes across generally as a multi-leveled affair affecting *the entire existence of the subject* and involving a broad range of spiritual and physical powers. Admittedly, mere frenzied delirium characterizes the early bands of prophets, and—of course— we should agree in principle that ecstasy can be a medium for communicating genuine revelation. Nevertheless, by reducing consciousness or at least personal control, ecstasy is not a fully human form for conveying God's saving message and becomes less prominent as time goes by. To be sure, we face an unusual psychological intensity, even abnormality, in Ezekiel's visions, ecstasy, shaking, dumbness and possible temporary paralysis (3:26; 24:27; 33:22 etc.). However, the classical prophets normally do not mediate the divine message through ecstasy, dreams or other such states but by consciously using their various powers. They look, listen, answer and deliver a message. Isaiah's vision in the temple ends thus:

And I heard the voice of the Lord saying, "Whom shall I send, and who will go for us?" Then I said, "Here am I! Send me." And he said, "Go, and say to this people: 'Hear and hear, but do not understand' " (Is 6:8f.).

Another case: The word of the Lord first questions Jeremiah about the things he sees before communicating the divine intentions (Jer 1:11, 13; see Amos 8:1f.). Here and elsewhere prophecy presents itself as a multi-leveled experience involving the whole person and a broad range of human powers.

As regards the items Chapter II considered under "the experience itself," we have already noted how the theme of newness pervades the prophetic stance and message. Another item: Like other experiences the prophetic experience does not exist in general. Usually the prophetic writings help to make this point by specifying the date and place of their origin. The Book of Amos begins: "The words of Amos, who was among the shepherds of Tekoa, which he saw concerning Israel in the days of Uzziah, king of Judah and in the days of Jeroboam the son of Joash, king of Israel, two years before the earthquake" (1:1). Isaiah names the date and place of the vision which communicated his prophetic call (6:1). Jeremiah indicates that the word of the Lord came to him:

. . . in the days of Josiah the son of Amon, king of Judah, in the thirteenth year of his reign. It came also in the days of Jehoiakim the son of Josiah, king of Judah, and until the end of the eleventh

year of Zedekiah, the son of Josiah, king of Judah, until the captivity
of Jerusalem in the fifth month (Jer 1:2f.).

For all his abnormality, the priest and prophet Ezekiel also provides details as to the date and place of his experiences (1:1–3). The prophetic
experience is nothing if not *concrete*. It happens at particular times, in
particular places, and to particular persons who must convey this or that
message to specific audiences.

    Lastly, the third section of the scheme on experience ("the conse-
quences of experience") clearly touches the prophets. What they experienced was to be discerned, interpreted and *expressed*. Let us pause for
a moment on the last point. The Nicene Creed ("the Holy Spirit *spoke*
through the prophets") reminds us that the prophets were speakers rather
than writers. Primarily they spoke and only secondarily did they write—
either by themselves or using a secretary, as Jeremiah seems to have done
with Baruch (Jer 36). Or else it was left to others (possibly disciples)
to collect, write out and publish the prophetic utterances. The prophets
themselves proclaimed the word—announcing God's saving intentions and
denouncing human failure. The prophetic message also got expressed
through symbolic gestures. Thus Isaiah acted out a threatening future
by going around naked like a prisoner-of-war (Is 20:2). Jeremiah wore
a yoke on his shoulders (Jer 27). He remained unmarried and childless—
to suggest the grim prospects that awaited Jewish parents and children
(16:1ff.). Hosea may have entered an unhappy marriage as a means of
communicating his word from the Lord. As well as expressing some message, all these symbolic gestures also mysteriously helped to bring about
what they represented. In that way the prophets shared in the dynamic
role of God's revealing word, which effects what it signifies.

    The last part of this book will take up the theme of inspiration. To
anticipate matters, we can relate the various kinds of inspiration by recognizing that the special divine self-communication to the prophets meant
this. They were inspired to speak and act, but—in general—not to write.
The inspiration to write down the prophetic utterances belonged rather
to those who came after them.

    The same point emerges also from the descriptions that Isaiah, Jer-
emiah and Ezekiel give of their vocations: they were all called to *speak*.
The lips of Isaiah were consecrated for that mission (6:6f.), while Jeremiah
received the word of the Lord in his mouth (1:9). Ezekiel, admittedly,
had to eat a scroll which was to fill his stomach (2:8—3:3). This image
suggests writing. Yet even in his case the predominant theme remains
speaking (2:4, 7; 3:1, 4 etc.).

    Much of what we have just been reviewing about the Old Testament
prophets—and in fact other material that appeared earlier in this chapter—must have raised for many readers the bothersome questions: Do

we really know that these things happened? The disclosure and inter-pretation of the divine name (Ex 3:14) could be no more than an ex-planation of the traditional name "Yahweh" made by later Israelites, retrojected into the history of Moses and there attributed to God. At other times it is likewise clear that the biblical writers (and the traditions they drew on) used the rubric "The Lord said to Moses" not on the basis of some special historical experience of God in their great leader's life but simply to ensure the authority of such things as the detailed moral legislation in Leviticus. As regards the prophets, can we now discern that their experiences (which all reach back more than two thousand years) authentically derived from God? Answers to such questions become even more problematic when we recall that the Old Testament was interested primarily in hearing the message of the prophets and not in examining their personal experiences as such. Let us, however, bracket for a moment these issues. Before leaving the question "*How* did/does revelation enter human experience?" we should attend to one final matter—the theme of *history*.

(e) Christianity is professedly an historical religion which believes the divine self-communication to have taken place normatively through a specific series of events and the experiences of a specific set of people. God's saving word came through the history of Israel and then—in a definitive fashion—through Jesus of Nazareth and the experiences in which he was involved. Christians now experience God's self-communi-cation reaching them through preaching, sacraments and other ritual ac-tions which interpret and re-enact those past events. The mediation of revelation and grace by means of the sacramental life, the Scriptures, the preached word and other channels remains essentially linked to the ac-ceptance of authoritative testimony about certain past acts of God on our behalf. Thus the remembered and interpreted past is deeply significant for the experience of revelation and salvation today. Belonging as they do to an historical religion, Christians recall, discern and express what happened "then" and "there," at given points in space and time, both to and through particular persons and groups of people. *History is the means par excellence* by which the divine self-communication has entered and continues to enter human experience. In short, transcendental rev-elation has assumed and continues to assume historical forms so as to constitute the history of revelation (and salvation).

But before dealing in detail with history, let me interject some re-marks about the experience of *nature* and the way the Scriptures sub-ordinate it to history as a means of mediating God's self-communication. The New Testament, being absolutely centered on the history of Christ and the origins of the Church, has little to say about experiencing God through nature (Acts 14:15, 17; Rom 1:18–23). Out of the little we have,

Paul's classic passage in Romans emphasizes human failure rather than the positive opportunity to know God through the created world. The Old Testament, however, is richer here. Job (38—39) poetically celebrates the Creator's power and intelligence which can be known and experienced through the world of nature. Some psalms praise the beauty and harmony of creation (19:1–6). The immensity of nature, and especially the vastness of the sea, mirrors God's absolute superiority (Ps 104). If these psalms are presented as prayers of *individuals* (19:11–14; 104:1, 33–34), natural phenomena can also mediate a *collective* experience of the divine presence. Thus cloud, thunder, lightning and smoke indicate God's presence to the people as they wander through the wilderness of Sinai (Ex 19:16–19). Some phenomena of nature accompany a theophany inserted into the story of the exodus from Egypt.

It will be useful to add two points about the Old Testament. First, we are not confronted with an intellectual deduction or an Aristotelian style of natural theology which argues from the world to the existence and attributes of God. Even Wisdom 13:1–9 envisages no such deduction but rather an experience of nature through which human beings can know the divine presence and enjoy a living contact with God.

Second, the Israelite experience of nature was subordinate to their experience of history. In Chapter II we saw that ancient confession of faith which summarized the saving history through which the people experienced Yahweh's concern and favor (Deut 26:5–9). This historical perspective prevailed over any divine self-manifestation through nature. Even the "account of origins" given in the early chapters of Genesis fits into the larger context of Israel's salvation history. Those chapters show us how the Israelites, on the basis of specific experiences of God in their own history, thought about the origins of the world and the human race. The stories found there answered the question: What must the beginning have been like for our past and present historical experiences to be what they are? The subordination of everything to the experience of salvation history went so far that even the *feasts* which dealt with creation and nature were tied to Israel's history. The feast of unleavened bread (which took place in the first month at the beginning of the barley harvest) was linked to the exodus from Egypt (Ex 23:15; 34:18). The harvest feast at the end of the year commemorated the time of wandering in the desert (Lev 23:42f.). Originally the Passover feast seemed to have been an offering made by nomads when they began their New Year's migration from the steppes into the agricultural land. This feast too was drawn into the story of the exodus from Egypt (Ex 12). For the Israelites the experience of God through history took precedence over any divine self-communication through the seasonal events of nature as such.

The Second Vatican Council went biblical in subordinating to history any experience of God through the created world. Vatican I had considered the "supernatural" revelation mediated through biblical history *only after* recalling the knowledge of God available through the created world (DS 3004). But Vatican II elaborated at length on the divine self-communication in history *and only then* reaffirmed in a brief conclusion the teaching of Vatican I on the revelation mediated through created reality (*Dei Verbum*, 2–6).

Let us now return to *history* (as experienced, remembered and reenacted) and clarify its place as *the means* for God's self-communication. In the Old Testament the profession of faith at the offering of the first fruits (Deut 26:5–10) and at the renewal of the covenant at Shechem (Jos 24:2–13) expressed the conviction that various key events in Israelite experience came about through the special intervention of their God. The Israelites saw and interpreted the exodus and other crucial events as Yahweh's deeds that revealed the divine design and intentions in their regard. After their deliverance from the Egyptians Miriam and the other women did not celebrate the courage and cunning of the Israelites nor the brilliant leadership of Moses. Their song highlighted Yahweh's act of salvation:

Sing to the Lord, for he has triumphed gloriously;
the horse and his rider he has thrown into the sea (Ex 15:21).

Yahweh was acknowledged as the real agent of the victory: "I am the Lord your God, who brought you out of the land of Egypt, out of the house of bondage" (Ex 20:2).

The Christians inherited from Israel such conviction about God's saving deeds and added what they themselves had experienced in Jesus' life, death and resurrection. They discerned and interpreted these later events as the climax in the divine activity on behalf of the human race. Peter's speech on the day of Pentecost (and further speeches in Acts) stressed the deeds of God:

Men of Israel, hear these words: Jesus of Nazareth, a man attested to you by God with mighty works and wonders and signs which God did through him in your midst, as you yourselves know—this Jesus, delivered up according to the definite plan and foreknowledge of God, you crucified and killed by the hands of lawless men. But God raised him up, having loosed the pangs of death, because it was not possible for him to be held by it (Acts 2:22–24).

The Nicene Creed and other professions of faith would embody the same belief: certain historical experiences, centered on Jesus of Nazareth, definitively manifested God and carried a decisive meaning for human salvation.

In *Dei Verbum* the Second Vatican Council classically formulated what the biblical history of revelation and salvation entails:

> The *works* performed by God in the history of salvation show forth and bear out the doctrine and realities signified by the *words;* the *words,* for their part, proclaim the *works,* and bring to light the mystery they contain (2; italics mine).

The two elements, word and event (or work of God), call for a little scrutiny.

The series of *events* or collective experiences in which God is represented as acting and which make up the history of revelation and salvation includes things which undoubtedly took place (like the deportation to Babylon, the ministry of Jesus and the destruction of Jerusalem) and episodes like Adam's fall which—to put it mildly—do not belong in the same way to secular history. The dissimilarities between the known factual status of, let us say, Abraham's emigration from Ur and Haran into Canaan and Jesus' crucifixion are startling. Nevertheless, revelation and salvation history encompass events which on any showing are genuinely historical: some kind of exodus experience, the reign of David, the return from Babylon, the preaching of John the Baptist, the crucifixion, the destruction of Jerusalem and so forth. In the Roman Forum the carvings inside the Arch of Titus still vividly assure us about the factuality of what, in their very different ways, the Romans, the Christians and the Jews experienced at the fall of Jerusalem in A. D. 70. At the heart of the biblical history of revelation and salvation lies a set of events which certainly occurred—to be experienced then by believers and non-believers alike and accessible now to common historical investigation, even if one's discernment and interpretation of these experiences embodies a specifically theological understanding which is shared only by believers.

The *word* lights up the revealing and saving values of events, which in some cases might otherwise seem merely anonymous and meaningless blows of fate. Thus the message of Jeremiah, Ezekiel and Second Isaiah discerns and interprets the Babylonian captivity—something which without their prophetic word could look like just another dreary case of a small nation overrun and deported by a major power. The divinely authorized word of interpretation lets such events of secular history be seen as acts of God in the history of revelation and salvation.

Which is finally the more significant means for the divine self-communication to human beings—the experienced event or the interpreting word? In recent years many theologians have put full weight on the word rather than on the events to be interpreted. They stress the role of reflection, discernment, interpretation and perspective—in short, the place of the word—as the key to the history of revelation and salvation. Through the presence of the interpreting word secular history becomes here and there transparent and conveys God's saving intentions. Two examples can illustrate this approach.

In a review of Robert Dentan's *The Knowledge of God in Ancient Israel* James Burtchaell remarks:

> Dentan asserts too facilely that God has acted in Israel's history. Nothing in Israel's history is that peculiar. Israel was a people that knew the same ups and downs which befell other nations. What made her peculiar was not her history [=the events as such], but her historical reflection, and one suspects that the same theological understanding could have been provoked by the history of Ilium or of Media.[11]

Stephen Neill likewise refuses to admit anything special about the events and experiences which constitute *Heilsgeschichte* or salvation history. The point of divergence from profane history is found in one's perspective: "*Heilsgeschichte* and secular history are the same history: each from a different point of view is the story of God's providential government of the nations."[12]

In these terms to share the same "historical reflection," "theological understanding" and "point of view" will enable us to see a particular stretch of (biblical) history as revealing and saving. The required perspective will then have been supplied. But the events and experiences themselves were in no way peculiar but the same as those which befell all people and all nations. Such an account of revelation and salvation history, however, leaves unanswered the questions: Why was this special prophetic and apostolic interpretation available for *these* historical experiences and events and not for those? Was there something about *these* historical experiences that both required and requires that theological reflection? The line that Burtchaell, Neill and others take up makes the word so predominant over the events which it interprets that these events as such lose any special significance. But the truth about the history of revelation and salvation is surely the opposite? Ultimately the word remains subordinate to the events and, specifically, to those events concerned with the person who stands at the center of that history. God's supreme act in Israel's history was to raise Jesus from the dead. Here action has priority over word, the effected reality over any interpretation of it. In the history of Ilium and Media or in the general story of "God's providential government of the nations" we find no other event which could properly compare to the first Easter Sunday and support the same historical reflection, theological understanding and point of view.

(f) What may well have been affecting those who press the role of the word over the event is their puzzlement about what could possibly be meant by *"acts of God."* For a century or more too many theologians have labeled certain biblical events "acts of God" but failed to explain how the term was being used and what it meant. Hence if this discussion of history as the means of the divine self-communication is not to remain patently incomplete, we need to tackle that term. Any account of it should embody at least the following four points.

First, to characterize some event as an "act of God" is to recognize there a special presence and a particular activity of God. There are various degrees of engagement on the part of God. Some events or series of events (as well as persons) reveal more of the divine concerns and interests than others. In this sense not all ages, cultures and histories have an equally immediate relationship to eternity. To deny that there exist such various degrees of engagement with the world and its multiform history logically leads to deism.

Further, the particular divine activity denoted by an "act of God" remains at least in some measure recognizably independent of the world and created causality. Thus the resurrection of Jesus manifests in a unique way a totally independent divine causality. Other happenings designated as "acts of God" may *also* be "acts of man" and entail a finely meshed array of human causes and agents. Thus the events which bring about the Babylonian captivity or the execution of Jesus involve fairly elaborate interactions from different human agents. Yet even in such events a certain degree of independent divine creativity remains.

Third, acts of God imply a religious claim and convey some moral values. Thus the ministry, death and resurrection of Jesus challenged and continues to challenge men and women to acknowledge the divine claim being made and to decide on new patterns of action. On the day of Pentecost Peter's proclamation of God's activity in Jesus' life, crucifixion and resurrection concluded with the call to repent and be baptized (Acts 2:38).

Lastly, the special freedom and unpredictability of an act of God implies an element of mystery. Acts of God are never unambiguously so. They remain concealed to the extent that people may see or fail to see these events as acts of God. Recognition is uncompelled. The factor of relative concealment allows cognitive freedom to persist.

3. Discernment

Example after example that has been used to illustrate the means and mediators of the divine self-communication must have provoked the question for many readers: Can we be sure that we are *discerning* correctly when we take these experiences to be reliably derived from God? How far can sound interpretation take us here? On the one hand, we may not sweep aside the historical reality of Amos, Isaiah, Jeremiah, St. Paul, St. Augustine and others—not to mention Jesus himself—who have provided material toward answering the question "How did/does God's saving revelation take place?" Yet, on the other hand, we may sometimes wonder whether we possess sufficient data to form a reasonable judgment or—if we have enough data—whether we are correctly reading the experiences. It seems unnecessary to indulge an enormous parenthesis to investigate every case. Close attention to one classic and difficult example, the prophets, can exemplify the major issues.

For the Old Testament the prophetic *message,* conveyed through words and symbolic actions, remains primary. From the message we *may* be able to infer something about the personal experiences that lie behind it, but precise and assured evaluations will be hard to come by.

For one thing, there is the chronological gap between the final form of the biblical text and the actual events in the lives of the prophets. Oral and written traditions intervene before the final edition of the various prophetic writings becomes settled. That complex process must obviously reduce any hopes about reaching easy certainties here. Further, if the prophets affirm the divine origin of their message and do so frequently by means of such traditional formulas as "Thus says the Lord," they normally show no interest in analyzing their experiences as such.

Third, these formulas are so brief and stereotyped that they hardly describe in any real sense the nature of the experiences to which they may in given cases refer. Sometimes they are simply traditional expressions for introducing an authoritative message rather than autobiographical statements about some lived experience of the prophet. "The word of the Lord" and "Thus says the Lord" indicate a message from God, but do not necessarily entail the claim that the prophets literally heard an inner or an outer voice speaking to them. Such conventional categories of announcement may be just that—conventional and nothing more. Likewise "to receive a vision" becomes a technical term for a prophetic revelation and by no means should always be taken literally. All of this is not special pleading to cope with an embarrassment over prophetic language and experience. The Old Testament as a whole teems with conventionalized expressions and images featuring the overthrow of heavenly bodies, God riding upon a storm, the shaking of the earth, the anguish of childbirth and the rest. It would be crass and extreme fundamentalism to presume that such language should alway be interpreted *au pied de la lettre.*

Our problem comes to this. On the one hand, we should not expect all prophets to deliver a message that in form (and content) strikingly diverges from both earlier prophetic messages and from the general religious language of Israel. It would be absurd to demand that kind of originality as *the* test of authentic prophetic experience. On the other hand, however, the fact that in the form and content of their messages later prophets draw on earlier messages and language, even if they introduce their own modifications, obviously leaves us with the question: To what extent are they simply taking over a tradition and not reporting their own personal religious experiences? Where do the traditional elements end and where does their personal experience begin? To sum up: To demand total originality from the prophets would be to deny that they are human beings born into a society with its religious traditions and language. Yet the more their message resembles what has gone before, the more inclined we will be to question the reality and authenticity of their personal experiences. How high a degree of such resemblance with the past can we tolerate without capitulating to our doubts?

Fourth, we have to contend with a frequent vagueness about the beginning, the end and the nature of prophetic experiences. Prophets *see* visions and *hear* the Lord's word. And the visions can contain auditive elements. For instance, the ninth chapter of Amos opens with a vision and a threatening message from God:

> I saw the Lord standing beside the altar, and he said:
> "Smite the capitals until the thresholds shake,
> and shatter them on the heads of all the people;
> and what are left of them I will slay with the sword;
> not one of them shall flee away,
> not one of them shall escape" (9:1).

The following verses continue to convey a severe judgment on the people. Are we to suppose that these verses also communicate the message received by the prophet during the vision with which the chapter begins?

Further questions arise when we recall how the frontier between what is seen and what is heard often gets blurred. Take the case of Balaam. With "open eyes" and seeing "the vision of the Almighty" he delivers "the oracle" of one "who hears the words of God" (Num 24:15f.; see 24:3f.). What we have here is properly no vision but a message—words that the Lord puts into Balaam's mouth (Num 23:5, 12, 16.). Samuel's experience as a boy in the temple at Shiloh is called a "vision" (1 Sam 3:15), but the vision in fact consists in his hearing God's call. Quite often the biblical text will slip into speaking about prophets (or others) having "visions" and "seeing" something or about God "appearing" or "showing" this or that (Gen 28:1; Ex 3:12 etc.), when the point at issue is not some visual experience. Talk about a vision or an appearance may simply mean that a communication from God has taken place. A promise or some other message has been received. For example, it would be a mistake to insist on the visionary nature of the experience in Genesis 12:7. Even if it speaks of an "appearance," the text focuses rather on the promise communicated to Abraham: "The Lord appeared to Abram, and said, 'To your descendants I will give this land.' " Isaiah reports a "stern vision," but it is a vision that has been "told" to him, an "oracle" and something that he has "heard from the Lord of hosts" (21:1f., 10). Alongside this blurring of the frontier between word and vision, we constantly find in the Old Testament and, specifically, in the prophets a tendency to play down the visual phenomena. What is heard predominates over what is seen.

Fifth, the *call* of the prophets not only essentially shapes their stories but also highlights the difficulties of discernment and interpretation. The prophets know themselves to be specially chosen and called by God. Amos simply states his call as a fact (7:14), without elaborating on how it took place. But with others like Isaiah, Jeremiah and Ezekiel, we have call-narratives which use common ideas and motifs to express the individual experience of the prophets and the personal authority they possess from God.

Ronald Clements classifies the prophetic call-narratives into two groups.[13] The first group which includes Jeremiah recalls also the call-experiences of Moses (Ex 3:1–4:9), Gideon (Jgs 6:11–14) and Saul (1 Sam 9). Here God overcomes an inadequacy and reluctance on the part of the person called. Members of the second group through some vision of God are summoned to join the deliberations of the heavenly council (for instance, Isaiah, Ezekiel and Micaiah-ben-Imlah in 1 Kings 22:5–28). God may be represented as specially equipping the prophet for the task, as in the case of Isaiah where we meet the cultic motif of a ritual cleansing (6:6–8).

Now in both groups the prophet is warned that his message will be rejected and he must endure opposition. This raises the questions: (a) Does such a warning truly and always belong to the original call-experience? (b) Or is it a reflection from the subsequent experience of rejection which has been retrojected back into an original call-experience? Such a prior warning, narrated as part of the call-experience, also happily meets the objection: If the prophetic message were from God, the people would have accepted it. With such a warning inserted into the call-narrative, the tables are turned and the people's refusal to listen only confirms the authenticity of a given prophet. (c) Or again has a warning about the hostility and opposition to be met with become simply a traditional way of talking about a prophetic call? New prophets are aware of being authentically called by God, but stand in a tradition which prompts them to use traditional motifs to describe their personal experience.

Finally, we find in the prophetic books a persistent awareness of the need to discriminate true prophets from *false* ones. Both in the history of Israel and elsewhere the possibility of falsehood looms over all prophecy. Has God spoken through *this* prophet? Does the divine authority and a genuine (and genuinely interpreted) experience of God stand behind his message? Conflicts between rival prophets can exacerbate the difficulty of discernment (1 Kgs 22; Jer 27—28). The theological reflections of Thomas Aquinas carry the problem even further. He declares prophecy to be a transient rather than permanent gift—what he calls a "motion" rather than a "habit."[14] We can put the point less solemnly: a true prophet could on occasions speak falsely, a false prophet might be found on occasions to be speaking truly, or else a true prophet might simply cease to prophesy. Here and elsewhere, one must mark prophecy off from the institutionalized role of priesthood. Many societies (including Israel) have reckoned men to be priests if they are born into a priestly family. Besides birth, other kinds of public evidence might establish priesthood. If challenged, a Roman Catholic priest today could produce a document from the bishop who ordained him. But such documentary evidence is never available to authenticate prophecy. How then can discernment take place?

Sometimes the Old Testament simply labels certain men as false prophets (Jer 27:14), without developing the criteria for this judgment. In places a true prophet's call and personal experience may be used to legitimate his mission and message (Is 6:1—8:18). But usually *truth and falsity in prophecy are identified through three criteria:* past tradition, present behavior and future fulfillment.

Loyalty to the inherited faith provides a major criterion for sorting out prophets. Traditional orthodoxy predominates even over the fulfillment of a prophetic sign. A heterodox message will not only unmask false prophets, but should carry drastic consequences for them.

> If a prophet arises among you, or a dreamer of dreams, and gives you a sign or a wonder, and the sign or wonder which he tells you comes to pass, and if he says, "Let us go after other gods," which you have not known, "and let us serve them," you shall not listen to the words of that prophet or to that dreamer of dreams.... But that prophet or that dreamer of dreams shall be put to death because he has taught rebellion against the Lord, your God, who brought you out of the land of Egypt (Deut 13:1–3, 5).

More specifically, Jeremiah urges one major lesson from the nation's religious past. Normally the true prophets pronounced words of judgment and predicted disaster. Speaking to Hananiah, Jeremiah says: "The prophets who preceded you and me from ancient times prophesied war, famine, and pestilence against many countries and great kingdoms" (28:8; see 26:16ff.). The bearer of bad news is more likely to be a true prophet. Bearers of good news can easily be false prophets, dominated by their audience and ready to make pleasing announcements. Jeremiah does not propose the word of woe as an absolute criterion, and he recognizes that a prophet might bring good tidings of great joy. Yet such joyful prophecies will have to be judged by their fulfillment: "As for the prophet who prophesies peace, when the word of that prophet comes to pass, then it will be known that the Lord has truly sent the prophet" (Jer 28:9).

Present life style also serves to test prophetic authenticity. False prophets will lead lives stained by moral evil (Jer 23:9ff.). Hence one knows that "they speak visions of their own minds, not from the mouth of the Lord" (Jer 23:16). Through Jeremiah God names a couple of false prophets (Ahab and Zedekiah) who "have committed adultery with their neighbors' wives" and "have spoken in my name lying words which I did not command them" (Jer 29:21, 23). Isaiah points to some prophets whose vision is blurred by drunkenness. He concludes that these will "stumble in giving judgment" (28:7).

In this way prophetic authenticity can be verified or falsified by the test of present moral conduct rather than by attempts to investigate the historical origins of a prophetic career and pass judgment on the experiences which gave rise to it. As William James put this approach: "By their fruits ye shall know them, not by their roots."[15]

Where immoral conduct unmasks the false prophet, obedience to the divine will leads true prophets into a life of suffering. This suffering comes as part of the prophetic vocation and is not simply the suffering that virtuous people can expect. Just as the prophets afflict the people with news of woe and words of judgment, so they themselves will suffer hostility and be persecuted persons (Amos 7:10ff.). Loyalty to his prophetic mission brings Jeremiah deep suffering at the hands of the people, the king, the princes, the priests and the "prophets" (20:1ff.; 26:1–24; 36:1–32). He is known as a genuine prophet by the fruits of persecution. To say the least, true prophets do not profit in the worldly sense from their vocation. Nevertheless, suffering fails to prove an absolute criterion. False prophets do not always prosper; they may even have to endure a violent death (Jer 29:21).

Lastly, the future and the fulfillment of predictions have their place among the tests of prophecy. True and false prophets will be revealed in retrospect. The death of Hananiah, for example, establishes the falsity of his message and the truth of Jeremiah (Jer 28:15–17). Similarly the subsequent death in battle of Israel's king vindicates Micaiah-ben-Imlah's prophecy (1 Kgs 22). It is along such lines that Deuteronomy offers a general rule for determining whether a given prophetic message comes from the Lord or not:

And if you say in your heart, "How may we know the word which the Lord has not spoken?"—when a prophet speaks in the name of the Lord, if the word does not come to pass or come true, that is a word which the Lord has not spoken; the prophet has spoken it presumptuously, you need not be afraid of him (Deut 18:21f.).

Here we should be aware that fulfillment of a prophecy was taken in a larger sense. It was not necessarily some precise prediction exactly realized.[16] For his part Ezekiel witnesses to his God-given confidence that in the long run authentic prophecy will be acknowledged as such. The Lord encourages Ezekiel:

> The people are imprudent and stubborn: I send you to them; and you shall say to them, "Thus says the Lord God." And whether they hear or refuse to hear (for they are a rebellious house) they will know that there has been a prophet among them (Ez 2:4f.).

All in all, the Old Testament yields a broad range of criteria by which to evaluate prophetic authenticity. Past, present and future factors suggest ways of discerning the experiences and message of the prophets. The Old Testament declines to turn any single criterion into *the* decisive test. Both this refusal to absolutize matters and the individual criteria themselves give an obvious plausibility to the biblical attitude toward discernment. Yet, once we have digested and agreed about these criteria and the other material on the prophets, what conclusions can we draw about these major mediators of the divine self-communication?

As Christian fundamental theology—no less than theology as such—is properly an exercise in Christian faith seeking understanding, we might be content to base a positive discernment of the prophetic experience on our belief in Jesus Christ. He entered the history of a people who had been prepared by a special call and lengthy divine self-communication. The experiences of the prophet and the subsequent prophetic writings formed a major part of that given within which Christ played his normative role. It is then impossible to reject the prophetic experience in the Old Testament and still have one's Christian faith whole.

Such considerations can prompt us to accept *in general* that the Holy Spirit spoke through the prophets. Yet it remains hard to settle specifics and confidently affirm just how, when and where given prophets received those personal experiences of God which constitute historical revelation. Various episodes in the life of Jeremiah, for example, and Isaiah's vision in the temple could well count among such specific instances. In such cases we would inevitably tend to put the questions: Did the prophets perceive an external object or hear an external voice? Or were their experiences rather a matter of objective but interior voices and images? And for that matter, what did Moses see when he saw God "face to face" (Ex 33:11)? We might decide to press analogies from the experience of Christian and other mystics. Whatever answer we give to such questions, we will need at least to be aware of one thing. These are *our* questions and *our* distinctions. People in the Old Testament never thought in such terms. We may finish up looking for exact answers when the data really cannot support such precision.

Ultimately it seems reasonable to maintain in general a special divine self-communication through the prophets, while allowing that particulars can be difficult to discern and interpret.

4. The Time of Revelation

A Christian faith that systematically reflects on the divine self-communication in human history must sooner or later grapple with the question: *When* did or do human beings experience that revelation and salvation which comes from God? One could fling out a whole flurry of sub-questions on the when and the where of the divine self-communication in history. But three items offer a way in: (a) the preparation in the Old Testament history, (b) the absolute climax of God's self-communication in Christ, and (c) the continuing presence of revelation and salvation. In short, we can take up matters *before* Christ, *with* Christ and *after* Christ.

(a) When we wind our way back through Israel's history to its origins with the patriarchs, the exodus and the period of the judges, we run across preparatory elements which mark those early stages in the history of the divine self-communication. At the outset the Israelites had recourse to the interpretation of dreams, the casting of lots and other means for discovering the divine will and intentions. In all this they resembled closely enough their pagan neighbors. The existence of *sanctuaries* affords an interesting example here.[17]

The early Israelites visited sanctuaries to learn God's good will and pleasure. In more or less clear terms a priest of the place would undertake to deliver some divine oracle or response. A number of such places of worship and consultation turn up in the stories of the patriarchs: Bersabee, Bethel, Mambre and Sichem. When she conceived and was suffering from pregnancy pains, Rebekah went to a sanctuary and there received (presumably from an attendant priest) a word from God:

And Isaac prayed to the Lord for his wife, because she was barren; and the Lord granted his prayer, and Rebekah his wife conceived. The children struggled within her; and she said, "If it is thus, why do I live?" So she went to inquire of the Lord. And the Lord said to her, "Two nations are in your womb, and two peoples, born of you, shall be divided; the one shall be stronger than the other, the elder shall serve the younger" (Gen 25:21–23).

We meet a similar, later phenomenon when the Israelites were wandering in the desert. The "tent of meeting" acquired the role of a mobile sanctuary, where principally Moses but also others could consult God:

> Now Moses used to take the tent and pitch it outside the camp, far off from the camp; and he called it the tent of meeting. And everyone who sought the Lord would go out to the tent of meeting, which was outside the camp. Whenever Moses went out to the tent, all the people rose up, and every man stood at his tent door, and looked after Moses, until he had gone into the tent (Ex 33:7f.).

The Book of Judges yields a third example which suggests the way in which sanctuary priests sought the divine oracles. It seems that they could have used an ephod or liturgical garment when consulting God or soliciting a divine response (17:5ff.). At the time of the judges new sanctuaries took over from those of the patriarchal period: Dan, Gilgal, Mizpah and Shiloh. Israelites visited these places of worship to learn God's answer to the problems of their lives.

We might, of course, bundle out of sight the sanctuaries and other such "primitive," pagan elements in the history of revelation and salvation. However, they do belong to that special history of divine self-communication which directly prepared the way for the coming of Jesus Christ. Besides, the sanctuaries let us glimpse one particular feature in the Jewish experience and understanding of God's revelation. Even if the Israelites resembled their pagan counterparts in consulting such sources of divine oracles, nevertheless, their practice diverged from other Near Eastern religions in one important respect. In the other religions some idol or divine object served as a major means for receiving revelations. Among the Israelites, however, images of God were officially forbidden and hence could not be used as instruments for soliciting some divine communication.

The cult of sanctuaries and other early practices exemplify the simple beginnings in which God respected the situation, habits and culture of the Israelites. From there they would be led through various experiences of the divine self-communication to a deeper and richer religious understanding.

Earlier in this chapter we noted that breakthrough to *new* experiences of God and *fresh* interpretations of their religious history which characterized the on-going story of the prophets. There, as elsewhere in Israel's history, we find the divine self-commnication dynamically and progressively unfolding. The multi-faceted history of the people became the means par excellence for conveying revelation and salvation. Of course, there could be religious decline alongside religious progress, failures to live out of collective and individual experiences of God, as well as fruitful conversions coming from those experiences.

The Letter to the Hebrews saw the Old Testament period as conveying through many mediators a fragmentary and imperfect divine self-communication until the "last days" came when God spoke "by a Son" (1:1f.). Nevertheless, for all its imperfections, that preparatory revelation had at least one remarkable result which should engage our attention: *its concept of God.*

Israelite experience bred a concept of God which set Judaism quite apart from other peoples. At first the Israelites reckoned with the gods of other peoples. But with increasing clarity they came to acknowledge the unique and exclusive place, functions and freedom of their God. The gap between Yahweh and the other gods opened up to the point that the Israelites denied the reality of other gods. The difference between Judaism and other religions was more than just monotheism. Echn Aton's *Song of the Sun* clearly acknowledged only one God. And the Greek philosophers reached the notion of the Absolute as Unmoved Mover. We spot the fundamental differences when we recall that Echn Aton's one god was the sun god. And over against the conclusions of Greek thought, Yahweh, if utterly transcendent, was experienced not as a remote Unmoved Mover but as a tender, loving God who called for exclusive love and loyalty from human beings and, especially, from Israel.

We would throw away any chance of really appreciating the Old Testament image of God if we ignored the extraordinary way it combined two elements: *majestic transcendence* and *a loving closeness*. If initially and partly associated with sanctuaries and other such places, Yahweh was experienced as transcending the limits of *space*. This God of the patriarchs not only encountered them in Haran, Canaan and Egypt but also transcended the usual national boundaries—bringing Israel on its exodus "from the land of Egypt, and the Philistines from Caphtor and the Syrians from Kir" (Am 9:7). Unlike the gods of other Oriental nations, Israel's deity was not identified in space as the sun or another heavenly body. The sun, the moon and the stars were among the things created by God (Gen 1:14–18). Yahweh also passed beyond the limits of *time*. Other Middle Eastern gods issued from chaos and various myths proclaimed their genesis. Israel's God, however, was known to be simply and always there, "the first and the last" (Is 44:6), the God who "in the beginning created the heavens and the earth" (Gen 1:1). The Israelites admitted neither a theogony nor an aging process for their God.

Despite this transcendence of space and time, however, Israel did not shrink from mythical language when speaking of the divine deeds. God crushed "the heads of Leviathan," "cut Rahab into pieces" (Ps

74:12–15; 89:10f.; Is 51:9f.), and came riding on a storm in a spectacular
scenario:

> Smoke went up from his nostrils,
>   and devouring fire from his mouth;
>   glowing coals flamed froth from him.
> He bowed the heavens, and came down;
>   thick darkness was under his feet.
> He rode on a cherub, and flew:
>   he came swiftly upon the wings of the wind
> Ps 18:7–10; see 29:3–10; 77:17–20).

Aristotle would have valued the transcendence of Israel's God, but he
could not have accepted the lively, mythical imagery of the psalmist. Israel's neighbors could have accepted such mythical language, but they
did not recognize a God who transcended space and time.

As regards sexuality, we likewise find a striking blend of elements
in Israel's attitude toward God. On the one hand, Yahweh had no spouse
and offspring and simply remained beyond the sexual activities typical
of ancient gods. But, on the other hand, Hosea and other prophets had
no scruple in talking of God as a husband who revealed a wounded but
tender love when his people acted like a harlot:

> Behold, I will allure her,
>   and bring her into the wilderness,
>   and speak tenderly to her (Hos 3:14).

Second Isaiah pictured God as "crying out like a woman in travail" (Is
42:14), or as a woman who gave birth to and carried Israel (Is 46:3f.;
see 49:15). Once again we run up against a remarkable combination: Yahweh was known to transcend sexuality, and yet the Israelites felt free
to introduce masculine and feminine imagery in describing God as mother,
father and spouse.[17a]

To sum up all this: The Israelites experienced Yahweh as a loving,
saving and tenderly devoted God. At the same time they had a most
elevated notion of their deity. Being so utterly transcendent, Yahweh was
not to be represented in any pictorial form. Divine images were strictly
forbidden (Ex 20:4f; Lev 19:4; Deut 4:15–20).

This highly elevated and yet intensely personal notion of God was
the finest product from the human experience of the divine self-communication in the Old Testament. To talk apologetic language: One could
style this notion a moral miracle that could only have come from authentic
experiences of God and was not to be explained through the "merely"

human powers of a tiny nation which enjoyed no philosophical or other special intellectual talents.

(b) Christian faith holds that God's saving and revealing self-communication came to its *absolute climax with Jesus of Nazareth.* The history of revelation and salvation had been moving progressively and irreversibly toward that goal. The many Old Testament mediators gave way to *the* Mediator of revelation and salvation. A complete and perfect self-communication of God followed on many partial and fragmentary communications. The earlier revelations were directed toward this point. *"Now* the righteousness of God has been manifested . . . the righteousness of God through faith in Jesus Christ" (Rom 3:21f.). This "now" was the goal of God's previous self-communication, and the future will be nothing but the future of this "now" in Christ.

In the New Testament record (which centers on the person of Jesus Christ), the experience which he had evoked and continued to evoke in others found a broad range of expressons. What Christ meant for the divine self-communication to human beings could never be adequately and exhaustively stated. Both the memory of their experience of him (shared by the core group of apostles) and the on-going experience of him (in the entire community of Christians) were multi-faceted and prompted a rich diversity of expression within a basic unity. If, for example, the Synoptic Gospels all stressed *the rule of God* as crucial to the experience of Jesus' ministry, they each had their own particular emphasis. Mark presented Jesus as *proclaiming* God's rule (1:14). For Luke, Jesus came bringing *the good news* to the poor and suffering (4:16ff.), while Matthew clung to the theme of a Master whose *teaching* would endure forever (28:19f.).

If we are to grasp how the New Testament remembered, discerned, interpreted and expressed what—or rather who—was experienced "when the time had fully come" (Gal 4:4), we need to descend to some particulars. Three examples taken in chronological order can serve our purposes: *Paul's letters, the Synoptic Gospels* and *the Fourth Gospel.*

It is perilously easy to make a treatment of Paul heavy with a mass of citations and references. Hence I wish here only to recall and sketch *some major ways* in which the apostle interpreted and expressed *the experience* of the divine self-communication in Christ.[18] I acknowledge the importance of Pauline themes which highlight the "object" revealed to and then preached by the apostle—the "Gospel" or "Mystery" which, expressed concretely, was and remains the person of Christ himself. The following pages, however, attend rather more to Paul's experience of that Mystery.

If we run through the Pauline vocabulary, we find few terms that do not bear fairly immediately—either positively or negatively—on that experience. Some (positive) terms (nouns like "knowledge" and "revelation" or verbs like "to reveal," "to appear," and "to manifest") obviously have a *revelatory* ring to them. Other (positive) terms and expressions (like "dead to Sin," "freedom," "reconciliation," "new creation," "newness of life," "being *in* Christ," and "the Holy Spirit given to us") suggest various *salvific* aspects of the divine intervention through Christ. The following passage from 2 Corinthians, a letter which is particularly rich in the language of revelation, highlights the revelatory side of things: "It is the God who said, 'Let light shine out of darkness,' who has shone in our hearts to give the light of the knowledge of the glory of God in the face of Christ" (4:6). Present and future salvation features more prominently in this verse from Romans: "If the Spirit of him who raised Jesus from the dead dwells in you, he who raised Christ Jesus from the dead will give life to your mortal bodies also through his Spirit which dwells in you" (8:11).

Paul's letters vigorously vindicate the view that both the language and the reality of revelation and salvation intertwine or—to vary the image—are but two sides of the one coin. Just as the Second Vatican Council moves easily from the history of salvation to the history of revelation, so the apostle slips from revelatory to salvific language. One example: When God reveals "the fragrance of his *knowledge,*" it is to "those who are being *saved*" (2 Cor 2:14f.). Those, however, who do not receive the Gospel are blind *and* on the way to destruction; their failure vis-à-vis revelation means a failure vis-à-vis salvation and vice versa: "Even if our Gospel is *veiled,* it is *veiled* only to those who are *perishing.* In their case the god of this world has *blinded* the minds of the unbelievers, to keep them from *seeing* the light of the Gospel" (2 Cor 4:3f.; see 2:15f.).

In the light of the analysis that has been given of experience, we could do two things with the data from Paul. We might, first of all, use that analysis to reflect systematically on the apostle's testimony. Point after point fits. Thus his initial (and continuing) contact with Christ was no second-hand business, but an intense experience of something immediately happening to him. If Paul reacted to that experience, in the first instance he knew himself to be acted upon. God "was pleased to reveal his Son" to Paul, in order that in turn the apostle "might preach" that Son "among the Gentiles" (Gal 1:16; see 1 Cor 15:8, 11). That basic experience of Christ affected the entire existence of Paul, gave his life fresh meaning and purpose, and opened him up to a new future. In short, what has been said about "the subject of experience," "the experience itself" and its "consequences" can be readily applied to the case of Paul.

Second, in the apostle's letters—as elsewhere in the biblical literature—"experience" and "to experience" can frequently replace "knowledge" and "to know" without real loss or change of meaning.[19] Two examples: In Philippians Paul's confession of faith and hope could be phrased as follows:

I count everything as loss because of the surpassing worth of experiencing Christ Jesus my Lord. For his sake I have suffered the loss of all things . . . that I may experience him and the power of his resurrection (3:8, 10).

The Letter to the Ephesians—and here it does not concern us whether the letter came directly from Paul or not—prays for a "deeper knowledge" *(epignōsis)* of Christ, a term that could be just as well translated "a deeper experience" of Christ (1:17).

Before leaving Paul, we can usefully single out four particular themes which bear on the nature of the divine self-communication "when the time had fully come": the *initial* encounter that brought Paul a life *in Christ,* in which he knew both the *"Trinitarian"* shape of his experience and what he called *"power-in-weakness."*

St. Paul knew his meeting with the risen Christ on the Damascus road to be a stunningly unexpected, utterly "abnormal" birth into new life, *the* experience which drastically reorganized all his values and shaped his subsequent existence. "Last of all, as to one untimely born," he recalled, Christ "appeared also to me" (1 Cor 15:8; see 9:1; Gal 1:11ff.). That once-and-for-all experience not only turned Paul's life around (Phil 3:7ff.), but also brought him into the ranks of the apostolic founding fathers of the Church.[20] That "last of all" encounter closed the series of appearances by the risen Christ which gave Paul and a limited number of others the unique, unrepeatable and non-transferable task of officially witnessing to the resurrection (Acts 10:40f.) and of founding the Church (Eph 2:20; Rev 21:14). No later Christians would ever again either have precisely the same experience or receive the same role as witnesses and founders. In that sense it is preferable to speak of bishops as successors *to* the apostles. "Successors of the apostles" easily implies that bishops play the same role as the apostles. "Successors to" would remind us that bishops do not follow on the apostles in the way, for example, that President Jimmy Carter took over from Gerald Ford and assumed an *identical* set of powers and responsibilities. We cannot say that of the bishops vis-à-vis the apostles.

But to come back to Paul: Through his Damascus road experience he joined a once-and-for-all group, the apostles "chosen by God" as "witnesses" to the risen Christ (Acts 10:40f.). The later books of the New Testament already look back to that group as confined to Christianity's period of foundation (Jude 3, 17). The one beatitude in John's Gospel distinguished between apostles like Thomas who saw and believed and those other, later disciples who are blessed because they have not seen and yet believe (20:29). The last chapters of that Gospel reveal a special awareness of a decisive shift in the Church's life that was practically complete: from the apostolic generation with its uniquely direct experience of Christ to all subsequent generations of believers who would know Christ in the experience of faith. In their art, liturgy, legends, theologies, and Church doctrines, Christians continued to endorse the conviction that the experience and responsibility of the apostles were unique and non-transferable, or at least were so in the sense we have indicated. Their never-to-be-repeated experience and responsibility eventually were expressed in the axiom that "revelation closed with the death of the last apostle" (DS 3421).

As we shall shortly see, this axiom (which the Second Vatican Council declined to include in the document on revelation) can be somewhat misleading. In a highly important sense revelation is not "closed" but continues. Moreover, their basic reception of God's saving revelation in Christ's life, death, resurrection and giving of the Holy Spirit was over *years before* any of the apostles died, let alone the last of them. They received the divine self-communication essential to their task when the risen Lord appeared to them and gave them his Spirit. Of course, the memory of that immediate and privileged confrontation with Christ in his paschal mystery endured powerfully and productively in their lives. But the experience was over, even if the apostles could never be finished with remembering, interpreting and expressing it. It is not too much to say that the experience which made them apostles had an *exclusive* and once-and-for-all character to it—rather like the death of Christ itself (Heb 9:12, 26).

Paul blamed the Galatian Christians for not understanding and living up to their experience of the Spirit (3:1–5). He accused the Corinthians of failing to express in their conduct the Eucharist which they repeatedly celebrated (1 Cor 11:17ff.). But he *never* reproached or belittled anyone for not sharing his fundamental encounter with the risen Christ. We nowhere find in Paul's letters such questions as these: "Are you not Christians? Have you not seen Jesus our Lord? Has he not appeared also to you?" Further, even in Paul's own case the post-resurrection appearance of the Lord was a unique event which happened "then" and was over and done with. In later life the apostle had ecstatic experiences of a "heavenly" nature and, when harassed by "a thorn in his flesh" (however we identify that particular problem), was personally confronted by the risen Christ (2 Cor 12:1–4, 7–9). But Paul did not recognize even such remarkable "peak" experiences as being on the same level as the Damascus road encounter which put him among the ranks of those whose public witness to the risen Christ founded the Church.

The *once-and-for-all nature of the basic apostolic experience*—for the "twelve" an experience that spanned Christ's life, death and resurrection and for Paul (and others?) an experience simply of the risen Christ—will focus subsequent reflections on revelation, tradition and inspiration. A firm grasp of this apostolic experience is of major importance for Christian fundamental theology.

Paul's experience on the Damascus road not only had a once-and-for-all character but also initiated him into existence *"in Christ,"* an expression which he seemingly took over from others and which described the reality that he now experienced *in common* with Christians at large.[21] Through his death and resurrection Jesus had become a kind of "inclusive" figure in whom believers knew themselves to be incorporated. Being "in Christ" came to form one of Paul's most characteristic ways of interpreting that experience he shared with other Christians (for example, Rom 8:1; 16:7; 1 Cor 15:22; Phil 3:8f.).

As we shall recall in a moment, the active presence of the Holy Spirit "within us" was another typically Pauline way of describing Christian experience and existence. Very occasionally Paul also spoke of Christ dwelling and living "in us" or "in me" (Gal 2:20). But normally he expressed the new communion of life not as a mutual indwelling (we in Christ and Christ in us), but as our/my existence in Christ—a one-way affair. Without losing his individuality, Christ had become through his death and resurrection a corporate person into whose life believers experienced themselves as drawn and inserted.

Both through formulations he adopted and the language he fashioned for himself, Paul gave voice also to the *"Trinitarian"* quality of that Christian experience which he shared with others. He reminded the Galatians of their enriched life in these terms: "God [the Father] has sent the Spirit of his Son into our hearts, crying 'Abba! Father!'" (Gal 4:6). Paul associated the experience of the indwelling Spirit not only with prayer (Rom 8:26) but also with the divine love (Rom 5:5), the spiritual gifts employed by different members of the community (1 Cor 12:4–11) and coming resurrection (Rom 8:11). In a "Trinitarian" way the apostle introduced his treatment of the particular gifts:

Now there are varieties of gifts, but the same *Spirit;* and there are varieties of service, but the same *Lord* [Jesus]; and there are varieties of working, but it is the same *God* [the Father] who inspires them all in every one (1 Cor 12:4–6).

Paul likewise gave a "Trinitarian" expression to the hope for resurrection which belongs to the Christian experience: "If the Spirit of him who raised Jesus from the dead [=the Father] dwells in you, he who raised Christ Jesus from the dead will give life to your mortal bodies also through his Spirit which dwells in you" (Rom 8:11). One last example: Paul closed his Second Letter to the Corinthians[22] with a traditional formula: "The grace of the Lord Jesus Christ and the love of God and the fellowship of the Holy Spirit be with you all" (13:14).

Undoubtedly we should shed any illusions that in Paul's letters we find a properly articulated doctrine of the Trinity. To mention only one point: A clear distinction between the person of (the risen) Christ and the person of the Holy Spirit remained to be worked out by later Church councils.[23] "Trinity" and "Trinitarian" can be misleading words here. Nevertheless, the divine self-communication experienced by the apostle and other Christians was of such a kind that they were forced to interpret and express it in terms of God (the Father), Son and Holy Spirit. There was a "Trinitarian" shape to the historical revelation and salvation experienced when the time came for God to "send forth his Son" (Gal 4:4).

Lastly, Paul's theme of "power-in-weakness" demands at least a brief look. In Second Corinthians he came as close as he ever did to anything like an autobiographical sketch of his life and mission. That long and very personal letter listed four times various painful experiences that had typified the course of his ministry (4:8ff.; 6:4ff.; 11:23ff.; 12:10). Paul called them "weaknesses" (12:9f.), but we might be advised to speak of "sufferings" and "vulnerability." Today "weakness" almost inevitably suggests moral failings. For Paul, however, Christ's crucifixion constituted the supreme example of "weakness"—not as a moral failure but as the fearful result of freely accepting vulnerability (13:4). Who could be more vulnerable than someone pinned to a cross?

A scrutiny of this theme in Second Corinthians reveals at least four major points. First, the apostle's painful, "trough" experiences were not uniquely special episodes (like an appearance of the risen Christ or heavenly ecstasies), but had a horrifying ordinariness about them:

> Five times I have received at the hands of the Jews the forty lashes less one. Three times I have been beaten with rods; once I was stoned. Three times I have been shipwrecked; a night and a day I have been adrift at sea; on frequent journeys, in danger from rivers, danger from robbers, danger from my own people, danger from Gentiles, danger in the city, danger in the wilderness, danger at sea, danger from false brethren, in toil and hardship, through many a sleepless night, in hunger and thirst, often without food, in cold and exposure (11:24–27).

If these experiences proved to be means for conveying the divine self-communication, they were not dramatically unusual events but continue to exemplify the sufferings and ill-treatment that generous, innocent and defenseless people frequently face in our world. Second, Paul was enabled to discern and interpret these events precisely as in their own way bringing and revealing the divine salvation to mankind. He understood that Christ's power to effect God's self-communication reaches its climax in such situations of extreme vulnerability. Hence Paul concluded: "When I am weak, then I am strong" (12:10). Thus, third, it was his painful "weaknesses" that cast him in the role of mediating, in subordination to the crucified and risen Christ, the divine revelation and salvation. The apostle's suffering existence meant just that:

> . . . always carrying in the body the death of Jesus, so tht the life of Jesus may also be *manifested* in our bodies. For while we live we are always being given up to death for Jesus' sake, so that the life of Jesus may be *manifested* in our mortal flesh (4:10f.).

By means of everyday suffering Paul disclosed and mediated to others God's revelation and salvation in Christ. Fourth, as a "law" governing the divine self-communication, "power-in-weakness" applied primarily to the apostle, but secondarily this "law" touches other Christians. In general it will hold good that the divine power is made perfect in human weakness (12:9).[24]

Paul's letters date from the late 40s to the early 60s. Then came the Synoptic Gospels: first Mark around 65 and afterward Matthew and Luke in the 70s or even 80s. However, their dating and order does not concern us here but only the question: What do these works from the apostolic Church communicate about the human experience of the divine self-communication when Jesus came on the scene? Where Paul focused on the way he and other Christians experienced the risen Christ, all four Gospels said something also about *Jesus' own experience.* As regards the *Synoptics* I want for the moment to take up only one theme: the "Trinitarian" aspect of what Jesus himself experienced and what others experienced of and through him—according to these records from the apostolic Church.

In a rich variety of ways Mark, Matthew and Luke portray Jesus as experiencing a profound and permanent dialogue of love with God his Father. A familiar intimacy ("Abba, Father dear") characterizes Jesus' life and prayer.[25] He invites others to share as much as they can in this deeply trusting and utterly obedient attitude toward his God. The parables show how Jesus reads the world off: the objects and events of daily life in ancient Galilee speak to him of his Father's presence and the growing impact of the divine power. Then in his preaching Jesus firmly, authoritatively and in his own right conveys the divine will and forgiveness. The Synoptic Gospels present a Jesus whose primordial and secure experience it is to be God's Son. He is both intimately bound to his Father and yet different from him. At the same time, here is a Jesus who is filled with the Holy Spirit (Lk 4:1) and from whom power comes forth to heal the sick. To sum up: During the ministry Jesus comes across as both experiencing for himself the Father and the Spirit and communicating this experience to others. He manifests himself as the Son of the Father, and his activity discloses the power of the Spirit.

Much of what has just been briefly recalled from Jesus' ministry corresponds to material invoked when the topics of implicit soteriology (the saving *work* of Jesus) and implicit Christology (the revelation of his *person*) are discussed.[26] Those topics focus the questions somewhat differently: *Who* is Jesus (Christology) and *what* has he done for us (soteriology)? Nevertheless, any answers to those questions will mean situating Jesus vis-à-vis the Father and the Holy Spirit.

The Trinitarian structure which in their informal way the Synoptic writers express through the story of Jesus' ministry emerges even more forcefully with his death and resurrection. In the Acts of the Apostles, as well as in the concluding chapter of his Gospel, Luke gives the resurrection a Trinitarian expression. The Father vindicates Jesus by raising him from the dead (Acts 2:24 etc.). The risen Christ communicates to believers the Holy Spirit he has received from his Father (Acts 2:33 etc.). In his own way Matthew also completes his account of Jesus in a Trinitarian fashion. The crucified and risen Lord commissions his disciples to preach to "all nations, baptizing them in the name of the Father, and of the Son, and of the Holy Spirit" (28:19). Both before and after Good Friday the revealing and saving divine intervention through Jesus of Nazareth takes on a Trinitarian shape.

Once again let me insist that I am *not* claiming that the Synoptic Gospels any more than Paul explicitly anticipate later teaching on the Trinity as three persons in one nature and so forth. Nevertheless, that teaching summarizes and (in its own terminology) makes explicit what the Apostolic Church through Mark, Matthew and Luke records about the "Trinitarian face" of Jesus' story. That is the way they have experienced the divine self-communication in his life, death and resurrection. This "Trinitarian" theme surfaces even more clearly with the later *Gospel of John*.

Origen observes somewhere that to understand the Fourth Gospel the reader must rest on Jesus' breast. The remark catches the *strongly experiential and prayerful quality* of the whole Johannine corpus. We can properly describe the Gospel as one long act in which the glory of God is experienced and contemplated in Christ. It begins with the community's testimony to their direct experience of the incarnate Word—"We have beheld his glory" (1:14)—and closes with Thomas looking at the risen Christ and confessing, "My Lord and my God" (20:28). Then the First Letter of John begins by proclaiming the experience of those who lived intimately with Jesus (1:1–3). The letter proceeds to spell out the two basic criteria (faith in the person of Jesus and effective love for others) which make it possible to discern the spiritual experience that brings authentic communion with God. The apostolic witnesses and the community ("we") testify to the role of these criteria in testing one's experience.

> We have seen [= experienced] and testify that the Father has sent his Son as the Savior of the world. Whoever confesses that Jesus is the Son of God, God abides in him, and he in God. So we know [= experience] and believe the love God has for us. God is love, and he who abides in love abides in God and God abides in him (4:14–16).

Lastly, the Book of Revelation begins with the writer's own experience (1:9ff.) when, being "in the Spirit on the Lord's day," he fell at the feet of the glorious Christ who encouraged him:

> When I saw him, I fell at his feet as though dead. But he laid his right hand upon me, saying, "Fear not. I am the first and the last, and the living one; I died, and behold I am alive forevermore. . . . Now write what you see, what is and what is to take place hereafter" (1:17–19).

The book invites its readers to contemplate in the unfolding of world history their Master, the glorious Christ who will be there at the end of all history as the light illuminating the heavenly Jerusalem (21:23). The text sweeps us from the experience of one Christian to what will be the experience of all.

Let us concentrate our attention on the Fourth Gospel itself.[27] Rudolf Bultmann and others have detected here a strong emphasis on the *revelatory* force of the divine self-communication. Even if the Gospel never formally gives Christ the title of "Revealer," the language of revelation abounds: glory (and glorify), light, signs, truth, witness (as noun and verb), the "I am" sayings and so forth. The Gospel uses only 1,011 words, an extraordinarily small vocabulary by today's standards and even by those of the New Testament. (St. Paul's vocabulary, for instance, includes well over 2,000 words.)

This small Johannine vocabulary is heavily revelational. The key words for expressing revelation recur constantly: glory (*doxa*) turns up eighteen times, glorify (*doxazein*) twenty-three times, light (*phōs*) twenty-three times, truth (*alētheia*) twenty-five times, witness as a noun (*marturia*) thirteen times and as a verb thirty-three times. The last example forms a striking contrast with the Synoptic Gospels: in all three Gospels witness as a noun occurs only three times and the verb only twice. Where the other Gospels call Jesus' miracles "acts of power" (*dunameis*), John turns toward revelation and speaks of "signs." Right from the outset (2:11) these signs manifest Jesus' "glory," which is not (as with the Synoptics) something reserved for his future (eschatological) condition (see Lk 24:26). According to John, Jesus enters into his definitive glorification through his death and resurrection (17:1 ff.), but the glory has already been disclosed through his earthly life and that theme serves to sum up his whole ministry (12:37–43). The "I am" sayings, which reveal various aspects of Jesus' person and work ("I am the good shepherd, the true bread, the light of the world, the way, the truth and the life" etc) culminate in the absolute "I am" (8:58) which recalls the divine self-presentation in Exodus 3:14. Jesus is the epiphany of God. Finally, the revelation which the Fourth Gospel attests transcends any "mere" matter of information. It communicates saving life and sets believers free from judgment, hunger and thirst. "Life" (*Zoē*) turns up thirty-six times, and that statistic highlights the salvific force of revelation.

All in all, John looks like the Gospel of revelation par excellence. And yet here too it is advisable to seek a higher terminology and speak of our experiencing in Jesus the epiphany of God and the fullness of life.

For one thing, at the level of translation "to experience" often conveys very satisfactorily what "to know" and "to have" are about. "Experience" has a fuller and more vibrant meaning than "know" which tends to restrict things to cognition. Where "have" can sound somewhat static, "experience" suggests a dynamic process. Thus the Samaritans who came to believe in Jesus say to the woman who met Jesus at the well and brought him to their notice: "It is no longer because of your words that we believe, for we have heard and experienced for ourselves that this is indeed the Savior of the world" (4:42).[27a] In the sixth chapter "having life" can be repeatedly translated as "experiencing life": "Truly, truly, I say to you, he who believes experiences eternal life. . . . Unless you eat the flesh of the Son of Man and drink his blood, you experience no life in you" (6:47, 53). We may render that solemn pronouncement from Jesus' last discourse as follows: "This is eternal life, that they experience thee the only true God, and Jesus Christ whom thou hast sent" (17:3). At the end the Gospel states its purpose:

> Now Jesus did many other signs in the presence of the disciples which are not written in this book; but these are written that you may believe that Jesus is the Christ, the Son of God, and that believing you may *experience* life in his name (20:30f.).

In all these passages "experience" substitutes for the usual "have" and "know." "Experiencing Jesus" would also (at least partly) express the meaning of "coming to Jesus," "believing in him," "seeing him," and "remaining in him."

This use of "experience" in translating John may have set some good Christian nerves on red alert. Let me, however, insist once again that "experience" does *not* have the soft or debased sense, let us say, of some "mere" sentimental feeling. Here and elsewhere the term should be understood in the strong and inclusive sense indicated by the analysis given in Chapter II.

When we struggle with John's Gospel, "experience" offers more than just an alternative translation for certain common verbs. "The communication of experience" sums up what the Gospel intends. First of all, the experience of Jesus himself bulks larger here than in the other Gospels. Except for one episode (6:15) he is never by himself, and with his different audiences he speaks repeatedly of one overriding experience: his permanent relationship with his Father. There is no escaping Jesus' profound sense of mutual self-giving: he is in the Father and the Father is in him (14:10). By manifesting his own glory Jesus is doing nothing else than consciously revealing *both* his origin and mission from the Father *and* his intimate communion of life with him. Hence he can sum up his ministry as the experience of having "glorified" his Father on earth (17:4).

In their turn believers will know Jesus by entering into his experience. To experience the saving revelation of God means their collective communion with the Father and the Son through the Holy Spirit—that reciprocal indwelling of God in them and them in God to which the last discourse repeatedly testifies. Thus Jesus promises this reciprocal self-giving: "You will know [= experience] that I am in the Father, and you in me, and I in you" (14:20). This "vertical" communion with the triune God entails a "horizontal" communion with other human beings. They are to be loved both *as* and *because* Jesus has loved and continues to love them (15:12). This divine love manifested in Jesus is not only the model for a communion of love with others but also makes such love possible.

The disciples (both those who knew Jesus intimately and the whole apostolic community) have experienced this profound communion with Jesus and with one another. John's Gospel piles symbol upon symbol (light, water, bread and so forth) to evoke and re-evoke this experience in its readers. Likewise in the opening verses of the First Letter of John, if the privileged eye-witnesses of the earthly and risen Jesus proclaim their experience, they do so in order to communicate it:

> That which we have seen and heard we proclaim also to you, so that you may have fellowship with us [= a collective "horizontal" experience]; and our fellowship is with the Father and with his Son Jesus Christ [= a collective "vertical" experience] (1:3).

At the beginning of this section on the "when" of the divine self-communication, I recalled the belief that *the absolute climax of that self-communication came with Christ.* Paul, the four evangelists and other New

Testament writers share this conviction but they single out different reasons for it. There is no such thing as *the* version which exhaustively accounts for the absoluteness of God's self-communication.

A future perspective surrounds the characteristically Pauline approach. What has been achieved and revealed through the events of Good
Friday and Easter Sunday forms the beginning of the end when God will
publicly intervene to bring the fullness of salvation. His resurrection has
made Christ "the first fruits" of the dead. He has thereby *already in-
augurated* the general resurrection, when death, the last enemy, will be
destroyed and God will be "everything to everyone" (1 Cor 15:20–28).
Nothing now lies ahead except the full gathering of that total harvest
which Christ has begun.

Matthew's Gospel makes much of Christ as *the* divine Teacher. Matthew never talks of the word of God coming to Jesus, nor does he represent Jesus in the style of an Old Testament prophet delivering his
message with a "Thus says the Lord." Luke writes of the word of God
coming to John the Baptist (3:2). But none of the Gospels ever use that
terminology of Jesus. He is *the* Teacher par excellence (Mt 23:8–10)—
much more than a prophet who delivers a message from God or a master
who teaches his disciples and can then leave them to the truth itself. This
divine Teacher is identified with the message he proclaims and will remain
with his disciples "always, to the close of the age" (Mt 28:20). This Teacher cannot be repeated, let alone surpassed.

John's Gospel holds out obvious possibilities for focusing on what
developed into the doctrine of the incarnation in order to answer the question: Why is Christ the absolute climax to the divine self-communication?
If "God so loved the world that he gave his only Son," we cannot expect
anything or anyone more. Here is the definitive communication of that
salvation by which we do "not perish but have eternal life" (3:16). The
Father cannot send anyone more effective as Revealer and Savior than
the only Son who is next to his heart (1:18). If the eternal, divine Word
"became flesh and dwelt among us, full of grace and truth" (1:14), God
has already shown us the deepest meaning of things and provided the
ultimate possibility for sharing as "born-again" children in the divine life
(1:12). God could not send another who would do more for us.

The Letter to the Hebrews comes close to this kind of Johannine
answer:

In many and various ways God spoke of old to our fathers by the
prophets; but in these last days he has spoken to us by a Son. . . .
He reflects the glory of God and bears the very stamp of his nature
(1:1–3).

In these terms Jesus Christ is clearly God's last word, *the* Revealer par excellence. Having "spoken" and sent this Son who "bears the very stamp" of the divine nature, God can have nothing more or greater to say to us. The absolute quality and authority of this revelation derives straight from Jesus' divinity and status as Son of God.

The Second Vatican Council in its document on revelation noted the absolute nature of the revelation Christ brought but in doing so it did not invoke the incarnation, the resurrection or Christ's role as *the* Teacher. The council turned rather to the theme of the new covenant (*Dei Verbum*, n. 4). Through Christ God has established a definitive and eternal covenant with humanity so as to mediate revelation and salvation until the end of the world. Here then is another way of elucidating the absoluteness of the divine action and self-communication in Christ.

To sum up: In the New Testament and later we find an interplay of motifs which justify identifying Christ's life, death and resurrection as the absolute climax in the human experience of God's revealing and saving activity. If different New Testament writers make distinctive contributions here, they are far from offering only one answer each. Paul, for instance, occasionally introduces the theme of the incarnation as bringing to a climax the divine work of revelation and salvation. He does not pursue the death and resurrection to the point of excluding or ignoring the significance of what was entailed when "God sent forth his Son" in the fullness of time (Gal 4:4). If John gives full weight to the incarnation, the Gospel also highlights the paschal mystery where one can contemplate and appreciate the final importance of what Jesus communicated in dying and rising (12:21 ff.; 19:37). Lastly, in the whole of the New Testament the Letter to the Hebrews provides the classic passage for expressing the once-and-for-all quality of the crucifixion and resurrection (9:26–28). This letter, to put it mildly, moves beyond the incarnation to indicate why, how and where the divine self-communication came to its unrepeatable climax.

Two statements can pull together much of the material discussed in this whole section on the New Testament. First, *when Christ came,* God's self-communication reached a complete and definitive climax. Second, Christians of the apostolic age—and especially Paul and the other apostles themselves—in experiencing that revelation and salvation through Christ did so, at least partly, in a unique and unrepeatable way that gave and gives their witness its special, normative quality. These two statements leave us with the question: What of those who came *later—after* that absolute self-communication of God and the apostolic experience of it?

(c) Any adequate reply to the question "When did/does revelation and salvation occur?" must then take into account *the continuing presence and power of that saving revelation.* William James remarks in *The Varieties of Religious Experience:* "A large acquaintance with particulars often makes us wiser than the possession of abstract formulas, however deep."[28] In line with his advice let us name some "particulars" where we find post-apostolic Christians experiencing the power and presence of God's self-communication. Saving revelation obviously continues when it reaches, brings to faith and renders holy an Augustine, a Thomas Merton or any other convert. The divine self-communication is present and at work when those who are already Christians grow "in Christ," know more fully his power in their weakness and enter more deeply into the life of the Trinity: through the sacraments, sermons, the reading of the Scriptures, loving activity with and for others, episodes of suffering and any other concrete means (of a dramatic or an everyday kind) that convey revelation and grace. Individuals experience this divine self-communication and so too does the community—through reading the signs of the times, and through collective experiences like a Church council, the election of a new pope and so forth. In short, wherever and whenever revelation and salvation are experienced, there the divine self-communication continues to take place.

The Second Vatican Council, while insisting on the complete and definitive nature of the saving revelation communicated through Christ, consistently underlines the continuing nature of this communication. In the Constitution on Divine Revelation the Council talks of "God as he reveals himself" (n. 5):

> God, who spoke in the past, continues to converse with the spouse of his beloved Son. And the Holy Spirit, through whom the living voice of the Gospel rings out in the Church—and through it in the world—leads believers to the full truth (n. 8).

In other documents God's self-revelation is likewise spoken of in the *present* tense (*Dignitatis Humanae*, n. 10; *Ad Gentes*, n. 13 etc), while the Council sees the Church as called to "reveal in the world . . . the mystery of its Lord until, in the consummation, it shall be manifested in full light" (*Lumen Gentium,* n. 8). Lastly, *Gaudium et Spes* presents together the revelatory and salvific aspects of the divine self-communication effected through the risen Lord: "Christ, who died and was raised for the sake of all, can *show* man the way and *strengthen* him through the Spirit in order to be worthy of his destiny" (n. 10). Once again it is a matter of a saving revelation that is taking place *now*.

Part of the challenge here is to find the most helpful terminology. We might use capitals for the divine self-communication that happened "then" through Christ's incarnation, life, death and resurrection and call it Revelation and Salvation. The self-communication of God that continues today we could style revelation and salvation. This distinction suggests usefully how the present religious experience of Christians draws upon and, as it were, always occurs under the shadow of what happened then in Christ.

Some authors have favored "immediate and mediate" as a technique for distinguishing between the "now" and the absolute "then" of revelation and salvation. This terminology, however, prompts misgivings. If we do not experience—and that means *immediately* experience—revelation and salvation, we simply do not receive either. As Chapter II pointed out, there is no such thing as a second-hand, indirect, mediate experience. Either God's self-communication directly and immediately touches us or it simply does not come to us at all. Behind this terminology, of course, lie some points of value. For example, Christ appeared to Paul and other apostolic witnesses of his resurrection, and *that* kind of immediate experience of the risen Christ remained special to them. Other Christians immediately experience Christ but not precisely in that way. Further, those who lived with Jesus during his ministry immediately experienced him in ways that others who know him now in faith do not. The "immediate/mediate" terminology undoubtedly embodies some truth, but we would pay too high a price for it. All too easily it implies that we do not experience revelation and salvation for ourselves but somehow take them over at second-hand from others.

In *Theology and Revelation*[29] I proposed "foundational" and "dependent" as terms which could be pressed into service to differentiate between the "then" and the "now" of revelation. Since writing that little book I discovered that Paul Tillich[30] had previously used similar terminology, but that, of course, does not make it automatically wrong. It remains no less useful.

The first Christians, and above all the apostles, experienced and testified to the *foundational* history of revelation and salvation. These founding fathers and founding mothers enjoyed the once-and-for-all experience of living intimately with Jesus, encountering him in his risen glory and becoming the basic witnesses to the resurrection. Revelation and salvation did not grind to a halt at the end of the apostolic era, but continued and continues in dependence upon the unique and normative apostolic experience of and witness to Jesus Christ. Thus the religious experience of post-apostolic Christians constitutes a *dependent* history of revelation and salvation. They know their experience of the divine self-communication to be tied to and derived from a series of historical events and persons—specifically, Jesus of Nazareth and the events in which he was involved. Christians see *their* religious history as founded in and dependent upon *his* history. Hence through preaching, sacraments, catechetics, art and other means they recite these past events, believing that the divine self-communication remains essentially linked with and interpreted by cer-

tain historical acts of God on their behalf to which the apostolic Scriptures
authoritatively witness. Thus baptism and the Eucharist recall Christ's
death and resurrection, events with which Christians now consciously
align themselves. Here and elsewhere the past becomes contemporary.
That foundational history of revelation and salvation is proclaimed from
which the present offer and reception of the divine self-communication
depend.

The later books of the New Testament already enshrined this sense
of depending upon the foundational experience of revelation and salvation
that came to the apostles and first followers of Jesus. The truth to which
the apostles witnessed was to be religiously "guarded" (1 Tim 6:20; 2
Tim 1:13f.; Jude 3). The apostolic Fathers distinguished themselves even
more clearly from the original apostles and looked back in dependence
upon the apostolic witness to which "nothing should be added" and from
which "nothing should be taken away."[31]

In short, a distinction between the *foundational* and *dependent* history
of revelation and salvation clarifies the relationship between the divine
self-communication "now" and its absolute climax "then" in Christ.

EXCURSUS:
SIGNS OF THE TIMES AND AUTOBIOGRAPHY

(1) The Signs of the Times.[31a]

In elucidating further the "particulars" of dependent revelation and
salvation, the contemporary theme of "the signs of the times" deserves
some notice. Pope John XXIII (especially in his encyclical *Pacem in Terris*) gave fresh support to the theme, the Vatican Council welcomed it
into its longest document (*Gaudium et Spes*), and one synod of bishops
after another (down to and including the synod of 1977) through the
official documents and the speeches of individual bishops has repeatedly
invoked and interpreted the signs of the times. They called on their fellow
Christians to ponder and assess movements within the Church (like the
charismatic renewal) and movements that touch large areas of human
life or even the world as a whole (like the functions and future of the
United Nations). The bishops in these synods have been taking their cue
from the Vatican Council which cited the signs of the times in many
of its documents: on priestly formation (n. 9), religious liberty (n. 15),
the roles of the laity (n. 15), the liturgy (n. 43) and ecumenism (n. 4).

If we retrace our steps to the New Testament, we find Jesus reproach-
ing his audience for failing to read the signs of their times—namely, those
indications in his person and work which pointed to the messianic climax
of divine revelation and salvation (Mt 16:2–4). But in that case the signs

of the times concerned the *foundational* history of revelation and salvation. Pope John, the council, the bishops and contemporary theologians, however, have attended rather to those signs which in their particular ways indicate God's intentions to reveal and save now: in short, *the signs of dependent revelation and salvation.* The central question is: Where in the world and its history today does God appear to be especially present and active?

The strong basis for such a theology of the signs of the times is scarcely deniable. First, God is Lord of all human history. Just as in the special *foundational* history of revelation and salvation there were "acts of God," events where God was particularly present and which therefore revealed more of the divine concerns, so in the *dependent* history of the divine self-communication there can be acts of God, signs that show where the Creator is more intensely engaged and working out the divine design. To indicate both the relationship and the difference, we could contrast the *Acts* of God in the foundational history with the *acts* of God in the dependent history of revelation and salvation. Second, events of contemporary history must somehow manifest the lordship of Christ and the working out of the divine redemption. Paul sees the whole of creation groaning in a history of suffering as it moves toward the fullness of freedom and salvation (Rom 8:18 ff.). Through Christ the history of the world unfolds as a history of cosmic and human reconciliation (2 Cor 5:18 ff.; Col 1:20 ff.). Through all the vivid scenarios and apocalyptic language the visionary who wrote the Book of Revelation invites the reader to contemplate the triumph of Christ in human history. It would be unaccountably odd to agree in theory that Christ's reconciling power is presently shaping the world's history toward the day of full and final salvation, and yet refuse to look for any visible signs of the profound development. Third, we argued above that the divine self-communication comes about through an endless variety of means. Hence we should break with any tendency to *restrict* the communication of revelation and salvation to the individual's history and minor episodes that fail to touch people at large. Collective as well as individual experiences convey the divine intentions and grace. That held true for the period of foundational revelation and salvation. There is no justification for arbitrarily deciding that now in the history of dependent revelation God cannot speak through graced events to groups of people and even mankind in general. A theology of the signs of the times respects the continuing divine liberty vis-à-vis the "how" of revelation and salvation.

What examples can be given to illustrate contemporary signs of the times? In *Pacem in Terris* Pope John pointed to various movements in the world: workers and women seek to participate fully in economic, political and other areas of human life. Former colonies aim at shedding the last vestiges of dependency and inferiority, so as to enjoy genuinely equal status in the world of nations. One could point to further signs like the widespread aspirations among youth for real justice and full freedom. Such phenomena which touch great sectors of the human race are seen as more than sociological changes of far-ranging impact. They serve as indicators of divine designs.

These typical examples, while they come across as strongly *positive,* imply a negative background. Full participation in the life of the world (including here the Christian Church) is still denied to women. Young people rebel against the injustice and lack of freedom that confront them. In many places workers continue to be treated as "things" which lack genuine human dignity and the proper range of rights. In other signs of the times *negative* elements move into the foreground: world hunger, the arms race, systematic use of torture, international terrorism, repeated ferocious (if small-scale) wars, environmental pollution, the reckless exploitation of natural resources, and the growth of the consumer society in both capitalist and communist countries. The hunger to acquire and possess governs that society which judges people by their performance and productivity. Successful personal achievement in competition with others brings the individual power and prestige but at the cost of division and violence. In our list we can include also *mixed* phenomena like Marxist movements which combine a number of false doctrines and presuppositions with legitimate human aspirations. (Perhaps the consumer society might be reckoned among such mixed phenomena?) Lastly, the contemporary world witnesses great changes in medicine, transport, communications, and many branches of science and technology. Such phenomena, often *neutral* in themselves, can bring dramatic changes in human possibilities and aspirations. At least in the Western world, for instance, medical science has drastically extended life expectations. How many theologians and Church leaders have so far reckoned seriously with retirement villages, old people's homes and the whole phenomenon of senior citizens among the current signs of the times? Undoubtedly there has been a massively generous response to this phenomenon at the level of pastoral and personal care. But does the growing population of senior citizens indicate anything about the presence and power of divine revelation and salvation? How do we read off this phenomenon in the light of faith?

By mixing positive, negative and seemingly neutral elements, the signs of the times or acts (lower case) of God in the present history of *dependent* revelation and salvation correspond to the Acts (upper case) of God in the *foundational* history of revelation and salvation. That history included events which ran all the way from the Babylonian captivity and the crucifixion to Jesus' miracles and resurrection. Some of these events entailed a large measure of evil and human sin. If out of love the Father "gave his Son up for us all" (Rom 8:32), Pilate, Judas and Caiaphas brought about the crucifixion through less than loving motives. For all that, Good Friday enacted and communicated the divine intentions to save the human race. Likewise today we can find the divine purposes being conveyed through episodes and situations in which evil bulks large and the (infinitely more powerful) reality of grace seems less apparent. What proved true at the stage of foundational revelation and salvation will prove true at the dependent stage.

Three further points of correspondence: Just as Acts of God like the crucifixion and resurrection carried revelation *and* salvation, so the signs of the times convey both the divine intentions and the divine grace. The word "signs" could mislead us here into thinking we are dealing simply with the means of (dependent) revelation. Second, the Acts of God implied a religious claim. The return from Babylon, the ministry of Jesus, his resurrection and so forth challenged men and women to respond and react in new ways. Likewise the signs of the times are more than nice messages to be deciphered and identified. When recognized, they are to be acted upon. Third, we noted how the classic Acts of God were not unambiguously so. People could fail to see these events as such. Recognition of them as Acts of God was never compelled. A certain degree of concealment and mystery always left room for cognitive freedom. That continues to be true of the signs of the times today. These dependent acts of God never force men and women to acknowledge what they are.

Having observed these correspondences, how do we go about discerning and interpreting those collective experiences we call the signs of the times—not to mention expressing and acting upon them? It is hardly fresh and original, but it may be useful to recall first the *difficulties.* We may be dazzled by mere flash phenomena and miss the real signs of the times. We could be pondering some trivial or local effects and neglect the significant causes that lie behind them. The deeper and more widespread the human aspirations are which produce these effects, the more likely they are to express the transcendental experience of God and to indicate the influence of the risen Christ through his Holy Spirit. (We will return to this point later when dealing with the discernment of traditions.) Or again we could be too anxious to hear answers and positive messages when through phenomena like national and international terrorism God is primarily putting a question to the non-terrorists. After all, the divine word in the Old Testament (as well as in John's Gospel) often takes the form of a question rather than a statement (for instance, Job 38:1ff.).

Further, we might correctly identify the significant movements in our world, and discern them rightly as carriers of the divine intentions, but fail to interpret them appropriately and hence not proceed to support the real designs of God. It is all too easy here to look around the twentieth century and criticize some American, German, Spanish and Ulster Christians for uncritically identifying the kingdom of God with certain historical events. We too may be fulfilling collective needs and supporting privileged positions by wrongly reading divine messages into our own set of events. Among the Old Testament criteria for authentic prophecy we recalled the principle "The prophet may not profit." *Mutatis mutandis,* this applies at the collective level to the nation, the Church or whatever the group is which reads the signs of the times. Our discernment and interpretation must confront the question: *Cui bono* (for whose advantage)? We could resemble those German Christians who rightly recognized Hitler's rise to power as the place to look. (How, of course, could they have failed to notice the momentous significance of National Socialism?) But unlike Dietrich Bonhoeffer and others they failed to grasp the real meaning of what was happening. The proper insight would have drastically called their lives into question.

By invoking the signs of the times, the Second Vatican Council was not blandly endorsing the trendy view which in fact goes back at least as far as the Roman proverb *vox temporis vox Dei* (the voice of the age is the voice of God). It is never as easy as that saying might suggest. What age ever literally speaks with one voice? The voices of an age, even the seemingly good voices expressing apparently good aspirations, can misrepresent the divine purposes. The Second Vatican Council believed that the voice and activity of God could be discerned and interpreted only after diligent scrutiny. If Christ set high store by the need to read the signs of the times, in his eschatological discourse he warned against the risk of deception (Mk 13:5, 21f.).

If these then are some of the pitfalls, how can we positively go about pinning down the divine intentions communicated through the signs of the times? At least *five pieces of advice* are called for. The first looks banal but is among the most important. To read the signs of the times we need to know the times. How can one who has no immediate contact with movements among workers, women and youth discern and interpret with any kind of assurance what they have never experienced for themselves but know only second-hand? There is something worse than comic about pronouncements on world hunger coming from those who have never missed a meal in their lives. Reading the signs of the times will prove an inherently elusive task for those who fail to know the times by experience.

Second, St Paul saw his suffering as a privileged place to look when he searched for the deepest meaning of his missionary experiences. This process of discernment led him to hear and accept the truth by which the Lord wished him to love: "My power is made perfect in weakness" (2 Cor 12:9). Just as the apostle interpreted his individual existence through his experiences of sufferings, so communities should follow suit and reflect on sectors of suffering as privileged carriers of the divine designs. Paul ended his Second Letter to the Corinthians by inviting them to "examine" and "test" themselves (13:5ff.) in the light of the personal discerning which the letter itself illustrated.

Paul brings us to the New Testament and the need to discern and interpret the signs of our times only after prayerfully reflecting on the New Testament as a whole. Any attempt to read today's signs without feeding on that record of God's foundational self-communication will never produce properly Christian answers. This requirement can be put more personally. As we review the major movements in our world in the light of the Gospels, we could well ask: How would Jesus read off these movements? Such a question takes seriously that being "in Christ" and his Spirit's presence within us which Christians from the beginning invoked to express their experience of intense communion with the risen Lord. *If* consciously drawing on this communion with Christ and his Father through the Holy Spirit *makes no difference* to our reflections on the signs of the times, the strong terms in which Paul, John and other New Testament writers describe the Christian experience ring horribly hollow.

Fourth, I suspect that engagement with many contemporary signs of the times will not produce positive answers but rather leave us with such questions as: How should world hunger and the population explosion challenge our expectations, modify our mind-sets and convert our values? Both in the period of foundational revelation and today God's word can take the form of a *question*.

Finally, *risk* cannot be excluded. It is fairly easy to identify and read off the signs of yesterday. But we can only expect a conflict of interpretations when we grapple with present reality and the shape of things to come. Interpreting the signs of the times demands an instinct not for what has been but for what is emerging and casting its shadows before it. Yet this instinct will not be able to justify itself to everyone's satisfaction. The acts of God today continue to leave room for cognitive freedom. Recognition is never compelled and hence conflict always remains possible.

2. Autobiography

Where reflection on the signs of the times deals with *collective* experiences of God's self-communication, the personal records of outstanding Christians from St. Augustine's *Confessions* down to Dietrich Bonhoeffer's *Letters and Papers from Prison* testify to the ways in which dependent revelation and salvation work on the *individual* level. Such autobiographical material yields clues about the conditions and nature of that continuing divine self-communication which is both experienced "now" and looks back to the unique apostolic experience of foundational Revelation and Salvation which took place "then."

Let me hasten to point out that I am *not* concerned here with "private revelations," those special divine communications to St. Margaret Mary and others which Roman Catholic theologians used to discuss within the framework of a propositional view of revelation.[32] That older theology insisted that such private communications could not add to the objective body of truths revealed before the death of the last apostle. Whatever the factuality and function of these private revelations, they did not increase that closed deposit of faith. Hence that manual theology, if it discussed some Christian autobiographies, focused on ecstatic visions, divine voices and other extraordinary elements in order to meet a possible objection. Did those private revelations enlarge the deposit of faith?

The question I wish to take up here is different. I am asking: What emerges about the divine self-communication if we study such autobiographical material, leave aside the extraordinary elements and—against the background of our analysis of experience—investigate the ways in which some remarkable men and women like St. Augustine, St. Teresa of Avila, Thomas Merton and Dietrich Bonhoeffer both (a) experienced *the acts of God* in their personal history and *the signs* of revelation in their lives, and (b) through their writings traced the progress of that saving revelation? These canonized and non-canonized saints make up a privileged group of Christians. They not only experienced more fruitfully than others the divine self-communication, but they also frequently enjoyed a special talent for expressing the ways God had spoken and acted in their lives.

Here I wish to take just one example: Dietrich Bonhoeffer and his personal experience of revelation and salvation as reflected in his prison writings.[33] What interests me here is not so much his *formal* pronouncements on revelation and salvation as the ways in which he was led by the Holy Spirit into a more profound experience of the divine self-communication. Hence I am not dealing as such with Bonhoeffer's explicit theologizing. The aim is rather to observe and uncover hints about the means which led to a deepening of his religious experience—that is to say, the ways in which dependent revelation and salvation worked on his individual level in the last two years of his life.

The language of Bonhoeffer's letters repeatedly suggests his being engaged in a revelational process, even if he only rarely uses strictly technical terminology to indicate this. Over and over again telltale verbs recur that show how he grows in understanding, how he reaches a more profound awareness of his relationship with God, and—in short—how he experiences revelation in those last two years of his life. He remarks that reading Stifter "makes one think of the things that really matter in life" (LPP, p. 50). He finds that the question of "what Christianity really is, or indeed who Christ really is, for us today" has been "bothering" him "incessantly" (LPP, p. 279). He speaks to Eberhard Bethge of what he has been "discovering" and "learning" (LPP, pp. 369f). "You see," Bonhoeffer tells him, "how my thoughts are constantly revolving around the same theme"—union with the crucified and risen Lord (LPP, p. 337). I am pulling in examples here almost at random. The significant verbs dot the letters: being "taught," becoming "conscious" of something, things being "brought home" to him, becoming "aware" of something, being "helped to a better understanding," and "realizing clearly."

Even when Bonhoeffer's language does not explicitly point to such revelatory experience, we can often glimpse his sense of meeting or having met the divine "Thou" (LPP, p. 217). On July 16, 1944 he writes to Bethge: "The God who is with us is the God who forsakes us." God "is weak and powerless in the world, and that is precisely the way, the only way, in which he is with us and helps us" (LPP, p. 360). Obviously Bonhoeffer is describing his own condition and the insights to which he has been led by his experience: here it is a matter of some insights that strikingly recall Paul's theme of "power-in-weakness."

Every few pages he records the conscious convictions which his communion with God has engendered. "*Metanoia,*" he assures Bethge, is "not in the first place thinking about one's own needs, problems, sins, and fears, but allowing oneself to be caught up into the way of Jesus Christ" (LPP, p. 361). For "us," "one" and "oneself" read "me." At once we can recognize what Bonhoeffer experiences in that mysterious interpersonal reality, the divine self-disclosure through Christ.

Bonhoeffer's letters also set out clearly both the given circumstances and the chosen *means* which trigger off insights, reinforce convictions and foster a revelatory and salvific relationship with God. The physical conditions of imprisonment, isolation and privation, the threat of death from bombing and the steady menace of his Nazi captors all play a role. These factors help to constitute the context which intensifies communion with the divine realities, as well as with Bonhoeffer's loved ones. In a letter to his fiancée he remarks: "It is as though in solitude the soul develops senses which we hardly know in everyday life" (LPP, p. 419). He reads the psalms daily, finds that the Bible takes on fresh meaning in his situation and illuminates the situation, experiences that favorite hymns yield strengthening enlightenment, and observes the effect which the sound of bells has upon him:

It is remarkable what power church bells have over human beings, and how deeply they can affect us. So many of our life's experiences gather round them. All discontent, ingratitude, and selfishness melt away, and in a moment we are left with only our pleasant memories hovering round us like gracious spirits (LPP, p. 73).

In short, bells become the means by which Christ exercises his healing revelation.

Memory often functions to bring things home to Bonhoeffer. Before his first Christmas in prison he recalls with gratitude the "perfectly lovely Christmases" which his parents had arranged:

> It's not till such times as these that we realize what it means to possess a past and a spiritual inheritance independent of changes of time and circumstance. The consciousness of being borne up by a spiritual tradition gives one a feeling of confidence and security in the face of all passing strains and stresses (LPP, p. 165).

The memory of hymns, especially those of Paul Gerhardt, proves comforting and illuminating.

In a special way it is Bonhoeffer's *prayer* which fashions the setting for his experience of God. His 1933 lectures on Christology had recognized the difficulty of finding Christ through historical knowledge, and had pointed to prayer as the place of Christ's revelation:

> If this way of knowledge is excluded, there remains just one more attempt possible to gain access to Jesus Christ. This is the attempt to be in the place where the person reveals himself in his own being, without any compulsion. This is the place of prayer to Christ. Only through the word of free self-revelation is the person of Christ, and thus his work, disclosed.[34]

Bonhoeffer's imprisonment becomes a life "before God," a constant turning in prayer to "the God before whom we stand continually" (LPP, p. 360). Through prayer Bonhoeffer keeps alive the sense of things: "In these turbulent times we repeatedly lose sight of what really makes life worth living.... The truth is that if this earth was good enough for the man Jesus Christ ... then, and only then, has life a meaning for us" (LPP, p. 391).

Thus far we have (a) glanced at the revelatory language of Bonhoeffer's letters, (b) noted how—even without using such language—he clearly records his experience of revelation, and (c) listed the internal and external conditions for such experience: prayer, memory, the communion with loved ones, his state as a prisoner and the rest. A broad range of positive and negative experiences—very ordinary as well as dramatic episodes—become the means which mediate the divine self-communication. Can we press beyond these points to grasp the dynamics of his experience? What are the structures of revelation as he encounters and interprets it? What particular shape does the divine self-disclosure take for him?

The pattern of *question and answer* emerges from a careful reading of his letters. Bonhoeffer yearns to discover the meaning of things (LPP, p. 301). His life seems "fragmentary and incomplete"—split up like houses demolished in the bombing. Yet he does his best "to keep in view how the whole was planned and thought out." He hopes that he "shall still be able to see" this (LPP, p. 215; cf. p. 219). He scrutinizes experience in quest of clarification (LPP, p. 277). God meets him no longer as "Thou" but also "disguised" in the "It." This leads Bonhoeffer to sum up the key element in his questioning: "In the last resort my question is how we are to find the 'Thou' in this 'It' (i.e. fate), or, in other words, how does 'fate' really become 'guidance'?" (LPP, p. 217). This admission comes in a letter of February 21, 1944.

The following month the questioning shifts from the fate-providence issue to express itself quite simply as that of *suffering:* "We need a great deal of correction on this point. . . . Suffering must be something different, and have a quite different dimension from what I've so far experienced" (LPP, p. 232). One month later the question moves from talk of fate, guidance and suffering to be formulated around the person of Christ. "What is bothering me incessantly," Bonhoeffer tells Bethge, "is the question what Christianity really is, or indeed who Christ really is, for us today" (LPP, p. 279).[35]

The *answer* takes shape. Bonhoeffer reaches a profound awareness of Christ's presence in his sufferings. In June 1944 he observes how his "thoughts are constantly revolving around the same theme"—that "Christ takes hold of a man at the center of his life." This means that "the Christian . . . must drink the earthly cup to the dregs, and only in so doing is the crucified and risen Lord with him" (LPP, p. 337). This insight into the harsh circumstances of his life persists and hardens. "Man," he declares, "is summoned to share in God's sufferings at the hands of a godless world" (LPP, p. 361). In all these passages we can simply substitute "I" for "the Christian" or "man." The use of the third person is no more than a thin veil through which Bonhoeffer's own inner experience is almost continuously visible.

His conviction about the divine presence in suffering reaches its classic expression in the letter to Bethge on July 16, 1944: God has been "compelling" Bonhoeffer to "recognize" his "situation before God. . . . The God who is with us is the God who forsakes us." Through prayer and suffering Bonhoeffer experiences a mysterious divine presence in seeming absence: "Before God and with God we live without God" (LPP, p. 360).

In 1933 Bonhoeffer had characterized as "the first statement of Christology" the proposition that "Jesus is the Christ present as the Crucified and Risen One."[36] Now as a prisoner doomed to die in the final days of Hitler's regime he comes to a final awareness of what Christ's presence in sufferings entails.

Obviously much more could be said about the revelatory and salvific experience reflected in Bonhoeffer's final writings: the healing quality of the insights which come to him, the genuine "elasticity of behavior" (LPP, p. 218) which made him so open to the revealing and sanctifying action of the Holy Spirit, the role of emotions in his deepening experience of God, the significance of the poetry which he found himself impelled to write (LPP, pp. 319ff.), and much else besides. Exterior circumstances and inner experiences converged to make Bonhoeffer modify his interpretation of himself and his world. He began to know consciously what he had "really" known all the time but had been unable to formulate.

This treatment of Bonhoeffer might have followed more precisely the scheme on experience proposed in Chapter II. For instance, his flexible willingness to face an uncertain future enacted in a high degree the openness for the unforeseen called for by that persistent feature of on-going experience, the element of *newness*. Or again the way Bonhoeffer set about scrutinizing his experiences exemplifies some major conditions for the successful *discernment* and *interpretation* of Christian experience: prayer, the use of the Scriptures, a powerful bond of love with others, and so forth.

This has been only a quick glance at Bonhoeffer's prison writings, but it does suggest the need to explore what the process of dependent revelation and salvation looks like in concrete cases.[37]

St. Paul spoke of the action of the Holy Spirit in guiding the sons and daughters of God (Rom 8:14). In John's Gospel Jesus promised that all those who hear him will be "taught by God" (6:45). "When he comes who is the Spirit of truth," he assured his disciples, "he will guide you into all truth" (Jn 16:13). The opening prayer in Ephesians proposed a similar growth into profound knowledge: "I pray that the God of our Lord Jesus Christ ... may give you the spiritual powers of wisdom and vision, by which there comes the knowledge (*epignōsis*) of him" (1:17).

All Christians should hope for such "guidance" into truth, and being "taught by God" can pray to find deeper experience, clearer vision and fuller grace—in short, a richer communion in the life of the Trinity. But Bonhoeffer and other men and women of high spiritual sensibility let us see more easily how the divine self-communication can profoundly shape a human life in this period of dependent revelation and salvation.

To conclude: This chapter has probed and grappled with a number of questions: *What* is revelation? What are the *means* and who are the *persons* involved in mediating God's self-communication? What criteria have been available to *discern* and *interpret* the experience of this divine self-communication claimed by prophets and others? *When* and *where* do we find God's revelation taking place? The answers took shape around Christ's life, death and resurrection: the absolute climax in the human experience of God's revealing and saving self-communication. That foundational experience continues to remain powerfully effective in this period of the dependent history of saving revelation when the signs of the times and the personal records of outstanding Christians (among many other things) manifest the saving presence and intentions of the risen Christ.

Up to this point the story of Israel and Christianity has largely monopolized our attention. If we stand back from that history, what of the divine self-communication experienced by non-Jews and non-Christians? Has Christian theology anything to say about other religions and the religious experiences of those who do not acknowledge the special divine plan realized in Jesus Christ? To those issues we now turn.

IV. CHRIST AND NON-CHRISTIANS

Vous annoncez un Dieu né et mort il y a deux mille ans, à l'autre extrémité du monde, dans je ne sais quelle petite ville, et vous me dites que toux ceux qui n'auront point cru à ce mystère seront damnés.

J. J. Rousseau

The Holy Spirit offers to all people the possibility of being made partners, in a way known to God, in the paschal mystery.

Second Vatican Council

The agenda of this book takes us next to the question of Christ's role in revelation and salvation. Granted that the divine self-communication reached its absolute and complete climax with his incarnation, life, death and resurrection, should we accept or vigorously oppose the belief that *all experience of revelation and salvation relates to Christ?* As regards the "where?" of God's self-communication, is it true that outside Christ there is neither revelation nor salvation?

Or should we agree, for instance, with Carl Braaten[1] who recognizes in Christ a universal role for salvation but not for revelation? In this view Christ is Savior for all but not Revealer for all. Only those who consciously know that their religious experience depends upon and is interpreted by the foundational experience of the apostles are related to Christ at the level of revelation. The others bypass Christ in receiving revelation. They genuinely know God but apart from Christ. In Braaten's view Christ may be absolutely necessary for salvation but only relatively important for the experience of divine revelation. He is the major mediator of revelation but not essential in that role for all human beings. Many can and do know God without his mediation.

We can express the problem this way: If, on the one hand, we maintain that outside Christ there is no revelation, what of those who profess to know God but who have never heard of Christ? It seems narrow-minded and downright untruthful to deny that the divine revelation is reaching them. But if, on the other hand, we admit that God is truly disclosed to them, we appear to tamper with the unique absoluteness of Christ's person and work. It looks as if he ceases to be universally significant for revelation and hence for salvation. It seems a desperate choice: either a bigoted refusal to face facts or a denial of Christ's unique place in the history of the divine self-communication.

The best way promises to be this: We can first examine the extent of Christ's role as Revealer. Then we can move to face that closely related theme: the experience of the divine self-communication among non-Christians and through non-Christian religions and ideologies.

I
CHRIST AS REVEALER

Any reflection on the scope of Christ's work as Revealer (and Savior) will turn chaotic unless we distinguish three issues: Christ as (1) the *goal* of revelation, (2) the *agent* of revelation (= the Revealer), and (3) the *object* of revelation (= the Revealed One).

(1) There should be little difficulty about accepting Christ as the universal *goal* of revelation and salvation. All human beings are called to be finally with Christ—being raised like him, knowing him and sharing his glory forever. Their ultimate destiny leads human beings toward Christ. As the Second Vatican Council put matters, "The Church believes that the key, the center and the purpose of the whole of man's history is to be found in its Lord and Master" (*Gaudium et Spes,* n. 10). The final purpose of human history is nothing less than sharing forever in the divine life. But that divine life will be mediated eternally by the risen Christ. In his glorified humanity he will remain the means by which the blessed know the Trinity and enjoy the fullness of salvation.[2] There can be no bypassing Christ when we come to the goal of revelation and salvation. He will be there for everyone as both the Revealer (= agent) and the Revealed One (= object).

(2) But must all revelation *here and now* come through Christ as *agent?* In its Constitution on the Church the Second Vatican Council described Christ as "the source of salvation for the whole world" (n. 17). But is he also the source and agent of *revelation* for the whole world? Can and does revelation come from God but not through Christ as the Revealer?

The New Testament appears to support the Braaten thesis. When Paul teaches in Romans that human beings can know God through the testimony of the created world and their own conscience, he makes no reference to Christ being involved as the agent or means of this knowledge (1:18ff.; 2:14ff.). When the Book of Acts speaks of the witness to God provided by the seasons and bounty of nature, it does so without invoking Christ (14:17; see 17:22ff.). What do we make of the people in the Old Testament to whom God's revelation had already come, as well as all the non-Israelites then and all the non-Christians who have lived after the coming of Christ? We have to reckon with millions of people who give every indication of genuinely knowing God and yet do not seem to receive this knowledge through Christ.

Nevertheless, we should maintain that Christ mediates revelation to all men and women. We can appeal here to the doctrines of creation, incarnation and resurrection.

Unlike the Old Testament, the New Testament does not have much to say on *creation*. But in the little that is said Christ takes over the role attributed by Jewish theology to the divine word and wisdom. He is acknowledged to be the agent of creation: "All things were created *through* him and for him. He is before all things, and in him all things hold together" (Col 1:16f.; see Jn 1:1–4, 10; Heb 1:3; 1 Cor 1:24; 8:6). For all their different nuances, these texts agree that through Christ all things were created. They celebrate him as the universal and exclusive agent of creation who preserves everything in existence, and as the model and goal of everything. The New Testament supports the conclusion. Whenever the created world and its history mediate a disclosure of God, those who receive this disclosure are in fact knowing God through Christ. As agent, model and goal of God's creation, Christ also brings about the revelation of God through the external world and the inner voice of conscience. Christ's agency is as broad and as old as creation itself. The created world has always borne the *vestigia Christi* (the traces of Christ), inasmuch as all things image forth the likeness of creation's agent. Admittedly only the eyes of faith will recognize in creation these *vestigia Christi* as such. But from the outset this study in fundamental theology has maintained the aim of reflecting systematically on what the eyes of faith see.

Apropos of the Son's role in creation, it is worth noting how some of the classical creeds of the Church could lead people astray into thinking that the Father alone creates, the Son alone redeems, and the Holy Ghost alone sanctifies. If the Nicene Creed does include one pertinent phrase ("through him all things were made"), the Apostles' Creed remains silent about the Son's creative activity. The New Testament, however, does not make such strict demarcations, as if Christ redeems us without being involved in creation.

Through his *incarnation* Christ moved into an historical solidarity with all human beings, as well as with the created world. He entered history to become everyman and the focus of the universe. Hereafter to know God through other men and women and through the world would be to know God through the incarnate Christ. The story of the last judgment in Matthew singles out strangers, hungry and thirsty people, the naked, the sick and prisoners to make the point: in meeting and caring for others, and especially those in need, we meet and care for Christ (25:31ff.). By his incarnation "the Son of God has in a certain way united himself with each man" (*Gaudium et Spes*, n. 22). Hence to know God through other human beings is to know God through the incarnate Christ.

The resurrection, without destroying the individual reality of Christ's humanity, transformed and freed it beyond the normal limitations of space and time. In his glorious humanity he has become present to people of all times and places. Hence in this risen state Christ can "show the way to" and "strengthen" every person through his Holy Spirit, offering "to all the possibility of being made partners, in a way known to God, in the paschal mystery" (*Gaudium et Spes*, nn. 10, 22). The omnipresent activity of the risen Christ universally mediates the divine life which is experienced as revelation and grace. To deny a universal role here is to belittle what happened to Christ in and through his resurrection.

Further, it does not require the eyes of faith to perceive that Christ's influence and message are spread widely through the world. What I have in mind here is not the enormous distribution of the New Testament, the statistics on Christian adherence or the fact that hundreds of millions of people have seen Zeffirelli's *Jesus of Nazareth*. Marxism, the official ideology of the Soviet Union and China, incorporates so much from its Christian origins that it can be styled a (secular) Christian heresy. The person, work and Gospel of Jesus Christ have likewise affected Islam and (modern) Hinduism. Whenever people know the ultimate truth about things through Marxism, Hinduism and Islam, they are—at least partly— knowing that truth through Christ. His impact clearly extends well beyond the boundaries of official Christianity to affect further sectors of humanity. Add too the fact that the four thousand million people alive today constitute half the human population that has ever lived. This entire argument from the world scene does not pretend to be stringent but simply to point to the visible evidence for Christ's broadly universal role in mediating truth.

Finally, salvation and revelation are too intimately connected to permit the thesis that Christ is universal Savior but not the universal agent of revelation. The experience of salvation affects the entire existence of the subject receiving it. It is implausible to throw a *cordon sanitaire* around human cognition, as if Christ's saving grace could be "invisibly active" (*Gaudium et Spes*, n. 22) in the hearts and lives of some people without *in any sense* affecting their knowledge. The divine self-communication which is offered to the whole person entails revelation and grace. One could put the point this way: Revelation is, as it were, salvation and grace for the mind and intellect. (As we have noted, this cognitive aura holds true even for contemporary theologies of revelation as interpersonal encounter.) Where the process of salvation affects human knowing and thinking, this means something in the order of revelation. In these terms Christ cannot be the agent of saving grace for all without also being the agent of revelation for all. His unique mediatorship between God and human being (1 Tim 2:5) involves both roles.

This argument might be expressed as follows: If all grace comes from Christ and if knowing God is a grace, then knowing God must also come from and through Christ. Otherwise we would have to deny *either* (a) that knowing God is a grace, *or* (b) that all grace comes from Christ. As all human beings in the present order of things are called to a supernatural destiny of sharing the divine life here and hereafter, knowing God can only be a grace. That all grace comes from Christ is clearly affirmed by the New Testament (Acts 4:12; 2 Cor 5:15; 1 Jn 5:11f. etc.), Christian tradition, official Church teaching (DS 2803; *Gaudium et Spes,* n. 10 etc.), and the consensus of all Christian communities today.

As regards the agent of revelation, a series of arguments converge on the same conclusion. There is one "true light" which enlightens everyone, and that light, whether accepted or rejected and whether consciously identified or not, is Christ (Jn 1:9). He is the one divine Word (Jn 1:1ff.) spoken eternally by the Father, which then in time and history mediates (directly and through subordinate agents) salvation and revelation to all mankind as the universal Revealer/Savior.

(3) What of the case for Christ as the universal *object* of revelation? Is all true religious experience Christological, so that one cannot experience and believe in God without experiencing and believing in Christ as the Revealed One?

The answer must be yes. If we know God, we are in fact knowing the Triune God. There is no God apart from the Father, Son and Holy Spirit. In any authentic religious experience we encounter a double reality: ourselves and the Trinity. However obscurely, the experience of divine revelation will always entail Christ as object along with the Father and the Holy Spirit. Every genuine acceptance of the divine self-communication is an acceptance of Christ.

At the three levels (of goal, agent and object) the evidence of Christian experience urges the conclusion: Christ alone is universal Revealer as well as universal Savior. Yet this is no fearful and threatening fact. His revelation, no less than his salvation, is there for all.

II
NON-CHRISTIANS AND CHRIST

Given that Christ is the universal goal, agent and object of God's self-revelation, how should we go about interpreting the religious experience of those who do not share in the history of Judaism and Christianity? Before proposing some systematic reflections on the divine self-communication to this vast number of people, we can set the scene by reviewing some facts from the history of Jewish-Christian experience and faith.

1. Some Biblical and Church Data

In Amos (1–2), Isaiah (13–23), Jeremiah (46–51), Ezekiel (25–32) and elsewhere in the Old Testament we run across prophetic oracles against foreign nations and cities. These oracles not only form a significant part of Jewish prophecy, but also are a backhanded way of recognizing Yahweh's concern with these cities and nations. Then we find positive data. Balaam is no Israelite and yet is acknowledged to be an authentic prophet (Num 22–24). Through that comic caricature of a prophet, Jonah, God's message brings the people of Nineveh to repentance. Significantly Jonah is sent simply to warn the Ninevites about the consequences of their sins, *but not* to call on them to abandon their religion and accept the faith of Israel. It is a moral conversion that the prophet has to proclaim, not a change of religion. The third chapter adds a nice touch to bring this out. When the Ninevites believe and cry out to "God," the text uses "Elohim," a more general name. Elsewhere in the story Jonah deals with "Yahweh," the God of Israel. But the prophet is not expected to press a Yahwist faith on Nineveh. They can truly hear the divine message and find salvation within the matrix of their own religion.

The sense that divine salvation is for all people turns up in Isaiah and Second Isaiah, even though this universalism takes a centralist form. Others must turn toward Jerusalem to find salvation (2:1ff.; 49:6, 22f.; 60:3ff. etc.). In general the prophetic rather than the historical books of the Old Testament enshrine a sense that Yahweh wishes to speak to and save the whole of humankind. Amos strikingly exemplifies this:

"Are you not like the Ethiopians to me,
O people of Israel?" says the Lord.
"Did I not bring up Israel from the land of Egypt,
and the Philistines from Caphtor
and the Syrians from Kir?" (9:7).

Here Yahweh is presented as the God not only of Israel but also of Ethiopia, which was traditionally regarded as a slave nation situated on the fringes of civilization. The Philistines and Aramaeans (here = the Syrians) ranked among Israel's worst enemies. Yet the prophet places the Philistine migration from Caphtor (= Crete) to Palestine and the Aramaean migration from Kir (the location of which is still unknown) on the same level as the exodus in which God brought the Israelites out of Egypt. Yahweh was also engaged on behalf of the Philistines and the Aramaeans, acting and revealing himself in and through their exodus.

Furthermore, we need to remember the "holy pagans" like the Queen of Sheba (1 Kgs 10) and Job who turn up in the Old Testament. Such non-Israelite individuals can enjoy God's friendship and favor just as much as whole groups of people. Through its covenant theme the flood story in Genesis affirms God's universal good will. A common phenomenon of nature, the rainbow, becomes the sign expressing the divine beneficence toward every living creature on the face of the earth. God says to Noah:

> This is the sign of the covenant which I make between me and you and with every living creature that is with you, for all future generations: I set my bow in the cloud, and it shall be a sign of the covenant between me and the earth (Gen 9:12f.).

We can sum up this evidence from the Old Testament. Yahweh's particular choice of Israel does not exclude the will to communicate with, be known by and bring salvation to other human beings. They can truly experience Yahweh's intervention on their behalf.

In the New Testament Paul recognizes that the external testimony of nature and the inner voice of conscience could lead people to know God (Rom 1:18–32; 2:13–15). Luke introduces holy pagans like Cornelius (Acts 10:1ff.) and testifies to God's universal concern for human salvation. If unknown, God is not absent but always the God in whom "we live and move and have our being" (Acts 17:22–31). A later book of the New Testament witnesses to the Christian experience and conviction that "God our Savior . . . desires all men to be saved and come to the knowledge of the truth" (1 Tim 2:3f.). In the historical context of the letter "truth" refers primarily to the truth of the Gospel. But when the passage was canonized as the classic biblical statement about God's universal saving will, the content of "the truth" became less precise. To be saved it would be enough to know and accept (at least with an implicit faith) the truth that God exists, rewards goodness and punishes evil (see Heb 11:6). All in all, however, we have to be content with hints from the New Testament about the state of those who do not hear the Gospel message and hence cannot embrace the Christian faith.

The Second Vatican Council drew material from traditional theology and contemporary experience to offer far more explicit teaching than any previous council on the communication of divine revelation and salvation to non-Christians.

(a) The Constitution on the Church echoed St. Paul in singling out conscience as the place where God speaks to all people (n. 16).

(b) The same constitution recognized the possibility and reality of salvation for all men and women of good will—even those who (through no fault of their own) do not know God explicitly.

> Those who, through no fault of their own, do not know the Gospel of Christ or his Church, but who nevertheless seek God with a sincere heart, and, moved by grace, try in their actions to do his will as they know it through the dictates of their conscience—those too may achieve eternal salvation. Nor shall divine providence deny the assistance necessary for salvation to those who, without any fault of theirs, have not yet arrived at an explicit knowledge of God, and who, not without grace, strive to lead a good life. Whatever good or truth is found among them is considered by the Church to be a preparation for the Gospel and given by him who enlightens all men that they may at length have life (n. 16).

Such sincere non-Christians are "moved by grace," "know" God's will "through the dictates of their conscience," display elements of "goodness and truth" in their lives, are in fact "enlightened" by Christ, and will find salvation. The Decree on the Church's Missionary Activity added that *faith* is available for such people: "God can lead those who, through no fault of their own, are ignorant of the Gospel to that faith without which it is impossible to please him" (n. 7). Divine grace invisibly relates all such persons of good will to Christ in his dying and rising: "The Holy Spirit offers to all the possibility of being made partners, in a way known to God, in the paschal mystery" (*Gaudium et Spes,* n. 22).

(c) The Declaration on the Relationship of the Church to Non-Christian Religions *(Nostra Aetate)* edged beyond merely general teaching not only to speak of Judaism and Islam but even to specify religions which in their origins were not visibly connected with the history of Christianity (Buddhism and Hinduism). These religions contain much that is holy and "often reflect a ray of that Truth which enlightens all men" (n. 2). *Gaudium et Spes* exemplified the right approach here by seriously reflecting on the complex experience of human beings in the modern world. *Nostra Aetate* followed suit by encouraging Roman Catholics to react positively to the elements of revelation and salvation found among non-Christians. In its closing message the 1977 synod of bishops in Rome exhorted catechists not only to maintain toward other religions "respect and understanding" but even to "develop an attitude which listens to these religions and discovers the *semina verbi* [seeds of the word] hidden in them" (n. 15). That entails going beyond the classic teachings of these other religions to know their spiritual experience and the ways in which their adherents interpret and express that experience.

2. Transcendental and Historical Experience

When we come to *reflect systematically* on the divine self-communication experienced by those who do not consciously and willingly align themselves with the biblical history of revelation and salvation, various possibilities present themselves.

First of all, we can introduce a distinction between the *general* (or universal) history of revelation and salvation and the *particular* (or official and special) history of revelation and salvation.[3] The whole of human history, if viewed from a revelatory and salvific perspective, forms the *general* history of revelation and salvation. In this sense revelation and salvation history are co-extensive (but not identical) with world history. The *particular* or *special* history of salvation and revelation is the story of the divine self-communication which was recorded once and for all by the books of the Bible but which continues to be remembered and re-enacted in the religious life of Christians (when they proclaim the good news about Jesus, celebrate the Eucharist and administer the sacraments), Jews and—to some extent—Moslems. This particular history of the divine self-communication is *special* for two reasons. It was officially and authentically interpreted by the prophets, Jesus himself, the apostles and others. The divinely authorized word discerned and expounded the meaning of events like the rule of King David, the Babylonian captivity, the ministry of John the Baptist, the crucifixion and so forth. But this special history of revelation and salvation meant that a series of events themselves were Acts of God—that is to say, events in which God was present and active in a particular way. The last chapter developed some implications of this special divine engagement.

Back in Chapter II we contrasted *transcendental experience* which constituted transcendental revelation and salvation with the *historical* revelation and salvation communicated through conscious religious experiences. What was stated there can be related now to the general and special history of revelation and salvation. That primordial openness to God which forms the *a priori* for all human knowing, willing and acting is the transcendental experience of the divine self-communication. But as the presupposition and condition for all specific experience it never exists by itself but always assumes some *historical,* categorical *(a posteriori)* form. For those who consciously stand within the history recorded in the Old and New Testaments, the transcendental experience of God's primordial communication takes historical shape as they share in that special story of revelation and salvation. For others the same transcendental experience must express itself in the general history of revelation and salvation. This can be illustrated by a diagram.

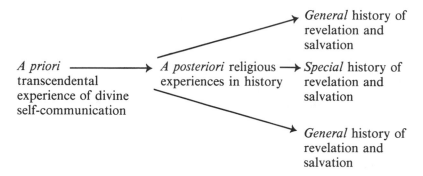

In reflecting on the general history of revelation and salvation we should not only consider individuals but also attend to Hinduism, Buddhism and other religions like the traditional religions of Africa and Papua New Guinea. *These religions historically objectify and socially institutionalize the transcendental experience of God's self-communication.* In doing so they may introduce elements of human error and depravity, but as historical institutions which objectify transcendental revelation they communicate revelation and put men and women in a position to decide for or against God. In the history of countless people it has been true: either they were to experience God in and through their religions or they could not do so at all. Their specific history, society and culture left them only that choice. Within the general history of God's self-communication these religions have proved authentic ways of revelation and salvation.

This scheme (general/special history of revelation and salvation + transcendental/historical experience) yields ways of answering the central question of this chapter: Can human beings truly experience God "outside" Christ (as agent, object and goal of revelation and salvation)?

(a) On the *transcendental* level the answer must be no. The primordial self-communication of God which forms the ultimate *a priori* for all human experiencing involves the Word of God. In every experience the God who is present, even if not explicitly acknowledged, can only be the *Triune God*—with the Word as the agent not only of creation but also of redemption. In the present order of things this transcendental experience is the primordial (supernatural) grace from the Triune God and as such is mediated by Christ who brings both the light of revelation and the life of salvation. He is actively present as agent (the Revealer), object (the Revealed One), and goal.

   (b) On the *historical* level of particular religious experience, Hindus, Buddhists, followers of Confucius, adherents of traditional religions and millions of others have known God and received salvation through their religious practices and their day-to-day lives, without Christ being explicitly envisaged or considered. The mediation of revelation and grace to them has not been on the level of *conscious* contact with the life, death and resurrection of Jesus. This history of their religious experiences has taken shape through their families, communities, sacred writings, worship, moral codes, the impact of great religious leaders and the rest. God has been genuinely present and active to bring those experiences into the general history of revelation and salvation, and that despite all those human elements which may be provisional, erroneous or downright perverse.
   Nevertheless, inasmuch as *the divine Word is present and active in the ultimate, transcendental horizon of all experience* and inasmuch as *all particular religious experiences remain conditioned by their transcendental horizon,* any specific divine self-communication in human history will in fact enact a saving dialogue with Christ—even if this is never consciously known. The divine Word actively influences the human history of religious experience at the transcendental *and* the categorical levels.
   Further, in the general (no less than in the special) history of revelation and salvation all the divine self-communication *before* Christ found its goal in the coming climax of his life, death and resurrection. *Since then* all revelation and grace has realized its point and purpose in the risen Christ, whose glorified humanity will mediate eternally the fullness of salvation in the vision of the Trinity. The entire divine self-communication in history points thus toward Christ as its focus and goal. For that reason also we can maintain that human experiences of God's self-communication always relate to and depend on Christ, even though only an explicitly Christian faith acknowledges this.[4]
   Undoubtedly some readers will be uneasy about referring to Christ *all* human experience of revelation and salvation. Is this no more than the traditional arrogance of Western Christianity which so often rode roughshod over other religions and their cultures and is here served up again in the guise of the transcendental/historical experience of the general/special history of revelation and salvation? It is very much the opposite, I believe. This approach, so far from denigrating the other world religions, encourages Christians to reverence Christ already present in them—transcendentally and historically. Christians do not simply bring to these others a Christ who has never at all been with them. Christ

is already there before the first missionaries arrive. The other religions and their cultures have proved the matrix in which God's self-communication through Christ has come about. All this should inculcate respect rather than arrogance in Christians who encounter these other religions. This approach may also encourage many Christians to relinquish certain settled values and standards when they see how Christ's saving revelation has worked itself out in these others. The European culture, through which Western Christianity has interpreted and expressed the special history of revelation and salvation, does not enjoy the absolute value which attaches only to Christ himself, *the* Revealer and *the* Savior. The cultural matrix for a sector of the *general* history of the divine-communication may well throw a critical light on and contribute to some cultural matrix which has served the *special* history of the divine self-communication.

A number of the Greek Fathers of the Church, when reflecting on the universal role of Christ in the human experiences of God, employed the notion of the *logos spermatikos.* In this vision of things the salvation which was offered to those living before Christ came through the *Word* of God who would be made flesh in the fullness of time. As agent of creation the Word was and is always present at least as a seed *(spermatikōs)* in every human being. Thus those who lived before the incarnation were nourished by the divine truth and set on the way of salvation—by the Word of God. This line of thought flowered with Justin, Clement of Alexandria and Irenaeus who saw the Old Testament prophets and the Greek philosophers as "Christians before Christ."[5]

3. Criteria for the "Semina Verbi"

Can we pin matters down somewhat? What criteria might we employ to spot (in Hinduism, Buddhism, other non-Christian religions of today and elsewhere) the *vestigia Christi,* the *semina Verbi,* the presence of the *logos spermatikos,* or however else we care to name the creative, revealing and redeeming presence of Christ?

We might examine other religions and ideologies at the level of institutions or at the level of the experiences of individual adherents. Either way we presuppose that the following positions have been established:

• that the definitive and complete climax of the divine self-communication came in and through Jesus Christ;

• that he is the goal, agent and object of *all* human experience of the divine self-communication in the special *and* general history of revelation and salvation, both transcendentally and historically;

• that he is the ultimate and decisive criterion for judging the entire history of revelation and salvation.

Hence to investigate (and state) criteria for discerning the *semina*

Verbi among non-Christians is to investigate (and state) criteria for authentic religious experience as such, and vice versa.

We are, of course, dealing here with conscious human experience; that is to say, this discussion focuses on the historical rather than the transcendental order. The following criteria serve to discriminate and evaluate experiences that are authentically religious.

(a) Such experiences will manifest a certain *profundity* that goes beyond the shallow flux of everyday experiences. In situations of unusual solitude, danger, surprise, joy and so forth people can be carried beyond the superficial level of ordinary existence to sense two things at the heart of their lives: on the one hand, their radical weakness, finitude and dependence, and, on the other hand, the meaning and strength that is given to them. In such episodes people know something of their absolute need and final values, even if the deepest reality is not explicitly identified as God.

(b) Genuine religious experiences will do more than simply help people to sense the ultimate dimensions of existence. They will *modify subsequent activity*. What has been consciously and profoundly experienced may be properly expected to have *consequences* that change the lives of those who personally claim to have experienced God or for whom such a claim is made. These changes can take the two basic forms of *hope* and *love*.

An authentic religious experience, whether precisely identified as such or not, means encountering the God "who is and who was and who *is to come*" (Rev 1:8). Here the divine "futurity" receives a special prominence. God will be truly and fully God for us only when the life of the final divine kingdom comes. The experience of such a God should encourage a basically hopeful stance toward life, even if this experience does not formally lead to a clear belief about life beyond death. As a minimum we can at least require that those who have been touched by the living God (who in fact holds out to us a full future) should somehow embody in their subsequent activity the conviction: "We are not facing an inevitable betrayal; existence is not inherently disappointing and finally absurd."

Alongside signs of a fundamentally hopeful attitude, genuine religious experience should induce care, compassion, and a generous openness to the needs of others. Any such experience will develop responsible love. Zen Buddhism deploys ten images to explain the nature of *satori* or profound illumination. The last image shows a man walking along a road into a city. The point is clear: One who has been genuinely illuminated will seek out other people so as to help them enjoy the same kind of illumination.

In short, this second criterion looks beyond the profound quality of experiences claimed to be religious to observe the hopeful and loving "behavior modifications" that such experiences bring in their wake.

(c) Third, there can be no substitute for testing alleged "vestigia Christi" or "semina Verbi" against God's historical self-communication in Jesus Christ himself. Authentic religious experiences can be expected to be *somehow Christological*—that is to say, to involve elements which hint at the creative, revealing and redeeming presence of Christ. This criterion demands that the religious experiences in question exhibit traces of his presence and power. Thus the experiences might in their own way show something of the paschal mystery and reproduce the pattern of Christ's power-in-weakness, or they might issue in teachings that bear similarities to the Gospel message.

Further, such experiences could bloom precisely through the impact of some outstanding religious leader, whose ministry can encourage us to extend Augustine's affirmation: "If Peter baptizes, it is Christ who baptizes. If Paul baptizes, it is Christ who baptizes." That principle attends to the presence of the risen Lord and affirms him to be the agent of grace whenever the administration of the sacraments takes place. As such the principle touches the *special* history of revelation and salvation. However, to the extent that various ideologies and non-Christian religions do in fact disclose hints of Christ's influence and message, we could, for example, say of certain leaders in the *general* history of revelation and salvation: "Here, where Gandhi speaks, it is Christ who speaks. Here, where Buddha teaches, it is Christ who teaches."

(d) Whatever the precise form involved, religious experiences that originate from God will show forth some orientation toward Christ. The historical divine self-communication in Christ, as we recalled in the last chapter, bore *a Trinitarian face* which—right from the writings of St. Paul—got reflected in the ways that the early Christians expressed their experience of God in Christ. The God communicated through that climax in the special history of revelation and salvation was a triune reality. There was and is no God apart from the Father, Son and Holy Spirit. Hence today we should expect some Trinitarian shape to the religious experiences that come to human beings in their own history and in their confrontation with the world of nature, even if these "vestigia Trinitatis" become recognizable as such only in the light of faith.

What is at stake here—we should remind ourselves—is *not* the primordial Trinitarian shape of the universe which Thomas Aquinas adverts to when he writes of the Trinity being represented in human beings "per modum imaginis" and in other creatures "per modum vestigii." Such talk about some "imago" or "vestigium Trinitatis" belongs to the level of that transcendental self-communication of God which forms the *a priori* condition for all human experience. This is true also of Augustine's psychological theory of the Trinity. He sees human knowledge and love as imaging forth the two processes by which the Father's act of thinking generates the Son, and the Holy Spirit is the mutual love of Father and Son. Here once again there is a concentration on the transcendental given which constitutes the *a priori* condition for the possibility of any human experience.

Our question is rather: Where in conscious, concrete experiences and their expression do we come across "vestigia Trinitatis" that would indicate authentic occurrences of historical revelation and salvation? Our quest for genuine religious experiences outside Christianity can rightly presuppose that, despite all the failures due to human depravity and misinterpretation, we will find traces of the Trinity. Wherever God is and is experienced, there is the Trinity *(ubi Deus, ibi Trinitas)*. Thus we can anticipate that, in some way or another, authentic experiences of the divine reality and their expression will bear a Trinitarian face. Examples suggest themselves for examination: the Trimurti or Hindu triad representing the three aspects of the Absolute Spirit (Brahma, Vishnu and Siva), the Yin, Yang and Tao of Taoism, and other religious experiences that speak of an absolute origin of things, some principle of meaning and order, and the unity of love. My aim here, however, is *not* to indulge an enormous parenthesis and argue several examples out in detail, but rather to point to an approach. "Vestigia Trinitatis" can serve to alert us to the presence of experiences that truly originate in God.

Such then are four criteria which can identify experiences that show the revealing and redeeming presence of Christ or, to put matters equivalently, that are authentically religious: the criteria of *profundity, consequences, Christological orientation,* and *Trinitarian shape.* These criteria ask: Do the experiences in question reveal ultimate, absolute elements at the heart of human existence? Do they modify subsequent behavior and make the persons concerned more hopeful and loving? Do they disclose some basic orientation toward Christ? Do they bear any "vestigia Trinitatis"? The first, third and fourth criteria look directly at the experience itself: Is it profound, Christological and in any way Trinitarian? The second criterion focuses on the aftermath of the experience: Does it bring ethical consequences that are deemed acceptable?

In applying these criteria, if we succumb to the impulse to investigate only the *teachings* of Buddhism, Hinduism and other non-Christian religions (and ideologies), we might be tempted to dismiss a great deal as mere deviant doctrine that fails to yield any signs of Christ's revealing and saving presence. The difficulty could be eased if we shift the focus a little from the spoken and written expression of experiences to consider also non-verbal expressions and, of course, the experiences themselves in their concrete reality. In the case of Christian teaching it has become a commonplace to recall the limitations inherent in even the most solemn Church formulations. They can never hope to express finally and fully the experience of God which reached its absolute and unsurpassable climax in Jesus Christ. Rahner's warning here has become a classic: "The clearest formulations, the most sanctified formulas, the classic condensations of the centuries-long work of the Church in prayer, reflection and struggle concerning God's mysteries—all these derive their life from the fact that they are not an end but a beginning, not goals but means, truths which open the way to the ever greater Truth."[6] My point here is this: What we admit about the gap between experience and expression in the case of Christianity should encourage us to allow for something similar in non-Christian religions and ideologies, instead of simply settling for their written teachings as the only place to look for possible "semina Verbi."

To conclude: This chapter has dwelt on the experience of God's self-communication among non-Christians in the general history of revelation and salvation. We can now turn back to the special history of revelation and salvation to examine the appropriate response called forth there by the experience of the divine self-communication: faith.

V. EXPERIENCING THE DIVINE SELF-COMMUNICATION IN FAITH

> *Well ... finally ... it is not a matter of reason: finally it is a matter of love.*
>
> Robert Bolt

> *Nemo credit nisi volens.*
>
> St. Augustine

More than two thousand years ago Socrates made his point: questions enjoy a certain priority over answers. Here, however, long interrogations are not needed and we can come quickly to the central question for this chapter: What is the believing experience of the divine self-communication like for those in the special history of revelation and salvation?

So far we have scrutinized the "what," the "how," the "when," the "where" and other aspects of God's revealing and saving self-communication. But this revelation and salvation do not, as it were, hang in the air. They reach their goal in human faith and grace. The divine and human roles are distinguishable but not separable. Hence it is natural to come across the language of mutuality and find contemporary theologians speaking of dialogue, encounter and communion. Similarly we catch St. Paul in his Letter to the Galatians moving easily from God's saving revelation in Christ (1:12, 16) to talk of the rise of human faith (3:23). The apostle understands revelation in its relationship to faith and vice versa. As he deals with strict correlatives, his theology of revelation/salvation will be his theology of faith and vice versa. Nevertheless, the divine self-communication is not identical with the human response to it. And so in this chapter we pause to dwell—even more than in the previous chapters—on the human side of things.

Our key question ("What is the believing experience of the divine self-communication like?") splits up into several sub-questions: (1) What is the *condition* of the human person who experiences the divine self-communication and reacts in faith? (2) Then what does this self-communication of God bring? (3) Finally, the heart of the matter: How does the response of *faith* to the divine revelation in Christ take place? What shape does it assume?

1. The Human Condition

Back in Chapter II we reflected on human experience at the historical and transcendental levels. That chapter opened up the social, historical, traditional and linguistic character of human beings.

Their bodily existence together in space and time turns human beings into *social* and institutional creatures. The good will of others sustains life. Affirmation by others fashions their self-identity. Right from the outset society shapes the understanding which men and women have of the world which they inhabit. Profound collective experiences mold the very existence and on-going life of nations and other societies.

Their space-time existence also necessarily means that men and women are beings of *history* and *tradition*. They not only make history and remember it (so as to re-enact and reinterpret it), but also interpret new experiences through the various traditions which fashion their collective horizon. Tradition always offers socially available ways of evaluating fresh episodes in which a whole generation shares. Just as given traditions may push a society into misinterpreting what happens, so the society itself can undergo decline as well as growth in its history. The social, historical and traditional existence of human beings can function with positive goodness or stumble under the pressure of evil.

Lastly, the second chapter attended briefly to the *linguistic* aspect of human existence. Men and women grow to maturity because they are addressed by others with words of affirmation and love. In turn through their language the flesh of personal experience becomes a word to others. From start to finish human life is essentially and deeply linguistic.

At this point we might decide to toil away at describing and explaining how society, history, tradition and language shape the human condition. But one could hardly manage to fit it all between the covers of a single book. Various articles suggest further lines of study for those so inclined.[1] Here it seems reasonable to presume at least a general agreement that men and women are social, historical, traditional and linguistic creatures. To prepare a way toward filling out the experience in faith of the divine self-communication, it appears more helpful to examine the human condition from this point of view: the *homo interrogans* or questioner in whose questions we can identify a "knower," a "decider," and a "hoper"—if you like, a *homo cognoscens,* a *homo decidens* and a *homo sperans.* The homo *cognoscens, decidens* and *sperans* matches, of course, Kant's classic questions at the end of his *Critique of Pure Reason* ("What can I know? What ought I to do? What may I hope for?") and suggest three basic areas of human questioning.

First let us look at and describe a little of what is entailed in calling the human person a *questioner.* We touch here a theme which goes back through St. Augustine ("I became a question to myself"), to Paul ("Who will deliver me from this body of death?"), to Socrates. The Greek philosopher established once and for all the fact that we will learn through our questions. Since then an endless line of thinkers have insisted that in the quest for knowledge and understanding, wisdom does not consist so much in giving the true answers as in asking the right questions.

We ask our questions because we *want* to *know* the truth and understand the meaning of things. Thus we are free and rational questioners, or we are not questioners at all. It takes *homo cognoscens,* a being of intellect, reason and free will to put questions. Later in this chapter we will need to weigh that mutual interaction between knowledge and freedom involved in faith's recognition and acceptance of God's self-communication in Jesus Christ.

No adult, of course, will hear and understand the Christian answers unless in some sense they have been willing to face these profound, ultimate questions which go beyond merely intellectual puzzles to touch the deepest needs and final values of human existence. Is the universe gracious or is it a computer programmed by an idiot? Does a life of love make sense? And then of course there are all the basic questions nicely summed up by the Second Vatican Council's Declaration on Non-Christian Religions:

> The problems that weigh heavily on the hearts of men are the same today as in the ages past. What is man? What is the meaning and purpose of life? What is upright behavior, and what is sinful? Where does suffering originate, and what purpose does it serve? How can genuine happiness be found? What happens at death? What is judgment? What reward follows death? And, finally, what is the ultimate mystery, beyond human explanation, which embraces our entire existence, from which we take our origin and toward which we tend (n. 1).[2]

On the one hand, these questions do not form some arbitrary list but spring from the nature of human existence that we constantly experience. On the other hand, however, they come down finally to the question of self and the question of God. As Bultmann, Rahner and others have rightly insisted, at bottom the question about God is the question about the human person and vice versa. We cannot raise profound questions about human existence without raising questions about God and vice versa. Augustine's prayer classically links together this ultimate search for oneself which is also the search for God: "Lord, that I might know myself! That I might know thee!" As Augustine realized through the troubled and elusive drama of his life, all our radical restlessness and self-questioning are only a thin veil concealing our search for God.

Further, the human person is not only a questioner who wants to know and understand but also a *decider* and a *doer* who asks: What ought I to do? Or perhaps better: What ought we to do in order to create a new social order? How should we live together in our linguistic community with its history, traditions and institutions?

Third, human beings are collectively and personally future-oriented through their hopes (and concomitant fears), so that they reach beyond themselves in a restless quest for what is yet to come. As they actually are, they suffer from a sense of incompleteness, remain dissatisfied with present reality and *hope* to be delivered from the broad range of evils which burden them. In countless ways men and women are afflicted by evil, above all by human sin which the New Testament sees as a much more urgent concern than human suffering. At present any salvation can only be provisional, and at all levels deliverance remains an open process. In the Bible no writer succeeds better than John in providing a lapidary expression of this incomplete state: "It does not yet appear what we shall be" (1 Jn 3:2). The promises and hopes mediated through nature and grace anchor human beings to the future, which is ultimately a future in Christ, the object, agent and goal of human salvation: "We have this as a sure and steadfast anchor of the soul, a hope that enters into the inner shrine behind the curtain, where Jesus has gone as a forerunner on our behalf" (Heb 6:19f.). The *homo cognoscens* and *decidens* is also a *homo sperans* who both yearns and works for better things and ceaselessly questions about the future: "What can I hope for?"

We can usefully relate these three notions (*homo cognoscens, homo decidens* and *homo sperans*) to the past, the present and the future. The knower reflects on past history and seeks to understand its meaning. The decider's interests touch present commitments. The hoper is concerned with the shape of things to come. The three basic lines of questioning from the *homo interrogans* span cognitive, ethical and eschatological matters, "what is past, or passing, or to come" (W. B. Yeats).

The focus of all this can be sharpened by modifying Kant's three questions to make them read: "What can we know of Jesus? What ought we to do about Jesus? What can we hope for from Jesus?" The captivity epistles offer texts that match these questions. In Colossians St. Paul (or someone of his school) prays for several Christian communities that they may "have all the riches of assured understanding and the knowledge

of God's mystery, of Christ" (Col 2:2).[2a] The same letter also expects
Christians to lead now "a life worthy of the Lord, fully pleasing to him,
bearing fruit in every good work" (1:10). Ephesians recalls "the God of
our Lord Jesus Christ" so as to pray: "That you may know what is the
hope to which he has called you" (1:17f.; cf. Col 3:4). Here and in innumerable other places the New Testament presents what is to be known,
decided on and hoped for, when Christian believers respond to Kant's
questions precisely by accepting the divine self-communication in Jesus
Christ.

But this is to anticipate matters somewhat. Before taking up the reply
of faith, we need to review some major features of the divine self-communication which enters human experience and invites an appropriate
reaction.

2. The Divine Self-Communication

Any reflection on the response of faith to *the divine self-communication in the special history of revelation and salvation* calls for at least
some summary answer to the question: What is that self-communication
itself supposed to be like? The previous chapters have in fact often been
in the business of offering replies to sub-aspects of that question. Here
we need to summarize some dominant features of those replies, add a
few details and, above all, focus matters for the key discussion on faith.
Once again Kant's three questions can serve our purposes here and allow
us to take up in turn what is to be *known* of God's self-communication
in Jewish-Christian history, what is to be *decided* on and *done* in face
of it, and what is to be *hoped for* through it.

(a) The faith founded in the special history of revelation and salvation
knows, first of all, that God's self-communication comes as a *gift* that
saves. It is due to the divine initiative that men and women experienced
and experience the presence of the living God. What Jesus says to Peter
in Matthew's Gospel applies to all people in their knowledge of God:
"Flesh and blood has not revealed this to you, but my Father who is
in heaven" (16:17). And this freely communicated revelation, as we saw
in Chapter III, is not merely informative but also effectively changes human lives as a healing and saving grace.

Further, the divine self-communication is always experienced by a
community bound together by language, other inherited traditions and
its entire culture. In Chapter III we noted the way that Israel's collective
experience of God settled down early into core credal statements, proclaimed with solidarity by the whole people. Similarly the First Letter
of John witnessed to what "*we* have heard, seen and touched" (1:1–3).
The Second Vatican Council emphasized the divine plan to encounter,

save and sanctify human beings "not as individuals without any bond or link between them, but rather" as "a people" (*Lumen Gentium,* n. 9). The Constitution on the Church in the Modern World returned to this theme of the "communitarian character" of the divine self-communication which respects and enhances the essential "solidarity" of the human race (n. 32).

Closely aligned with its social dimension is another "law" of the divine self-communication. In both the Old and the New Testament the community's eyes are drawn to *history* as the place where God's saving revelation progressively occurs. It is not that the Jewish-Christian tradition pushes nature away on principle, as if it had and could have nothing to do with revelation and our free response to it. We simply do not experience history in sharp isolation from nature. Gordon Kaufman writes:

> All historical events take place within the context of natural process and order, and involve the movements and reordering of physical bodies and material objects of many sorts. Moreover, many natural events—one need think only of rainfall and drouth, earthquake and disease, birth and death, etc.—have significant historical consequences. It is impossible to speak of history as though it were a realm of freedom and decision entirely separate from nature.[3]

The world of nature has its role to play in the divine self-communication and, as we observed in Chapter III, the Old Testament indicates this more forcefully than the New Testament. Nevertheless, as carriers of the divine intentions the unfolding events of human history always rise above natural phenomena.

Chapter III also called attention to the fact of faith that every experience, as well as every person, has the potential to convey God's revelation and salvation. The divine self-communication can take place through an endless variety of *means* and *mediators*. The same chapter dwelt on the problem which surfaced for the Israelites and remains with us: *discernment*. What criteria can we devise to identify, for example, authentic prophetic messages from God?

Lastly, the One who comes to be known in answer to the question "Who is God?" is the Triune God. The Father, Son and Holy Spirit reveal the profound source, meaning and goal of all reality and history.

At the same time this revelation of God indicates also the nature and destiny of the human person as being called here and hereafter to a profound communion of love with the Trinity. In the special—and for that matter in the general—history of revelation and salvation, any knowledge of God always brings also self-knowledge. This is not to return to the Protagorean principle that "man is the measure of all things," including divine things. Rather it is to recognize that the experience of self inevitably accompanies all experience, above all when we face and probe the divine mystery.

This is classically exemplified by the history of Israel up to its climax in Jesus Christ. While the divine self-communication dynamically and progressively unfolded, the self-knowledge of human beings flowered as well. Through all the ups and downs of life on a national and a personal level, any growth in the experience and knowledge of God went hand in hand with an increasing human self-awareness. It was not merely God who was revealed but concomitantly human beings. They were shown up for what they were. It took the encounter with divine revelation for men and women to be disclosed in their ultimate poverty, sin and need, as well as in their ultimate grandeur. Precisely through meeting the risen Christ St. Paul came to acknowledge the evil of his own former life and his utter dependence upon divine grace (1 Cor 15:8–10; Gal 1:13–16; Phil 3:4ff.). The case of Dietrich Bonhoeffer showed us how in the final two years of his life that saintly man knew himself more profoundly, as his experience of the divine revelation deepened.

(b) God's self-communication also entails things *to be decided on and done,* inasmuch as it makes drastic claims on us to live in new ways. The gift creates an obligation and calls for our personal involvement. To echo the initial scheme on human experience in Chapter II, we should be alive and responsive to what is happening to us. We ought to react in line with the way we have been acted on by God. Thus the divine call and revelation which come to St. Paul open up and merge into his mission to the Gentiles (Gal 1:16; cf. 1 Cor 15:8ff.).

Here we can spot a startling difference between the divine self-revelation and "revelations" that form the stock-in-trade of popular journals and everyday speech. Often such "revelations" about public figures, government actions and suburban scandals do not bring—or are not understood to bring—any call to action. Still less do they prove particularly saving and sanctifying to their recipients.

(c) Third, the saving self-revelation of God entails things *to be hoped for.* In Chapter III we reviewed some ways in which the Old Testament prophets constantly summoned the people to be open for the new future which God held out to them. One sense of the Spanish and Portuguese word "revelar" suggests this unfolding history of promise that invited human hope. As well as meaning "to reveal" the verb also means to develop a film. Something like that happened in the history of Israel. Yahweh's intentions for his people and for human beings generally developed clearer lines until the whole picture emerged in "the glory of God on the face of Christ" (2 Cor 4:6). A history of obscure and limited divine self-communication reached its hoped-for goal with Christ, in whom all the divine promises found their "yes" (2 Cor 1:20).

If Christ was the climax of revelation and salvation, nevertheless the divine promise which provoked human hope did not stay put there. On the one hand, the revelation conveyed through the Christ-event left matters still "shrouded as it were in darkness" (DS 3016). The mysteries of God and of the human person remained and in a sense were even heightened. On the other hand, salvation was not yet total and complete. Paul needed to write of our being saved "in hope" (Rom 8:24). If the apostolic generation enjoyed a once-and-for-all experience of the divine self-communication climaxing in Christ, this experience pointed beyond itself to the coming fullness of the divine kingdom.

If "now is the day of salvation" (2 Cor 6:2), we must still hope for the day which will bring the future of this "now" in Christ. That divine self-communication to come will be a person-to-person encounter in the fullest possible sense. It will be a continual, direct, face-to-face knowing in which God will stand revealed with full clarity and intimacy. By way of contrast present revelation falls short of anything like complete disclosure and must be characterized as partial and obscure. Likewise present salvation is given only in a qualified sense. The full saving self-revelation of God remains a matter of divine promise to be accepted in human hope.

3. The Response of Christian Faith

What has emerged so far in this chapter has been but a preliminary to the question that follows: What is involved in shifting from experiencing the offer of the divine self-communication to actively accepting it? Or, more briefly, what is faith like?[3a]

(a) Faith is a "response term" in two ways. First of all, faith responds to one's essential self-questioning, to the three basic questions of *homo interrogans:* "What can I know? What ought I to do? What may I hope for?"

In faith I hear and *know* the good news about Jesus' death and resurrection (1 Cor 15:3–5), those events in which the self-communication of the Triune God reached its unsurpassable and normative climax. Here I find the heart of *what* I believe, the *"fides quae,"* the *orthodox content* of faith, which is transmitted from the past by the apostolic witnesses (who in a special way experienced Christ) and which forms the heart of the Christian *confession* (Rom 10:9). In the history of revelation and salvation (and, above all, in the crucifixion and resurrection of Jesus) faith confesses the special divine intervention and presence.

Faith responds to the second question by present *commitment, ortho-*

praxy or *"fides qua."* Where the *fides quae* is a "believing that," this *fides qua* means a "believing in." It is "the *obedience* of faith" (Rom 1:5), the event of personal surrender to the God encountered now in and through Jesus Christ. The content of faith or *fides quae* would never have arisen and makes no sense without the act of "believing in" or *fides qua*.

Third, faith answers the question "What may I hope for?" by its *confidence* that the future rests in God's hands. The divine promise invites a confident hope of resurrection to glory: "If we have died with Christ, we believe that we shall also live with him" (Rom 6:8).

The answer to the second question ("What ought I to do?") finds its *base* in faith's answer to the first question ("What can I know?"). It finds its *future* in faith's answer to the third question ("What may I hope for?"). We will return shortly to the way the answers (and questions) mutually involve each other.

Along these lines we can interpret faith as *a response to Kant's three questions.* Perhaps someone has long ago pointed out the neat correspondence between those questions at the end of *The Critique of Pure Reason* and the three basic dimensions of Christian faith (as it is experienced, interpreted and described by St. Paul). However, I am not aware that attention has so far been drawn to this correspondence.

Be that as it may, Kant's questions could do with a little adjustment. To indicate the intersubjective and transsubjective condition of humanity we should speak of *homines interrogantes* (rather than *homo interrogans*) and modify the questions accordingly: "What can *we* know? What ought *we* to do? What may *we* hope for?" At all three levels—of confession (about the past), commitment (in the present) and confidence (for the future)—faith does not bypass the social nature of humanity; from the outset faith is a shared community experience. Ultimately "we believe" rather than "*I* believe" is the appropriate response to the questions of *homo cognoscens, decidens* and *sperans.*

Faith is also a "response term" inasmuch as it expresses the human response to the questioning God *(Deus interrogans)* who is personally present in Jesus Christ and asks: "What are you looking for?" (Jn 1:38). The confession, commitment and confidence of faith bring a new center in God. Knowing in the Holy Spirit the Father who raised Jesus from the dead (Gal 1:1) means construing and interpreting the world and its history in the light of the first Good Friday and Easter Sunday. Present commitment entails centering our love and loyalty in God, so that this primordial affection proves decisive for the values by which we live. Lastly, an appreciation of God's personal fidelity grounds a confident hope in resurrection. This confession, commitment and confidence show what the believer is looking for.

A classical way of handling "credere" suggests the triple nature of faith's personal response to the divine self-communication in Christ. "Credere Deum/Christum" (believing God/Christ) entails confessing that God *has acted* in stated ways. "Credere Deo/Christo" (giving faith to God/Christ) indicates the *present* self-involvement of faith's commitment. "Credere in Deum/Christum" (believing in God/Christ) refers to the future which faith confidently expects *will come* from God.

(b) The account so far given of faith has the aesthetic satisfaction found in some unitary treatment. Faith responds to the three basic questions of *homo interrogans* by its confession, commitment and confidence. The Nicene Creed nicely suggests the three elements: confession ("became incarnate," "suffered death," "rose again" and so forth), commitment ("we believe"), and confidence ("we look for the resurrection of the dead and the life of the world to come").

All of this treatment may, of course, only serve to intensify the built-in difficulties: Why should one respond in faith? *How does this response take place?* What prompts human beings to make this confession and commitment and to profess such a hopeful confidence?

One answer emerges readily enough from St. Paul's letters. The *preached word* and an *interior illumination* make it possible to acknowledge in faith the divine self-communication in Christ. Faith comes from hearing the external proclamation (Rom 10:17; Gal 3:5). But it is not simply the public persuasiveness of the preacher which brings faith about (1 Cor 2:4f.). When through the ministry of Paul and others human beings come to "the knowledge of the glory of God in the face of Christ," this is due to the power of the God who once said, "Let light shine out of darkness," and who is now illuminating the hearts of believers to give them this knowledge by, as it were, a new act of creation (2 Cor 4:6). The human acceptance of God's self-communication is a divine work to be compared with the original act of creation (2 Cor 5:17). When believers see the glory of the Lord, this happens because the interior, invisible action of the Holy Spirit has made them free to do so (2 Cor 3:17f.). As Paul experiences and interprets his Christian existence, it takes the *creative* and *liberating* action of God to bring about faith.

To sum this up: Preaching (in all its forms) recounts the community's experience of the divine self-communication. Interiorly grace prompts hearers to accept the good news, open themselves up to the experience and enter the community of faith. But can we press beyond this rather formal account to say something about the respective roles of reason, freedom and imagination? How does *homo cognoscens, decidens* and *sperans* reach faith? The question can be reversed. Where and how does faith insert itself into human existence? As the interior presence of divine grace associated with the exterior presentation of the Christian message does not bypass our human powers but operates through them, we can now reflect on the rational and imaginative use of freedom in one's path to faith.

4. The Role of Reason

(a) Some Christians, it must be admitted, have not been particularly concerned with the rational character of faith—whether it is matter of people coming to believe for the first time or remaining believers. According to Kierkegaard's classic formulation in his *Concluding Unscientific Postscript,* faith is "an objective uncertainty held fast with the most passionate inwardness." In Karl Barth's view we have no right—when faced with the divine revelation—to raise questions, seek reasons and weigh evidence. This revelation puts us into question, so that the only proper attitude must be one of obedient acceptance. Barth renounced reason, and in the spirit of *"credo quia absurdum"* he called for an irrational commitment.

> What could be more irrational and laughable, ridiculous and impossible, than God's words to Abraham?. . . Moreover, all the articles of our Christian belief are, when considered rationally, just as impossible and mendacious and preposterous. Faith, however, is completely abreast of the situation. It grips reason by the throat and strangles the beast.[4]

Some years ago I attended a course on ancient history in which the lecturer began the section concerning the rise of Christianity by quoting Franz Werfel's words about Lourdes: "For those who believe no explanation is necessary. For those who do not believe no explanation is possible." In these terms one either acknowledges in faith that God's saving purposes were at work in the foundation and spread of Christianity or one simply does not see it that way at all. No evidence could or should be produced to justify faith's vision. It is simply misguided to seek such legitimation.

Nevertheless, views that disdain the rational aspect of faith are *neither fully human nor properly Christian.* Back in Chapter II we saw how experience has a multi-leveled structure and involves all our human powers, mind and reason included. People come to believe when in the midst of life's experiences they encounter the good news about Christ. Knowledge and understanding will necessarily have at least a minimal place in that move toward faith. Further, experience entails discernment, interpretation and expression, all of which processes are inconceivable apart from human reason.

Secondly, to exclude reason from the sphere of Christian faith turns faith into an irrational *sacrificium intellectus* which fails to respect what creation and redemption mean. A blind, uninformed faith is an affront to God who creates human beings in the divine image as rational *homines cognoscentes*. Their power of reason discloses their divine origin. It would then seem unaccountably odd if intellectual knowledge and rational reflection played no part in the act of faith by which human beings submit to God and gratefully accept the divine self-communication.

Furthermore, faith in the God who creates and guides human history assumes its precise shape (in the special history of revelation and salvation) through acknowledging the climax of the divine self-communication in Christ's incarnation, life, death and resurrection. That redemptive climax requires no blind decision which strangles reason. After all, the Johannine beatitude on faith (Jn 20:29) does not run: "Blessed are they who have no rational grounds whatsoever for their faith and yet have believed." Rather the blessing goes out to those who lack the powerful, direct evidence that confronts Thomas and yet profess the same faith in Jesus as their Lord and God. Earlier in John's Gospel, if Jesus insists on the Father's divine "attraction" which invites our obedient submission, he does not describe faith as follows: "No one can come to me unless the Father draws him in a state of utter uncertainty and blind commitment that dismisses all evidence, reasons and explanations (6:44).

Ultimately it is a question of rightly recognizing the role of reason for faith—making neither too little nor too much of it. Here the language of "leaping" will only lead us astray, no matter whether we insist that the decision of faith is not a leap into the dark but into the light, or that faith is no leap from the dark but from the twilight. "Leaping" too readily suggests abandoning something: a boat, a building, one side of a stream, the solid ground and so forth. But Christian faith does not call on us to abandon anything good, let alone the light and guidance of reason. Hence it seems closer to the truth if we speak of faith as a risk, an adventure or a journey in which reason enjoys an essential, if limited, role.

Present experience and past history point to grounds of faith which reason examines and checks. The Christian community can be experienced as a plausible and attractive religious option. The evident goodness found among many of its members and other signs like miracles of healing testify now to a divine endorsement. Moreover, history provides key grounds for faith. Earlier we looked at that remarkable group of people, the Hebrew prophets. Then too the Old Testament concept of God comes across as a kind of moral miracle. Historical reason may reach a deep center of conviction when it ponders the life, death and resurrection of Jesus, the one whose story lies at the heart of Christian claims.

(b) Yet in all of this search to ground faith in experience and history, human reasoning—no matter whether it remains explicit or becomes fully elaborated—will certainly never find irresistible and overwhelmingly clear evidence and publicly demonstrable proof. The truth of the Christian confession will not be settled by simply scrutinizing the reasons, historical and otherwise, and producing "knockdown" arguments that satisfy everyone. We can go astray by demanding comprehensive and compelling guarantees for our reason, instead of being content with those grounds which are available. Any "merely rational" approach which aims at an impartial investigation and a purely objective assessment of the evidence falls down in several ways.

First, a "merely rational" approach to the Christian confession of God's self-revelation in Christ makes the mistake of aiming to put aside *subjective dispositions* as sources of unfortunate interference. In the name of intellectual honesty such an approach wrongheadedly tries to suppress these dispositions and capitulates to the illusion that it can study the confession of faith in an "unprejudiced" and thoroughly "objective" manner.

In Chapter I we noted how Gadamer and others have convincingly challenged what he calls "the prejudice against prejudice." He rightly argues against any allegedly "rational" effort to wipe out presuppositions and begin experiencing or studying anything from allegedly neutral grounds. There is simply no such thing as an experience free from all preconditioning and subjective expectations.

Social influences of all kinds shape the way we enter into and interpret fresh experiences—in this case our hearing some presentation of the Christian confession. Our own *personal* attitudes, values and whole mind-set modify every experience and its interpretation. Here we dare not erase the point made in Chapter II: Both the collective horizon of society and our individual horizon will shape and color any experience, above all when we face a message that promises to deal with our ultimate bewilderments and satisfy our deepest needs. Here, if anywhere, there can be no such thing as a purely "objective," neutral and non-interpreted experience.

To sum up: On the one hand, subjective dispositions could play havoc with us if we remain stubbornly unaware of them. But, on the other hand, they have an essential role when we experience anything—and especially when we are confronted with a faith that offers a profound center of conviction on which to base our lives.

The second thing wrong with a more or less "purely rational" presentation of their faith by some Christians is this: They tidy away the fact that the *evidence* from the past (and present), if "taken by itself," does not constrain people to accept the Christian confession. Such evidential considerations lend a certain credibility but remain limited in their force. We noted a key question regarding the Old Testament prophets who presented their message as the word of the Lord. Can we prove that at times those prophets really did encounter God in some special way and receive a divine message? Was it something more than the prophets saying in a loud, authoritative voice: "Now, I'm telling you"? Back in Chapter III we also observed the element of concealment involved in acts of God such as the Babylonian captivity, the crucifixion of Jesus and his resurrection. In some cases we might feel satisfied that it would be absurd to deny that certain alleged acts of God like the crucifixion took place. But can historical evidence *also* establish that this event carried the significance for revelation and salvation that Christian faith sees in it? In other cases, such as the resurrection, assessing the arguments for and against notoriously leads to no general agreement that the event even happened—let alone bore this or that significance.[5]

The ministry of Jesus exemplifies the way that sheerly rational examination of the evidence is not enough. Like (and even more than) the prophets before him, the best Christian preachers after him and outstanding leaders in other religions, Jesus presents his message in imaginative, symbolic language. Those who prize logical argument or even see mathematical proof as the ideal have to face the unpalatable truth: parables, symbols, myths and metaphors remain untranslatable or at least not fully translatable into rational discourse. Jesus' parables and imaginative language cannot simply be translated into such discourse and so become material for straight logical argumentation. Further, the Gospel writers may make much of his miraculous activity but they are aware that even the most striking miracles would not and will not compel belief (Jn 11:48; 12:37). No miracle proves the Christian faith in the way that a conclusive scientific experiment might establish some truth.

Even after the resurrection and the coming of the Holy Spirit the early Christians have to admit that God is not yet manifested unambiguously and irresistibly. The limited nature of the divine self-revelation means that this revelation can be overlooked, misunderstood and become the occasion of scandal and contradiction. At best it can be said: "Now we see in a mirror dimly.... Now I know in part" (1 Cor 13:12). At worst the Christian message can look like an affront to human ideas (1 Cor 1:18–2:8)—"a stumbling block to Jews and a folly to Gentiles." It is not merely that this message is accessible only through the testimony of witnesses: "God raised" Jesus of Nazareth "on the third day," declares St. Peter, "and made him manifest; not to all the people but to us who were chosen by God as witnesses" (Acts 10:40f.). The very Gospel itself can appear strange and deserving of mockery (Acts 17:32). Paul admits that the "wisdom" which he offers is not "of this age": "We impart a secret and hidden wisdom of God." To describe his message he uses the words of Isaiah: " 'What no eye has seen, nor ear heard, nor the heart of man conceived, what God has prepared for those who love him,' God has revealed to us" (1 Cor 2:6f., 9f.). The strange paradox of the divine self-communication centers on this. When Christ was "made sin" and hung "cursed upon the tree," "God was in Christ reconciling the world to himself" (Gal 3:13; 2 Cor 5:18–21). This confession of faith runs counter to human ways of thinking and helps to explain why people may remain unmoved by its presentation.

To sum up: The *evidence* for the Christian confession is *limited,* while the very *content* of that message may come across as strange, repellent and certainly not compelling and self-authenticating. Hence it is no surprise that many do not leap headlong to embrace the Christian faith which must then co-exist with competing religions and world views.

In the third place, if (from historical investigation and other sources) full, "objective" evidence for the truth of the Christian message were available, *faith would be ruled out.* A mass of evidence that to everyone's satisfaction totally supported the Christian confession would reduce faith to the necessary conclusion of an argument and forget that it is free commitment. If it were *merely* a matter of reason alone, we could run the evidence through a computer and have our assured conclusion. However, unless it remains a free option, faith is no longer faith. Absolutely tangible guarantees and "knockdown" proofs would rule out, and not rule in, faith. The limitations in the evidence leave room for faith. There is enough evidence to make a proper claim on us but not enough to take away freedom. This freedom of faith goes beyond the freedom involved, let us say, in accepting the existence of flying saucers or dismissing as silly dreams all the reports about visitors from outer space. It is the freedom required for a personal relationship: in this case the relationship between the believing self and the risen Christ to whom allegiance is given.[6] We will return to this point shortly.

Fourth, a "merely rational" understanding of faith forgets that we need *to go beyond the evidence.*[7] In a clear sense we cannot wait until all the evidence is in. We do not know, for example, how many people will continue to accept the Christian confession nor what course the community with faith in Jesus will take. But as actors in the world now we must choose, stake ourselves on our attitude toward him, and answer for ourselves the questions: What kind of life will be possible on the basis of such faith? Will it enable us to deal creatively and productively with our world?

This "going beyond the evidence" entails both *cognitive* and moral freedom. Believers will freely "know" the reality of Jesus and the Christian message about him even as they freely "ac-knowledge" his claim on them. It is open to them to ignore the truth and not honor the claim. This recalls a point made in Chapter III apropos of Acts of God. The believer recognizes in events like the return from the Babylonian captivity and the death of Jesus a special presence and a particular activity of God.

Knowing these events for what they are entails acknowledging their religious claim and deciding on new patterns of action. In short, an Act of God, when known as such, invites allegiance and involvement.

Committed "rationalists" of all kinds, of course, set their faces against any going beyond the evidence. One Cambridge scientist, W. K. Clifford, put this way the case for staying within the limits of evidence alone: "It is wrong, always, everywhere and for anyone to believe anything on insufficient evidence."[8] This sweeping generalization is obviously vulnerable to the question: What counts as *insufficient* evidence? The standards for deciding that sufficient evidence is available vary enormously from person to person and from case to case. Moreover, as regards faith in Christ and other personal relationships, we primarily believe (in) someone rather than something. Hence Clifford's assertion should be confronted with a question: Is it wrong, always, everywhere and for anyone to believe *someone* on what *others* might consider insufficient evidence?

So far these reflections on *the role of reason* in the human being's response of faith have taken a "yes-but" form. Yes, we need to uphold this role against those who deny or minimize it. But—faith may not, therefore, be reduced to a merely rational transaction. Yes, faith is *reasonable;* it can point to evidence in support of itself. But—faith is not *rational,* at least not rational in the sense of being able to provide totally comprehensive and utterly conclusive arguments for its position.

However, the discussion must be taken further. It is not enough simply to say that reason (historical and otherwise) plays an essential but limited role for faith. As we shall see, we are not dealing with some Cartesian conjunction of reason *and* will (or understanding *and* free decision), in which reason supplies some arguments but leaves the will free to make its option. Faith does not leave reason, will and—we should add—imagination in isolation but brings them together so that they influence each other in an integrated, reciprocal fashion. The knowing, deciding and hoping of the *homo cognoscens, decidens* and *sperans* belong together in the one act of faith. To this we now turn.

5. Knowing, Loving and Imagining

Robert Frost remarks somewhere: "What a man needs is the courage to take a chance on his own discriminations." Here the poet singles out the decision of the will and the discerning of the mind. To these we should add two other factors: the human imagination and that divine assistance which makes possible the response of faith. "What a person needs is the divine light and strength which will support the courage to trust one's imagination and take a chance on one's own discriminations." Empowered by grace, people respond to God's self-communication in Christ with the rational confession, free commitment and hopeful imagination of faith.

To put matters equivalently: The confession of truth is actuated and accompanied by self-commitment and expectant confidence. Let us give some further shape to these reflections.

First of all, we need to establish the interaction of confession and commitment, or of knowing and deciding/loving. There are several ways of tackling this. To begin with, faith is more than simply confessing a set of truths or affirming some objective facts which happen to look reasonably plausible. Besides recognizing certain things as true, faith means committing oneself by accepting *a personal relationship* with Jesus Christ. Entering any personal relationship always requires an element of risk and the exercise of freedom. In taking on a lasting commitment like marriage one normally knows something about the other person, the factors involved and the likely development of the relationship, *but not everything.* The relationship is accepted despite a lack of total knowledge. It begins and grows as the intriguing result of reason and risk or—to use Frost's language—the product of discrimination and courage.

From beginning to end Christian faith is dominated by the fact that it constitutes a personal relationship to Jesus of Nazareth, who has been revealed as Son of God and Savior or, in other words, as God's truth and grace (Jn 1:14). This faith includes a confession *of* Christ as crucified and risen, not just a confession of some good news "out there" and "back there" about a death and a resurrection. It brings a commitment *to* Christ, not just a general commitment to live according to some new and attractive ideals. It entails a hopeful confidence *in* Christ, not just an unspecified hope in a future resurrection that floats free of its origin in him.

To bring out the fact that Christian faith means confessing Jesus Christ, being committed to him and having confidence in him, we can modify two words used above (orthodoxy or orthopraxy) and coin a third so as to speak of faith's three dimensions as *Christodoxy, Christopraxy* and *Christoelpis* (hope in Christ). Yet whatever terminology we decide to adopt, one thing is clear. Its particular relationship to Jesus Christ sets Christian faith apart from faith as a general human phenomenon, even (or especially?) when it takes the form of the kind of "atheist's faith" briefly mentioned in Chapter I.

Believers know the truth of their Christian confession by dwelling in Christ and sharing his consciousness of divine sonship (Rom 8:15; Gal 4:6). They personally "convert" to him with their head *and* heart. They go beyond the doctrines and reasons that make up the content of their confession *(fides quae)* to relate to the person of Jesus who has intervened in the history of the world and in their personal history. Their confession proves self-involving *(fides qua).* Knowing its truth entails "ac-knowledging" and obediently accepting Jesus Christ (and themselves in the light of Christ).

John's Gospel powerfully presents the drama of the human person face to face with Christ. Believing in him or refusing to believe in him will decide the point and outcome of one's life. But reason alone will not bring about this personal relationship of faith. The opponents of Jesus know the Scriptures (5:39), but hatred (8:40ff.) rather than love accompanies their scholarship. They deploy intellectual resources which make them superior to people like the Samaritan woman or the man born blind. But being closed to the possibility of "acknowledging" Jesus, they will never know him.

Ideally faith's personal relationship entails a radical and total confession of the truth about Jesus and a full commitment (in trusting hope) to his person. But obviously there are plentiful limitations and imperfections which affect any human confession and commitment. If the God revealed in Jesus Christ *should* be the object of our unconditional love and absolute devotion, we can be painfully aware that our allegiance to his person is less than total and our assent to his truth trails along hesitatingly.

Nevertheless, *all this falling short of the ideal only serves to confirm the essence of faith as a personal relationship.* A fresh and innocent personal relationship may gather strength, grow weak or even cease altogether. This is all part of the contingent nature of human life. Despite its firm confession, commitment, and confidence, faith always remains precarious and vulnerable. And this is because in personal relationships, as elsewhere, human beings spend their lives "trying things on for size" and remain open at every point to change, growth and collapse.

Some reflections on *knowing and deciding* or *knowing and loving* offer a second way of tackling the interaction of confession and commitment. Rahner expresses the mutual influence in a simple, luminous way: "Free decision does not merely follow from knowledge; it also influences the latter."[9] In other words, if we commit ourselves after accepting the reasons and seeing the truth, we also accept the reasons and see the truth *because* we are already freely inclined to do so. Personal commitments follow from *and also* shape our knowing. This is not to assert that freedom is simply reducible to knowledge or vice versa, but to recall the volitional moment of knowledge. When we dealt with the link between the spiritual practice and critical theory of the theologian (in Chapter I), we noted the direct connection between understanding and (willing) practice. There we argued against the belief that the more uncommitted we are, the better we will understand. Of course, we should not go to the other extreme and maintain that vehement commitment *proves* the truth of something. The twentieth century has repeatedly thrown up cases of people ready to risk and give their lives in the service of some demonic absurdity. Nevertheless, experience shows that we will truly know and understand other people through our commitment to them. In the sector of interpersonal relations (and elsewhere) we know the truth by dwelling in it.

Hence when it is a matter of our knowing God, the risen Christ, a partner in marriage or some other person or thing of profound personal importance to us, *we do not first know God,* the risen Christ or the partner in marriage in some "neutral" way, *and only then decide* whether we will love, hate, or act in this way or that. Free decisions always go hand in hand with such personal knowing.

The relationship of knowing and deciding can be put this way: *The use or misuse of freedom will determine to some extent the knowledge which we are open to receive and the reasons we are ready to appreciate.* A sincere desire to know the truth, a humble openness to reality and—in general—the moral state of our mind will affect the operations of our reason. To quote John's Gospel: "Everyone who does evil hates the light and does not come to the light. . . . But he who does what is true comes to the light" (3:20f.). Moral deviation will block our knowing the truth, just as genuine love will make it possible. To recognize the divine self-revelation, human beings must be ready to turn freely from their sinfulness. Hence they are not so much told (either by the Old Testament prophets or by Jesus himself) "See the truth" or "Read history correctly" as "Repent, do the divine will, and receive God's merciful grace." The reality of God's self-revelation will remain an unintelligible puzzle to sinful men and women to the extent that they refuse the gift of conversion. Hence Rahner rightly stresses how the ultimate realities "can become the object of explicit knowledge only to the extent that this knowledge fits into the structure of the love for which man has opted in his concrete conduct."[10]

This brings us to the interaction of *knowing and loving.* According to the traditional adage "Nihil volitum nisi precognitum," we desire and love something because we have already seen and known it. But interpersonal relationships and other areas of human experience show how the influence can also run in the opposite direction. We will know the truth—and especially the truth about persons—because we already love them: *Nihil cognitum nisi prevolitum.* Love predisposes us to see. Those who do not love will fail to see the truth. In Aquinas' lapidary phrase, "Ubi amor, ibi oculus" (Where there is love, there is vision).[11] Knowing and loving remain inseparably together—in function of each other.

We can assemble all this around our theme. The commitment of love both depends upon and makes possible the confession of faith. We not only freely decide to commit ourselves because we already see the truth of Christian faith, but also we see and confess that truth in the light of love. Knowing the truth prompts us to make our option of love. At the same time, the option of love enables us to leap into the light of truth. It is a case of "both/and" rather than the "either/or" implied by

Robert Bolt's words: "Finally it is not a matter of reason; finally it is a matter of love." As St. John realized with blinding clarity, if we lovingly believe *in* Jesus, we will come to the truth and believe *that* he is Son of God and vice versa.

So far we have dwelt on the interaction between knowing and deciding/loving. It is high time to let *the imagination of hope* enter the discussion. This imagination also belongs to those permanent structures of the human person which render faith possible when the exterior word and the interior promptings of the Holy Spirit invite someone to believe in Christ. The imagination of hope sets one free to leap forward to the final purposes of the whole scheme of things. The *homo cognoscens* will see and confess the truth not only because *qua homo decidens* he or she is drawn by and committed to the good, but also because *qua homo sperans* he or she imaginatively and confidently anticipates in hope a personal future with God. Under the impact of present love and future hope, faith sees meaning in the historical "data" about Jesus' life, death and resurrection. In faith's knowledge (and in fact in all human knowing) there is a moment both of free option *and* of an imagination that seizes something of the future. Conversely, by finding the truth the confession of faith supports the leap of love and the imagination of hope. In brief, the human response of faith to the divine self-communication in Christ reveals a deep, mutual interaction between knowing, deciding *and hoping.*

Sadly enough, it is often a negative situation which serves to illustrate the influence of hope upon knowledge and decision. Pain, frustration and bewilderment can reach the point where people can no longer master despair. Their hopeless weariness brings a loss of nerve and an inability to understand reality. Genuine despair lacks courage for living and finds existence pointless. If they totally lack the imagination of hope, they will neither see and confess the truth nor commit themselves in love.

Thus we are in a position to appreciate the elements of *risk* and *mystery* in the act of faith. The risk of faith consists in the leap of love and the imagination of hope. Loving and imagining are risky enterprises never to be justified simply on the basis of known facts or clear and distinct reasons.

Then the element of mystery persists. Our own lives, the lives of other people and the world of literature constantly confront us with that mysterious process by which men and women make their decisions. In *Burnt Norton* T. S. Eliot wrote:

Footfalls echo in the memory
Down the passage which we did not take
Towards the door we never opened
Into the rose-garden.

Why did we decide not to take that passage, open that door and go out into the rose-garden? At the climax of Iris Murdoch's *The Sandcastle,* why does the hero remain seated at the dinner table instead of rushing after the girl he has fallen in love with? What happens when people make this kind of decision which can shape their lives either for evil or for good? Free decisions, especially ones that make or break a human life, can never be *fully* explained even to oneself, let alone to another.

All the more does a sense of mystery hover over the free decision to believe in Jesus Christ. Faith brings a mysterious experience of self-commitment in which—led by the Holy Spirit in the depths of their being—men and women take their fundamental option intelligently, yet freely and so uncompelled by any reasons or other factors.

6. A Plan

At this point it could help to summarize our reflections schematically.

Homo Interrogans	Time Sign	Response of Faith	Deus trinus autocommunicans Deus loquens et agens
Homo cognoscens What can I know?	Past	Confession:Ortho-(Christo)doxy	Acts of God: climax in paschal mystery
Homo decidens What should I do?	Present	Commitment: Ortho-(Christo)praxy	Call to communion with God
Homo sperans What may I hope for?	Future	Confidence: Ortho-(Christo)elpis	Promise of a future with God

As one who knows, decides and hopes, the human person comes under the influence of the *external* presentation of the Christian message and the *internal* divine illumination. The free act of faith becomes possible. The human questions find in Christ the divine answer. Three additional comments will help to fill out the material indicated in this plan.

First, the divine self-communication expresses itself in the Acts of God, the call to the free commitment of faith and the word of promise for the future. We can relate this account of the *Deus agens et loquens* (= *invitans et promittens*) to the heart of the good news. The death and resurrection of Jesus Christ brought *the* definitive divine Act of revelation and salvation on behalf of the human race. With the first Good Friday, Easter Sunday and Pentecost, the Father raised his Son from the dead (Gal 1:1; Rom 1:3 etc.) to send us the Holy Spirit (Rom 5:5) and hold out to us the promise of future resurrection (Rom 8:11). This climactic divine deed constitutes the center of faith's confession (Rom 10:9). It calls now for an obedient commitment "from the heart" (Rom 6:17) which makes us "walk in newness of life" (Rom 6:4). It forms the foundation of a confident hope for the final reality of resurrection (Rom 6:8).

Second, at bottom the response of faith is an act of *identification*— in two senses. The Christian message both interprets Jesus himself and promises to interpret definitively human existence. By accepting this message and thus answering the question "Who do you say that I am?" believers identify *both* Jesus (as the one who gives ultimate meaning to their lives) *and* themselves in the one act of faith. In coming to him they also come to themselves in a profound act of self-identification. Thus two things happen. In *identifying* Jesus as *the* truth and grace of God, they consciously *submit* to him, enter into a communion of life with the Trinity, and *abandon* the future trustingly into the divine hands. And at the same time they know and possess themselves in their full dignity.

We noted above how a long line of Christian thinkers have understood questioning about God to be inseparably connected with any ultimate questioning about oneself. Depth experiences and crucial turning points in our lives confront us with the mystery of self *and* the mystery of God. Hence when faith occurs, we simultaneously identify our existence in a new way. Experiencing and knowing God revealed in Jesus Christ entails experiencing and knowing oneself in a fresh light.

Third, in what ideally aims at being a total and unconditional acceptance of Christ, believers find a *personal certainty* which can co-exist with the recognition of theoretical difficulties. As we have seen, the reasons supporting the Christian message remain limited and at points its contents can come across as strange. Nevertheless, faith's personal relationship with Jesus yields a lived certainty unlike more "objective" certainties such as those of mathematics and the natural sciences. It is a special kind of certainty in that it finds the ultimate meaning of human existence to be decided, lived and expressed through *this* personal relationship. By identifying Jesus and themselves in the act of faith, believers become certain of him and themselves, even if like Paul's "hope against hope" (Rom 4:18) their personal certainty must cope with theoretical and "objective" uncertainties.

Throughout this chapter I am painfully aware that here and there respectable "oughts" may have been transmuted into an objectionable "is" or "will be." Faith, perhaps more than any other theological theme, tempts one to move from what one thinks *should* be the case to statements about what *is* or *will be* the case. A scheme coherent in itself may not correspond fully to the facts. Readers can decide whether the overall scheme is verified in their own experience of faith. But before closing the chapter it seems advisable to append a coda (which will take up some obvious objections) and add an excursus on the particular issue of faith and history.

7. A Coda

Like all neat schemes the version of faith given in this chapter may have gone too far in tidying up reality to make it conform to a clear and typical pattern. Hence I want now to qualify matters, meet some objections and recognize one alternate approach.

(a) One problem about using *Kant's three questions* has already floated to the surface: the contented individualism that sells short the social dimension of human knowledge, action and hope. It may have been better to have spoken of "homines interrogantes" and restated the questions as: "What can we know? What should we do? What may we hope for?" Moreover, these questions could easily encourage us to stress human activity and downplay the divine initiative. When we recall God's loving self-communication, it would be more accurate to ask: "What can we *receive* by way of knowledge about the divine acts of revelation and salvation, support now for the option of love, and courage for the future?"

However, in the context of faith one advantage peeps through if we retain the "I" of Kant's questions. They can serve to bring out the way in which the act of faith remains "my" act and allows of no substitute. Even though faith is always a divine gift which comes through the power and light of the Holy Spirit, in the decision to believe no one can be represented by another. St. Paul experiences and speaks of the Spirit dwelling in us (Rom 8:9, 11 etc.) and praying in us (Rom 8:26). But there are limits to this language. The apostle never says: "The Holy Spirit believes in us." Faith may be a gift but it can only be *my* act.

Another problem with Kant's three questions: We risk misrepresenting their original sense by introducing them into our scheme of faith. For example, where he aimed to find a *scientific* theory and base for knowledge, the confession of faith expresses a knowledge of the heart: "If you confess with your lips that Jesus is Lord and *believe in your heart* that God raised him from the dead you will be saved" (Rom 10:9). Nevertheless, the questions remain useful and illuminating. We can honor and preserve their original form, provided we do not allege that we intend to use them precisely in Kant's sense.

Finally, Kant's questions may overstress the spiritual side of the human person as one who knows, decides and hopes. What of the human person as one who through his or her bodily existence experiences *feelings* of fear, depression, joy, sexual desire, hunger and so forth? Would the basic condition of men and women be more clearly indicated by such questions as "How do I feel? What do I fear? What may I yearn for?"

In short, would we do better to concentrate on the *homo patiens* rather than interpret the human person as a free and rational questioner?

Obviously it would be absurd to ignore feelings. They animate and endow our existence with life. As we saw in Chapter II and elsewhere, they belong in any adequate account of human experience, religious or otherwise. Nevertheless, no matter how our feelings color and affect our knowing, deciding and hoping, they cannot substitute for them. In identifying Christ and ourselves in faith, each of us acts primarily as *homo cognoscens, decidens* and *sperans.*

(b) A further question: The reference to *past, present and future* respects the historical nature of human existence. At the same time, however, will it distort reality by associating knowledge (confession) with the past, decision (commitment) with the present, and hope (confidence) with the future? Obviously human knowing does not merely concern the past but reaches out also to present and future matters. Likewise hoping is not "confined" to the future. Christian hope finds its basis by remembering the divine promise communicated once and for all through the life, death and resurrection of Jesus. Moreover, it makes sense for an individual to declare: "I hope *to have received* forgiveness for my sins." Lastly, the believing commitment of a figure like Abraham maintains a strong relationship to an invisible and as yet unrealized future (Gen 12:1–4).

Nevertheless, a certain time signature does characterize, albeit not exclusively, the thrust of faith's knowledge, as well as faith's decision and confident hope. In the Old Testament the people's confession of faith looked back to recount the Acts of God which had manifested the divine intention to save and cherish them (Deut 26:5–9). Similarly the New Testament confession of faith remembers and acknowledges what God *has done*—particularly in the death and resurrection of Jesus (Rom 10:9; 1 Cor 15:3ff.). Further, it should hardly provoke dissent to note that faith's commitment centers on what should and can be decided upon and carried out here and now. Lastly, we should not hedge faith's confident hope around with too many qualifications and avoid the clear-cut fact that as such it expects what is to come.

(c) A third difficulty concerns the choice of the last word to complete the triad: "confession," "commitment" and "confidence." It is clear that confidence deeply qualifies both confession and commitment, and hence may not be able to set up on its own as a reasonably distinct aspect of faith's response. To begin with, it is because we confidently trust the apostolic witness to Jesus' resurrection that we can make our confession of faith: "Jesus is risen. Jesus lives." Likewise believers freely decide now to commit themselves because they have confidence in the present divine call reaching them through the Church's proclamation.

Beyond question, confidence intertwines with confession and commitment. This is part of that mutual reciprocity and interaction of these three moments in the one act of faith on which we have already dwelt. Nevertheless, a German Protestant tradition (kept alive, for example, by Pannenberg[12]) which practically reduces faith to *fiducia* rightly senses one thing: the special but not exclusive link between faith's trusting confidence and the future. St. Paul presents his classic example of faith, Abraham, in a manner that highlights the peculiar connection between the believer's confidence and what lies ahead (Rom 4:18–22).

(d) Another issue should be faced at some point. This chapter has considered the faith of those who respond to the divine self-communication as they experience it in the *special* history of revelation/salvation. But what is to be said about the faith of those who belong to the general history of revelation/salvation? If all these millions of men and women share the same human condition and the same basic orientation toward God (transcendental experience), to what extent will their response to the divine self-communication as they consciously experience it resemble the faith-response of Christian believers?

The Lord's account of the last judgment singles out what human beings do or fail to do for others (and especially those in need) as *the* basis for making that judgment (Matt 25:31–46). This highlights the second division of faith, *commitment.* Obviously any such fundamental option for or against the practice of a caring love will be conditioned by what one can *know* and by what one is in the position *to hope for.* The loving commitment of those who have never heard the Christian message cannot be consciously motivated and shaped by faith in Jesus Christ. The actual form in which they answer the questions "What can I know?" and "What may I hope for?" will be limited by the possibilities of their religious and cultural context. Their convictions about the ultimate nature and destiny of human existence will influence and be influenced by their commitment. We cannot maintain a mutual interaction between confession, commitment and confession in the case of Christian faith and then refuse to recognize it in the case of other faiths. At the same time, of course, all faith-responses will take shape as some kind of confession, commitment and trusting confidence—in answer to the three basic questions which come with human existence itself.

(e) A further objection can be expressed this way: Has this chapter set out a self-validating circle of ideas which *cuts up the dynamic, living reality of Christian faith?* Does the plan wrongly divide up elements which exist only in a lived unity?

One should agree that such an existential whole as faith cannot be split into several fragments as if they were separable items that could enjoy a life of their own. It is *one* act when in faith we experience and accept the mysterious presence and nearness of God. However, by distinguishing several moments and dimensions we may be enabled to understand better that complex unity which is faith.

(f) Perhaps the most serious challenge to the analysis which has been given of faith touches the triad: *faith, hope and love.* The three basic attitudes constitute together a total response to God's loving initiative in Christ. Before God's revealing and active word human beings respond by knowing God in *faith,* affirming what God has done (in the past) and assenting to the content of their confession. God's love invites a response of *love* which here and now submits itself obediently to the divine will. The divine word of promise calls for a trusting *hope* that finds its absolute future in God.

In other words, should we eliminate the triple division of faith into confession, commitment and confidence (which look respectively to the past, present and future), substitute faith, love and hope, and deploy that scheme as follows? The *confession of faith* assents to the truth about God's self-communication in human history. The *option of love* consents to a personal relationship with Jesus, our risen and present Lord. The *imagination of hope* anticipates the future promised through his death and resurrection.

There is much to be said for this alternative. It introduces, for instance, the possibility of relating the "horizontal" and "vertical" dimensions of human life. We all have a basic need to believe and be believed in, to hope and be hoped in, to love and be loved—and all of this on the horizontal level of our relationship with other human beings. A failure of faith, hope and love in these interpersonal relationships can stand at the basis of difficulties in faith, hope and love toward God. Positively, faith, hope and love in our "vertical" relationship with the Triune God should permeate our "horizontal" relationships with other human beings, and vice versa. No other book in the New Testament has stressed this more than the First Letter of John. In its vision believing, hoping and, above all, *loving* should characterize our personal response to God *and* to our brothers and sisters in the human family.

All in all, we should not pull back from frankly accepting faith, hope and love as a rich alternative for describing the appropriate human response to the divine self-communication.[13] At the same time, however, faith as such remains a legitimate "heading" for dealing with that response—*provided,* of course, that we follow the example of the Second Vatican Council (*Dei Verbum,* n. 5) and *understand faith comprehensively* as a confession, commitment and confidence which constitutes the "yes" of the whole person to the climax of God's revealing and saving activity in the incarnation, life, death and resurrection of Christ.

(g) The reference of God's "revealing and saving activity" brings us to the last point in this coda. Inevitably the concentration on *faith* as the proper human response to God's self-communication has involved attending more to the divine self-*revelation.* As correlatives, faith and revelation draw attention to each other.

Nevertheless, revelation *and salvation* belong together as inseparable elements in God's self-communication. Of course, if we take up that self-communication *precisely as disclosed,* we will call it the divine revelation which invites human faith. But the essential unity of those two elements must not be pushed aside. In faith the believer finds in Christ not only a Revealer but also a Savior, the Son of God who draws near in love. The confession of our faith acknowledges Christ crucified and risen to be supremely significant for our salvation. The divine call goes out to sinful people and invites them to submit to Christ the Lord and live now a life of love. Then faith looks forward confidently to a future resurrection through which will come a full deliverance from evil. Thus salvation touches all three dimensions of faith's response to the divine self-communication: confession, commitment and confidence.

At the level of the community the experience of the divine self-communication and the response of faith lead to shared expressions of faith: creeds, dogmas and other forms of teaching. These common confessions form the theme for the following chapter. But before taking up that theme, I want to insert an excursus on the issue of faith and history.

EXCURSUS:
HISTORICAL KNOWLEDGE AND FAITH

Only the metaphysical can save, never the historical.
Johann Gottlieb Fichte

What role or roles does *historical* knowledge play in the genesis of Christian faith?[14] Not to raise the question would be disturbingly at odds not only with this present chapter but also with earlier material. Chapter III recalled the fact that Christianity is professedly an historical religion which recognizes certain events of history as the means par excellence by which the divine self-communication has entered and continues to enter human history. Then this chapter has presented faith as a *reasonable* commitment which, even if it is not exclusively rational, points to historical evidence and confesses what it believes about certain past events as Acts of God.

Christian faith cannot do without historical knowledge. Yet how much historical knowledge does it need? And who provides the believer with the necessary knowledge?

That fallen father of modern exegesis and theology, Rudolf Bultmann, answered these questions by drastically reducing the amount of historical knowledge needed for faith to the assertion "that Jesus came," and decreeing that the historian as such can never be involved in the process by which even this minimum reaches the believer: "Faith, being personal decision, cannot be dependent upon an historian's labor."[15] In this view (which has its roots in Lessing and the Enlightenment), the certainty of faith's decision could not depend upon the uncertainties of historical knowledge. The rationalism of the Enlightenment helped to provoke later irrationalism. Bultmann himself is dead, but the issue of historical knowledge and faith remains alive and highly complex. Let me content myself here to stating and briefly expounding several theses.

1. *Christian faith cannot exist without some historical knowledge.* The amount of historical knowledge enjoyed by those who come to faith for the first time obviously varies a great deal, just as does the amount of such knowledge involved in the on-going life of believers. Nevertheless, some such knowledge must be there—at the very least the kind of minimum contained in the Apostles' Creed and implied by the basic sacraments of baptism and the Eucharist. Believers may in fact derive this minimum from "an historian's labor" or may pick up their knowledge in less solemn ways. After all to depend on (some) historical knowledge is not necessarily to depend on (professional) historians. But in all cases faith's personal relationship to Jesus Christ means being able to say something about history, at least his history.

2. *Christian faith does not depend simply on historical knowledge.* As this chapter has already pointed out, faith—if it requires some exercise of reason—depends and draws on things that go beyond reason and, specifically, that go beyond historical reason. Without the grace of an interior divine illumination that accompanies the external presentation of the Christian message, no amount of historical knowledge—even the most extensive and sophisticated kind of knowledge—will bring about faith. The professional historian enjoys no such head-start over others in the race for faith. Moreover, faith entails a loving commitment and a hopeful imagination which freely goes beyond the limited evidence and enters a personal relationship with Christ. "Mere" knowledge, even the most critically acquired knowledge, so long as it remains bereft of grace, love and hope, can never result in faith.

To sum up: Faith is neither based simply on historical knowledge nor a mere prolongation of such knowledge, as though the critical investigation of history could by itself establish and maintain faith. Christian faith may not exist independently of historical knowledge, but it cannot be reduced to it.

3. *The historical knowledge of believers is affected by the loving commitment and hopeful confidence made possible by the external proclamation and the internal grace.* This chapter argued for a mutual interaction between knowing, loving and imagining. Love, for instance, facilitates knowledge, just as knowing makes it possible to love the thing or person already known. This holds good also of historical knowledge. Believers will know the historical truth and see meaning in the history of Jesus because they love him and find in him the object of their hopes—and vice versa, of course. They commit themselves to him in love and trust after they have come to know something of him and his history. Thus the *historical* knowledge of faith also exemplifies the principles "Nihil volitum nisi precognitum" *and* "Nihil cognitum nisi prevolitum."

4. *The certitude of faith's historical knowledge is part of its total certitude.* Faith's certitude at the level of its historical knowledge comes in for routine censure from skeptics. How can faith justify its firm historical claims? What this censure presupposes is that the assurance of faith about matters of past history can be detached from other elements and studied by itself. However, faith's firm answer to the question "What can I know?" belongs to the *one* act in which it answers as well those other questions "What ought I to do?" and "What may I hope for?" by giving its confident allegiance to the person of Christ. Ideally the believer should go all the way *both* with a firm confession of the historical truth about Jesus *and* a full commitment (in trusting hope) to his person. As the act of faith exists only as a lived unity, its certitude qualifies its commitment and confidence as well as its confession.

As regards faith's certitude, it has been usual to make high claims for an objection which goes back to the Enlightenment: How can the absolute assurance of faith depend on knowing events from the past, when such knowledge is always open—at least in principle—to some degree of doubt and revision? Three replies are called for here. (a) "The absolute assurance of faith" depends partly *but not* simply and exclusively on knowing events from the past (thesis two). (b) If such knowledge remains liable to doubt and revision, the commitment and confidence of faith also remain vulnerable. The knowledge and confession of faith are not the only things to worry about. (c) It is a solemn form of cheating to isolate the element of (historical) knowledge, stress its precariousness, insist on faith's assurance being absolute and unconditional, and then pit the precariousness of the knowledge over against that assurance. Historical knowledge is not always that precarious, and—alas—the assurance of faith does not always reach such a pitch of unconditioned absoluteness.

This last reply can do with a little more discussion. The objection fabricates an excessive gap between the "absolute" certitude of faith and the relative and probable results of historical investigation. But surely faith, for all its firm commitment, confession and confidence, remains deeply vulnerable. The only style of life open to us can be no more than tentative, experimental and contingent. There is nothing especially shocking about the fact that with respect to our Christian faith we are always trying things on for size, as we must do in "other" areas. In this endless process of trying things on for size, Christians are at the mercy of history in much the same way as they live at the mercy of reality itself, above all the human reality of other people. In a large variety of ways we rely on others. And one of these ways touches our knowledge of the special history of salvation and, in particular, the life, death and resurrection of Jesus. If we trust that the progress of historical science will not destroy our contact with what we have accepted as the historical ingredients for faith, we are no more giving way to a reckless confidence than when we trust that other changes will not show us that we have been relating to domestic, economic and other sectors of our life in an utterly mistaken fashion. Life would be intolerable if we had to live under the persistent fear that we could be confronted with the startling news that reality is not what we have taken it to be. We admit that it may be logically possible that we have been deluded, but we are confident that it is not so.

Ultimately what I am arguing for here is the view that the confession of faith involves an historical risk. And two important riders must be added at once. Faith does not depend simply upon historical knowledge (thesis two). And the historical risk is part of the general risk of reality as the believer understands reality.

5. *If faith's historical confession weakens or ceases, this will affect the other elements of faith, and vice versa.* It is simply a fact of experience that Christian believers can waver and cease to confess, for example, that Jesus lived, died and rose to bring salvation to the world. They may do so because they judge that historical research has disproved the resurrection or even the existence of Jesus. Or they may make no secret of the fact that they now lack the nerve to maintain either the obedient commitment of faith or a hopeful attitude toward the future. Such failure in commitment or confidence will tamper with faith's confession, and vice versa. Things which hold men and women back from full love and total trust can sap the firmness of their faith, as much as can doubts about the validity of the basic (historical) confession indicated by the Christian message. In short, faith is neither totally made (thesis two) nor totally unmade (this thesis) at the level of the historical confession which responds to the question "What can I know (about the past events of salvation history)?" At each of the three levels of confession, commitment and confidence faith remains humanly vulnerable.

6. *The historical confession of faith moves from the particular to the universal, even as faith's commitment and confidence moves from the universal to the particular.* On the one hand, when faith confesses that "Jesus is Lord" because it believes "that God raised him from the dead" (Rom

10:9), it knows that through his concrete, historical existence Jesus has come to enjoy a universal and absolute function as the Revealer and Savior. This confession can be summed up in the words "Jesus (the particular person from Nazareth) is the Christ (the Lord of the universe)." On the other hand, the questions which give rise to commitment and confidence start by taking a general form: How should a human life be shaped? What may be expected from life and hoped for after death? Such open questions about the nature and destiny of human life find their specific answer in a confident commitment to the particular person of Jesus.

We can put matters this way: The confession of faith moves from the historical (Jesus) to the "metaphysical" (Christ the Lord). Faith's commitment and confidence, on the contrary, move from the metaphysical (questions about the nature and destiny of human beings) to the historical (the answer to these questions in the particular human story). The confession, by being rooted in history, corrects any flight to a set of vague generalities. By recalling the need to face universal issues, faith's commitment and confidence counter the temptation to reduce Christianity to some kind of mere nostalgic interest in the history of Jesus. In brief, faith finds salvation in both the historical (Jesus) and the metaphysical (Christ).

This chapter with its coda and excursus may have appeased somewhat our "rage for order" about faith, that human response to the experience of the divine self-communication. However, before moving beyond that experience, we need to put in one further theme: the community's formulations to which faith gives rise.

VI. SHARED STATEMENTS OF FAITH

> *A statement of faith does not become true because it is put into practice or untrue because it is not put into practice.*
>
> Edward Schillebeeckx

> *What matters ... is how a revelation once given (and definitively given) continues to meet later generations of believers.*
>
> William Reiser

Among the basic ways Israel and later the New Testament Church responded to the divine self-communication was by the construction of common confessions of faith.[1] These could take full and detailed form like the credo found in Deuteronomy 26:5–9 ("A wandering Aramean was my father ..."), or else remain extremely brief like that basic Christian affirmation "Jesus is Lord." Right from its origins the post-apostolic Church followed this practice, and it has continued to produce shared statements of faith as an essential part of its response to the revealing and saving self-communication of the Triune God. These formulations of faith stem from the community's mission to proclaim the good news effectively to every generation.

Inasmuch as these statements derive from the *human* experience of the *divine* self-communication, they are always both anthropological and theological. Even when at the explicit level they primarily state things about the divine reality, they will always at least implicitly say something about the experience and commitments of human beings. Thus confessing the "Creator of heaven and earth" speaks also of the unconditional obedience toward God demanded of rational creatures as well as hinting at the human experience of the divine power and presence in the works of nature.

This chapter examines such statements of faith from four angles: their *function* in the Christian community, their *meaning*, their *truth* and the varying nature of their *authority*.

I
THE FUNCTIONS OF FAITH STATEMENTS

In the post-apostolic Church shared statements of faith have taken indefinitely varied forms: from the Nicene Creed, through the medieval professions of faith, the Augsburg Confession, the Council of Trent's teaching on the sacraments, to the Second Vatican Council's Dogmatic Constitution on the Church *(Lumen Gentium)* and the three documents that have come from the Anglican-Roman Catholic International Commission (hereafter ARCIC) on the Eucharist (1971), ministry (1973) and authority (1976). In the course of nearly two thousand years of Christian history so many shared statements of faith have appeared that it would be impossible even to put a list of their titles between the covers of one book. They have differed in length, in the "area" of faith they considered, in the authoritative status which they claimed, in the number of believers directly or (much more often) indirectly involved in their making, and in the response that they subsequently elicited. Despite the enormous variety of these statements of faith, we can, nevertheless, sort out certain major functions which they persistently fulfill. There are two pairs of words around which we can organize an account of these functions: confession and commitment, description and prescription.

1. Confession and Commitment

Those who produce or endorse new formulations to express their experience of the divine self-communication—whether they be bishops at the Council of Nicaea (325) declaring Christ to be "consubstantial" with the Father or the members of the ARCIC publishing their Windsor Statement on the Eucharist—not only confess what they claim to be the case about the reality of God, human beings and the world but also testify to their own personal commitment. On the one hand, they affirm that such and such, for instance, holds true about Christ's existence and the mystery of the Eucharist. Their statements of faith have an informative value. On the other hand, they also express their personal response in the face of this truth. If they point to the reality of Christ's divine origin or to that of the Eucharist as presence and "memorial," they also commit themselves to appropriate decisions and actions on the basis of their claims about these realities. Thus the confession of Christ as "consubstantial" with the Father entails praising, worshiping and entrusting one's life to him. Likewise the various affirmations made by the Windsor Statement imply a personal commitment to eucharistic practice.

Hence any interpretation of faith statements remains essentially impoverished unless it attends to the connection between confessions of objective belief and subjective commitments to certain patterns of behavior. What the speakers affirm to be true they also accept as a focus of personal values. What is held to be true *in se* (in itself) also gives shape to what is valuable *pro nobis* (for us). Thus statements of faith express attitudes of the *whole* human person. In acknowledging some aspects of the divine self-communication the believers commit themselves accordingly. To confess "Jesus is Lord" is more than a statement *about* his post-mortem existence and status. It expresses (or should express) an unconditional commitment to the risen Savior. Adults, for example, who come to believe in Christ and wish to enter the Christian community by receiving baptism do two things in pronouncing the Apostles' Creed: they confess what they now see to be true and they commit themselves to this new way of life.

Of course, the levels of confession and commitment can vary indefinitely. The degree of personal conviction with which, for instance, the bishops at a council endorse the final statements can vary greatly. The sheer fact that they give their votes to some joint documents hardly offers sufficient evidence to conclude *either* to a universal (high) state of interior belief *or* to exterior practices shared wholeheartedly by all. Thus the pronouncements on the sacraments from the Council of Trent (1545–63) do not as such allow us to argue that such pronouncements enjoyed an equal force in the thinking of all the participants and pointed to a uniform way of acting. Inevitably the quality and level of real confession and commitment will be infinitely varied.

Furthermore, we should not expect the two elements of confession and commitment to be equally present always. Of course, each element will be present to some degree. Shared statements of faith will never unilaterally *either* merely communicate the claim of a neutral observer *or* simply express an intention to follow a certain course of action. Such "pure" orthodoxy and orthopraxy will not occur. Nevertheless, one or other element can predominate. For example, some common statement of faith may aim at pledging a group to certain patterns of action rather than offering a detailed confession of the reality which faith acknowledges. Thus the Council of Trent insisted that "in the three sacraments of baptism, confirmation and orders there was imprinted on the soul a character, that is to say, a spiritual and indelible sign" (DS 1609). The bishops at Trent committed themselves to preserve the orthodox practice of not administering these three sacraments a second time to any who had already received them. Their main aim was not to describe in detail the sacramental "character." But this brings us to the next pair of words which help to indicate the principal functions of faith statements.

2. Description and Prescription

Besides confession and commitment we could also use the notions of "description" and "prescription" to elucidate somewhat the nature of shared statements of faith. Such statements offer more than sheer information about the divine self-communication—certainly much more than purely theoretical information, if such a thing exists. Statements of faith make truth claims about God, human life and history, and they do so in such a way as to invite others to react appropriately to these saving truths. These statements enjoy *both* a descriptive function as they seek to make sense of the world *and* a prescriptive function as they encourage certain policies of behavior. Let us take two examples: the Chalcedonian Definition (451) and an article from the Augsburg Confession (1530).

The key passage from the Council of Chalcedon runs as follows:

> We all with one accord teach men to acknowledge one and the same Son, our Lord Jesus Christ, at once complete in Godhead and complete in manhood, truly God and truly man, consisting also of a rational soul and body; of one substance with the Father as regards his Godhead, and at the same time of one substance with us as regards his manhood; like us in all respects, apart from sin; as regards his Godhead, begotten of the Father before the ages, but yet as regards his manhood, begotten for us men and for our salvation, of Mary the Virgin, the God-bearer; one and the same Christ, Son, Lord, Only-begotten, recognized in two natures, without confusion, without change, without division, without separation; the distinction of natures being in no way annulled by the union, but rather the characteristics of each nature being preserved and coming together to form one person and subsistence (DS 301–02).

On the one hand, as with similar faith statements, we must not ignore the cognitive intention of the various assertions made. The council fathers wished to state something about the structure of reality. Of course, their account did not purport to be a full description, let alone an adequate explanation, of Christ's reality. Nevertheless, we would distort the nature of their teaching if we analyzed it as no more than "crypto-commands, expressions of wishes, disguised ejaculations, concealed ethics."[2] On the other hand, however, the council fathers were doing more than merely describing the person of Jesus of Nazareth. They wished to direct their audience to acknowledge religiously the mystery of the God-man so that their faith in Christ might be renewed and they might be brought into closer union with him.

Article Four from the Augsburg Confession states:

> They teach that men cannot be justified in the sight of God by their own strength, merits or works, but that they are justified freely on account of Christ through faith, when they believe that they are received into grace and that their sins are remitted on account of Christ who made satisfaction for sins on our behalf by his death. God imputes this faith for righteousness in his own sight (Romans 3 and 4).[3]

Here again Melanchthon and other Lutherans did not draft and publish these and the other statements that make up the Augsburg Confession simply because they wished to expound the truth as they saw it, but without caring whether their readers accepted the Confession and acted accordingly. Rather they reported how they believed things to be, precisely with the intention of regulating and renewing the lives of their audience. In effect they both stated, "This is the nature of justification," and enjoined the faithful, "Receive justification as God's free gift." The prescription is at the very least implicit in the description. Through this and its other articles the Augsburg Confession wished to guide proper Christian practice as well as to offer illumination for the mind.

With both the Chalcedonian Definition and the Augsburg Confession apparently straightforward statements ("Christ is one person in two natures" and "Men are justified freely on account of Christ through faith") are used to do more than simply present or recall information. This happens, of course, in contexts other than the faith statements of Christians. P. F. Strawson points out:

> There are many different circumstances in which the simple sentence-pattern "X is Y" may be used to do things which are not merely stating (though they all involve stating) that X is Y. In uttering words of this simple pattern we may be encouraging, reporting or warning someone; reminding someone; answering, or replying to, someone; denying what someone has said; confirming, granting, corroborating, agreeing with, admitting what someone has said. Which of these, if any, we are doing depends on the circumstances in which, using this simple sentence-pattern, we assert that X is Y.[4]

If we are in the mood for history, we can easily recall those whom the statements from Chalcedon and Augsburg were encouraging, reproving or warning, answering or replying to, denying, corroborating or agreeing with. In such terms it seems thoroughly reasonable to maintain both the descriptive ("stating") and prescriptive ("encouraging" etc.) functions of Christian statements of faith.

Over the twenty centuries of Christianity which function has predominated in statements of faith—the descriptive or the prescriptive? Let me not hedge my answer with qualifications and avoid a clear-cut judgment. Both in earlier and later Church history statements of faith have proved more successful at guiding conduct, warning the faithful against aberrations, encouraging lines of commitment—in short, at prescribing things than at really describing ways in which human beings have experienced and continue to experience the divine self-communication. Often these confessions of faith have been informative only in a vague and abstract way. At the heart of the Chalcedonian Definition four negatives balance each other carefully—"without confusion, without change, without division, without separation." Even if such statements point to and affirm certain realities, they do not describe them in detail, let alone completely. (It was left to some pre- and post-Reformation theologians to answer "everything you wanted to know about Christ" and attempt thorough descriptions of his reality.) The same is true of the Augsburg Confession. Even its champions will hardly claim that it takes us very far in describing what the experience of justification is really like.[5]

It would then be difficult to sustain the case that even the most solemn formulations of faith succeed in being highly informative. Do Christians *know* more about the reality of Jesus Christ, justification, sacramental life and the Scriptures after hearing the Chalcedonian Definition, the Augsburg Confession and the teachings of the Council of Trent? These and later statements of faith can describe some aspect of the divine self-communication more precisely than it had been described previously, but they do not normally work as if they were totally fresh pieces of information confronting the eye of the mind like new photographs that have suddenly arrived. They clarify something or recall some truth rather than offer information for the first time. Faced with a situation of controversy, the Council of Chalcedon authoritatively decided in favor of certain terms for describing Christ's reality. That council did not present fifth-century Christians with vital pieces of information about Christ and their experience of him which had hitherto remained unavailable. More than a thousand years later the Council of Trent insisted on retaining seven sacraments, attempted to clarify the nature of justification, laid down the canon of Scriptures, and in general tried to cope with the urgent questions of the day. All in all, it offered precise reminders, pastoral directions and terminological decisions much more than truly informative descriptions about various aspects of the divine self-communication in Christ.

Let me throw in one final observation before leaving the ways in which faith formulations function as confession/commitment and description/prescription. These functions can enjoy a mutual priority and exert a mutual influence on each other. On the one hand, a shared experience of and commitment to Christ preceded the solemn clarification—through Nicaea and subsequent councils—of what the Church believed and wished to say about his reality in relationship to the Father. Likewise the practice of the Eucharist had continued for more than a thousand years before Lateran IV (1215), the Council of Florence (1439–45) and the Council of Trent progressively pronounced on the nature of the Eucharist. Here long experience of the Lord's eucharistic presence and power anticipated elaborated theory. On the other hand, such statements of faith can provide commitment with a greater self-awareness and clarity, which in turn will reinforce a stronger and more profound experience of Christian living. "Theoretical" descriptions can transform practice. At every level the lived experience and the statements of faith enjoy a mutual impact. This carries an important implication for the meaning of faith statements. When they are removed from the situation of Christian life and experience, they do not necessarily lose all meaning. But their full meaning will be acknowledged and confessed only in the context of total commitment.

II
THE MEANING OF FAITH STATEMENTS

On the meaning[6] of faith statements—as with their functions—I disclaim any attempt to say everything, but I will try to say something and say it accurately. In any case the discussion of the Scriptures in the last part of this book will add further material on meaning, truth, authority and other issues treated in this chapter. Of course, we are concerned here with shared faith statements which have been fashioned by various individuals and groups in the post-apostolic Church. None of these statements, even the most authoritatively proclaimed and widely accepted, rises to the level of the inspired Scriptures. Nevertheless, there are far-reaching similarities in the respective ways that both the biblical and the post-biblical statements of faith discern, interpret, express and remember the human experience of the divine self-communication which reached its definitive climax in Jesus Christ. Hence what is left out here can be put in later.

1. Some False Moves

What did the Chalcedonian Definition, the Augsburg Confession, the 1971 ARCIC (Windsor) document on the Eucharist, and other statements of faith *mean*? What was being said in what was said? Three lines of approach can be quickly discarded: the identification of the meaning of these statements with their (a) causes, (b) intended purposes, or (c) *de facto* effects.

To claim, for instance, that the Windsor Statement "meant" the defeat of Evangelicals and the victory of Anglo-Catholics does nothing more than affirm things about the impulses which gave rise to that document. The effort to trace interlocking causes which produced some such statement may be interesting and important. But as such the causality line fails to pin down the meaning of the statement in itself. We must revert to the question: What did the Anglican (and Roman Catholic) representatives on the ARCIC intend to convey by their prouncements on the Eucharist? What did they wish to communicate by their common text?

We would likewise evade the central issue if we remained content to point to aims, objectives and purposes. We might agree that Luther and Melanchthon adopted moderate expressions in the Augsburg Confession (presented to Emperor Charles V) because they *meant* to hold out an olive branch to the Catholic party. Nevertheless, we need to ask what they understood and wished to convey by their utterances about justification, faith and good works, the sacraments, abuses in the Church and the rest. Three things need to be said here. They intended (i) to bring the emperor and other readers to think that they strongly believed certain things, (ii) to activate or reactivate such beliefs in their audiences, and (iii) to bring about as a natural consequence certain results—for instance, some measure of peace with the Catholic party through the milder and less offensive language they adopted. Here it would be playing with words to gloss over (i) and (ii) and allege that (iii) constituted "the meaning" of the Augsburg Confession. *Motivation must not be confused with meaning.*

Third, we might maintain that the Chalcedonian Definition and the council's approval of Pope Leo I's teaching meant the posthumous vindication of Flavian, the dead patriarch of Constantinople. But we cannot draw from this historical judgment the conclusion that Leo "meant" just that by his "Tome." Leo's actions and writings helped to bring about such a vindication. But it would be false to reduce his meaning to such *de facto* effects.

2. What Was Meant

Once we put aside causes, consciously intended purposes and *de facto* effects, what should be said about the meaning of faith statements? At the very least this: We would lapse into messy and imprecise answers if we failed to distinguish between what such statements *meant* then and what they might *mean* now.

From past generations of Christians we have inherited numerous faith statements which as such indicate what they said. But what was meant in what was said? What meaning(s) did they intend to express through these words?

The challenge becomes more acute if we recall several interrelated commonplaces. Both then and now meaning can be conveyed by some action unaccompanied by words—for instance, by carving a particular style of crucifix, raising a clenched fist or giving someone a warm hug. In any case conveying meaning is always more than *just using words.* Non-linguistic elements such as the choice of time and place will play some essential role to help render the spoken and written words meaningful. Finally, while meaning may be embodied in chosen formulations like the words of a creed or a conciliar "canon," the meaning cannot simply be identified with these words in and of themselves.

After these cautions what can one say about the meaning(s) of inherited statements of faith like the Chalcedonian Definition, the Augsburg Confession or *Munificentissimus Deus,* the solemn definition by Pius XII of the Virgin Mary's assumption into heaven? Two moves are essential here. First, we need to put the statements back in history and relate them to the precise experiences which generated them. What were the questions and challenges that faced the authors of these faith statements? What were the experiences which they decided to express in these terms?

Second, once we have retrieved as much as possible about the particular circumstances which lay behind the statements in question, we need also to scan the general language usage of the times. At the end of the *Phaedrus* Socrates may rightly warn us that words cannot simply be shifted from place to place and retain their meaning unchanged. Nevertheless, if the meaning of words is determined at least partly by general usage, there is at any given period a certain constancy in usage, and this general usage helps to establish meaning. The use of terms like nature *(physis),* justification, sacrament and sacrifice may be varied, vague and extraordinarily complex in theological, ritual and other situations. All the same, attention to current usage will go some way toward settling the meaning of faith statements. Such general usage and the public conventions governing the recognition of words have always indicated to a degree what authors of faith statements wished to convey. Strawson is reassuring: "We may expect a certain regularity of relationship between what people intend to communicate by uttering certain sentences and what those sentences conventionally mean."[7] Even with material from the distant past we should require firm evidence before agreeing that some statement expressed a hidden meaning which differed from the conventional sense indicated by linguistic usage then.

Another way of enunciating much of what has just been said is this: Faith statements from the past like other statements had their meaning in their context—or, rather, their contexts. There was the immediate context constituted by the questions faced or raised by the authors of the statements, the answers they formulated and the experiences they wished to express. Then there was the wider context constituted by the whole structure of the age and especially by current linguistic usage. A scrutiny of both the closer and the wider contexts will point to the things that the authors of faith statements intended to affirm back there and then. In the spirit of Pilate's "Quod scripsi scripsi" we can say: What they meant they meant. Their meaning, which may at times be extraordinarily difficult to pin down, serves in principle as a fixed point of reference in the past.

Here, however, one needs to face a problem which is regularly slipped over: the difference between faith statements coming from one author like a Pope and those coming from such groups as ecumenical councils of the Church. We can easily mount an operation to ascertain, for example, the original meaning of Pius XII when he solemnly proclaimed the Virgin Mary's assumption into heaven. The context, general usage of theological language and public conventions governing the recognition of such language indicated what he wished to convey. Neither here nor elsewhere do we face a special handicap from the fact that solemn teaching from the Popes never offers an infallibly guaranteed account of its meaning. (If in fact such an account were added, we would require a further infallibly guaranteed account of the account, and so on *ad infinitum.*) In general what a Pope and other individuals intend to communicate by saying or writing certain sentences regularly corresponds to what such sentences *conventionally* mean.

In the case of conciliar and other shared statements of faith it becomes much more problematic to speak of "the" original meaning of those pronouncements. What are they agreeing upon and believing in common by accepting the same set of words? Let me put the question this way: Suppose we had managed to buttonhole several bishops as they left the Council of Chalcedon, the Council of Trent or Vatican I and then questioned them about the statements to which they had just given their approval. Let us imagine that we could have interrogated some Tridentine bishops about certain sections of their 1547 decree on the justification of the unrighteous, or several Chalcedonian bishops about their teaching on Christ's "two natures." They would all have offered some paraphrase but would not have said precisely the same thing. Identical items in the conciliar documents would have evoked from them somewhat differing interpretations.

Should we then speak of various intentions or minds of the bishops rather than of "the" intention or mind of the council? The one conciliar statement could convey varying shades of meaning to the very authors of the common text. The aftermath of Chalcedon showed how Church leaders were not perfectly united in their interpretation of what the conciliar definitions meant. The fact that the Moslems soon overran the "Monophysites" has tended to obscure the seriousness of these differences. Any attempt to represent Chalcedon as conveying "a set of clearly agreed-upon, least-common-denominator, clear and distinct ideas"[8] to express *one* common meaning would fly in the face of the historical evidence.

Conciliar definitions of faith arose normally as compromise statements after long debates and were frequently left somewhat ambiguous to allow for a range of meanings. In defining papal infallibility at Vatican I some bishops clearly attached the strongest possible sense to the affirmation that "the definitions of the Roman Pontiff are irreformable of themselves and not by virtue of the consent of the Church" (DS 3074). Other bishops understood these same words in the weakest possible sense. Given that such conciliar statements are the products of committees, it looks dubious to speak confidently of *one* original meaning. A certain ambiguity or latitude of legitimate interpretations seems to discourage us from offering a simple answer on either side. We may not read the most rigorous meaning into the words, nor may we try reductionism and give them the weakest possible sense. From the outset conciliar statements of faith—at least on questions that have been in dispute—normally display an ineradicable plurality of meaning. Some clearly definable "original meaning" simply cannot be caught in a net of words.

To sum up the problem: Sharing the same set of words never guaranteed of itself that one clearly defined meaning would be fully shared by those groups of Christians who agreed to endorse together various statements of faith.

Nevertheless, one should not force matters and overlook the degree of shared meaning which undoubtedly did exist. To begin with, like those individuals who produced faith statements the groups also committed themselves to abide by the current usage and conventions of language. Unless they indicated otherwise, we must presume that their shared sentences must, at least in general, be understood according to the conventional sense of the times. Second, often enough councils drafted their faith statements when various distortions threatened Christian life and practice. In thus directing their formulations against what they took to be heterodox positions, they were frequently more explicit in the meanings they ruled out than in those they affirmed. Thus when the long controversy over the relations between the human and divine elements in Jesus Christ eventually brought the Chalcedonian Definition, we find four negatives nestling at the heart of this statement. The one person of Christ exists in two natures "without confusion, without change, without division, without separation." The council directed "without confusion" against Eutychianism and "without division" against Nestorianism.

One should not, of course, exaggerate the point that conciliar definitions have communicated shared meanings and intentions inasmuch as they were ruling out rather than ruling in certain meanings and terms. The Christian leaders at Chalcedon had positive information to convey in describing Christ as one person in two natures and thus wishing to express their experience of the Lord in a fuller way than had been available before. Nevertheless, the common meaning which such conciliar satements intended to communicate often came to this: "In the light of our faith experience we disagree with such and such a belief and find this or that terminology false or misleading." Thus at times the shared meaning simply took a negative form.

Third, over and over again statements of faith, especially the most solemn creeds and definitions emerging from councils, have not been very specific. When calling Christ "of one subtance with the Father" the Council of Nicaea did not enter into details. The less said and specified, the less meaning—shared or otherwise—to be communicated. In other words, since many statements of faith coming from the highest leaders in the Church have enjoyed only a *low specificity* in their content, a fairly minimal unity on the part of the authors would allow us to claim that some common meaning had in fact been shared.

Fourth, on many occasions in the course of Christian history an individual or committee has explained in some detail the sense of a text which the whole group was about to accept. Thus at the First Vatican Council Cardinal Gasser in a four-hour speech expounded the meaning of the constitution on papal primacy and infallibility *(Pastor Aeternus)* which—with some minor changes—the majority went on to approve. At the Second Vatican Council the theological commission played a similar role by indicating what the various documents *meant*—above all in their final, revised form—before they were voted upon and accepted. Wherever such procedures were followed, we can more readily affirm that there was some shared meaning when the group approved the common statement of faith—and that despite the differing paraphrases which some participants later offered.

Finally, there are always limits to the paraphrases which the authors of a common statement of faith can subsequently put out. On the one hand, the various signatories may detect stronger or weaker senses in the text, expound differing shades of meaning and come up with interpretations that have family resemblances to each other but are not totally identical. On the other hand, however, their original agreement to issue together that common statement has set limits to their possible paraphrases. They did jointly commit themselves to a text whose meaning was at least partly determined right there and then by the conventional usage of the language adopted. At times the interpretation of such common texts offered later by some members of given groups departs so far from the original statements that these subsequent paraphrases, whatever their value, cannot be accepted as versions of *what was meant then*. Rather these ex-participants have shifted from what the statement originally meant to what "it now means to me."

3. What It Means

Toward the end of his eschatological discourse in Mark's Gospel Christ declares: "Heaven and earth will pass away, but my words will not pass away" (13:31). However, he is never represented anywhere in the New Testament as assuring his followers: "Your words will not pass away." To put this in other terms: In the life of the post-apostolic Church even the most solemn and authoritative statements of faith cannot remain independent of historical change and form a kind of transtemporal and transcultural medium for preserving and transmitting various meanings concerned with the experience of faith. One cannot in that way objectify and, as it were, fix and freeze meanings for all time.

This point holds true even if we press the distinction between (a) the *meaning(s)* intended by those who authored the faith statements and (b) the precise *formulations* they chose. What they meant then and what we mean now do not totally coincide, as we shall see. And this is all the more the case if, as normally happens, the precise wording is maintained when past formulations are read and interpreted now. The historical conditioning that shaped the original experience of the divine self-communication which culminated in the coming of Christ also affects the dependent experience of that saving revelation of God in the on-going life of the Church. That subsequent experience, its interpretation and its expression in faith statements remain radically shaped by history.

Thus the historical nature of human existence lies behind the distinction between what a faith statement meant and what it means. To begin with, like all other structures in the Church's lived experience the making of faith statements remains an open affair. After the Council of Nicaea (325) had affirmed against the Arians that Jesus is divine ("of one substance with the Father"), that statement showed up differently when later councils set further statements of faith alongside it. Constantinople (381) reaffirmed the *homoousios* of Nicaea and—against the Apollinarian denial of Jesus' soul—added that Jesus is fully human. Then Ephesus (431) taught that Jesus' two natures (*physeis*) are not separated and Chalcedon (451) asserted that his two natures are not confused with one another. All these later statements inevitably colored and affected the way in which the Nicene Creed continued to be read and interpreted. It meant more to later readers when further conciliar expressions of faith in Christ took their place alongside it.

The faith statement from Nicaea formed part of an open, growing system and did that not just because later councils added further words and sentences. Within the total complex of human history Christian experience has constantly been modified, as language shifts occurred, cultures altered, particular traditions grew and declined, and fresh challenges at the political, social, economic and explicitly religious levels had constantly to be faced.

Take language, for instance. Just as divine inspiration did not exempt the Scriptures from being conditioned by the changing states of human language, so the on-going guidance of the Holy Spirit in the post-apostolic Church has not made faith statements, even the most solemnly authoritative ones, unique exceptions to the general mutability of human language. No less than biblical language, the language of Christian individuals and groups could never rise above historical relativities to some stable heaven but has always remained contingent and changing. Hence using the "old" words in new contexts will only mask the shifts and accretions of meaning that are taking place.

When we recall the nature of language and other items that make up the whole historicity of the human condition, the conclusion imposes itself. Any faith statement through which Christian leaders or groups—of whatever standing or authority—have expressed their experience of the divine self-communication in Christ will have taken its place as something partial and provisional within a total Christian and human structure which is constantly growing and shifting.

Naturally the question "What does it mean?" concerns our reading here and now of some past statement of faith and finding meaning in it. Let me set out what I take to be involved in this process.

(a) Any such statements of faith will in one way or another direct us *back* to the climactic event of God's self-communication which holds together all subsequent generations of believers: Jesus Christ in his life, death, resurrection and giving of the Spirit. All Christian professions of faith refer directly or indirectly to that event, even if they always fall short of expressing its reality.

(b) At the same time, statements of faith which we read today also point *forward* through all the history of the Church and world (which history *will* in its turn help to determine and shape the meaning of those statements) to the *eschaton*. Only at the end when the work of the Holy Spirit in guiding the community of believers is over and the whole history of the Church and world is complete will particular expressions of faith like the Nicene Creed have their meaning totally, fully and finally determined. Until then some statements of faith can only serve as provisional pieces of knowledge which in their different ways anticipate the whole of Church history and its end.

(c) Whenever we hear, ponder and understand some inherited statements of faith, they signify something to us and provide us with enlightenment in the face of our questions, or—to put matters another way—*meaning happens.* When all is said and done, two things are involved here. We *both* discover *and* create meaning; we both receive sense from and make sense of such traditional Christian texts. Let me comment briefly on some aspects of this process.

When they were first formulated, these statements of faith, even longer ones like the Augsburg Confession and the documents from the Council of Trent, said *relatively few things.* If the divine reality—to put it mildly—transcends the sum total of all actual and possible faith statements, all the more is this true of some individual statement or set of statements. The historical Christian confessions have said relatively little about the Triune God who is revealed and communicated to us through the life, death and resurrection of Jesus.

Nevertheless, something was always said and some meaning was there to be discovered and appropriated later. Indeed, the authors of a faith statement often said *more* than they intended or realized. Michel Foucault develops this point persuasively:

> We know—and this has probably been the case ever since men began to speak—that one thing is often said in place of another; that one sentence may have two meanings at once; that an obvious meaning, understood without difficulty by everyone, may conceal a second esoteric or prophetic meaning that a more subtle deciphering, or perhaps only the erosion of time, will finally reveal; that beneath a visible formulation, there may remain another that controls it, disturbs it, and imposes on it an articulation of its own; in short that in one way or another, things said say more than themselves.[9]

Changes in the context ("the erosion of time") can reveal such surplus meanings.

Besides the changes in the outer, public context which will partly determine what some inherited faith statement means when read today, there is the total personal history which any individual brings to the reading of such texts. Those deeper experiences that have woven the web of our inner lives, our inherited assumptions, the questions which spontaneously arise for each of us, and the insights which particular religious analogies can provoke for us—these and other factors will affect us as we conceptualize and formulate for ourselves the meaning conveyed by traditional statements of faith. The endless variations in personal history, no less than the course of public history, mean that these statements will never enjoy an identical reception by everyone along perfectly pre-defined lines.

When we read and personally appropriate the text of some faith statement, it finds its proper goal. In this process of fulfillment there are two distinguishable, though not genuinely separable, moments. We *both* discover something of its earlier, original meaning *and* creatively articulate its significance for ourselves today. The whole process could be called *personally paraphrasing.* Our personal paraphrases will express what these texts *now* mean *to us* and *for us.* Whenever the personal paraphrasing fails to take place, traditional statements of faith will remain for us at best noble but irrelevant monuments from the past. It is only such internalizing which can make them more than merely venerable and interesting ideas.

In paraphrasing them for ourselves we will always be conscious of some gap between what we believe them to mean and what we say. This gap between the meaning we glimpse and grasp and what we actually say should always prompt us to take matters further and never abandon the task of reconceptualizing and reformulating the meaning of such texts. If the paraphrasing responds to the question "What do these texts mean?" every answer calls for new questions. The results can only be provisional.

(d) Before leaving the issue of meaning, we might usefully note two minimal *limitations* on our personal paraphrases of inherited faith statements. The first limitation concerns the past; the second concerns the present.

First of all, to what extent does our interpretation of what the text in question now means need to be consistent with what its authors meant then? At the very least, I would hold, our interpretation will never entail a fundamental and blatant conflict with what they intended. The cultural context has changed dramatically, new questions have emerged at every level of human life, and the texts themselves can have undergone a long history of interpretation, but it would be strange to the point of paradox to claim that Article Four of the Augsburg Confession now means justification simply through personal achievement, or that the Council of Trent's decree on the Eucharist (DS 1635ff.) in no sense now means the real presence of the risen Christ. Granted everything that needs to be said about the historicity of human existence, it seems absurd to maintain that what a given statement of faith meant then and what it means now could be strictly contradictory. Different, yes, but mutually exclusive, no. Linguistically and historically there will always be some link between what a text of faith meant then and what it could mean now. A total turnaround in meaning such that what the text now means contradicts what it once meant does not appear feasible. *At least* in this minimal sense *what was meant* exercises a control over what a text now means, and this sets a limit on the freedom of our paraphrases and creative reinterpretations of that text.

It may help to dwell a little more on the linguistic and historical link. Shakespeare expressed some basic human experiences so well that his texts affected and even shaped all later English language, literature and culture. In a somewhat similar way formulations of faith—at least the great ones like the Chalcedonian Definition—articulated in a classical way the heart of the matter and, so far from merely surviving on some library shelf, have shaped the subsequent linguistic confession and practical commitment of the Christian community. Finding and fashioning some meaning from these texts which would be simply irreconcilable with what we can establish as their original meaning seems excluded.

The second limit on personal paraphrasing touches the necessity of respecting the intersubjective or transsubjective meaning of inherited faith statements. What particular texts mean now—be they the Nicene Creed, Trent's decrees on justification or the Thirty-Nine Articles—must be more than some merely private significance for me alone. These texts have come down from groups of past Christians to be read and interpreted today by those who wish to take them up. Yet if my interpretation has literally nothing in common with that of my contemporaries, I would appear in this matter to inhabit a totally (and impossibly) private world, cut off both from the contemporary context and from that common inheritance which brings me these traditional statements of faith. In such a case I would certainly not be "joined to others in the search" for meaning and truth.

(e) Finally, certain pastoral implications of all this should be recalled. If we read some ancient formulations of faith, we may have to answer the question "What do they mean?" by admitting, "Not very much." Not even the most solemn statements from the greatest councils of the Church can be guaranteed to have lasting clarity and force. If they are to continue communicating meaning and retain authority, they will need to be re-interpreted and re-expressed.

In 1964 the first encyclical of Pope Paul VI, *Ecclesiam Suam,* included among the desirable characteristics of the Church's dialogue with the world the fact that "it does not hold fast to forms of expression which have *lost their meaning* and can no longer stir men's minds."[10] The following year in *Gaudium et Spes* the Second Vatican Council noted the conceptual and linguistic diversity with which the Church has expressed the basic Christian message. It affirmed that this constant search for "suitable terms" is no less important "nowadays when things change so rapidly and thought patterns differ so widely" (n. 44).[11] Then in 1973 a declaration of the Congregation for the Doctrine of the Faith, *Mysterium Ecclesiae,* touched on the same point in observing that "the meaning of the pronouncements of faith depend partly upon the expressive power of the language used at a certain point in time and in particular circumstances"—

presumably at that point in time and in those circumstances when the pronouncements in question were first formulated. Hence among the "ancient dogmatic formulas," while some can "remain living and fruitful," provided there are "suitable explanatory additions that maintain and clarify their original meaning," other such formulas have simply given way "to new expressions" (n. 5).

To sum this up: Whenever contemporary readers or hearers discover little or no meaning in inherited formulations of faith, it is high time for the Church's teachers and theologians to fashion better formulations.

III
THE TRUTH OF FAITH STATEMENTS

When we ask Pilate's question "What is truth?" about shared statements of faith, many options open up to us as regards both the procedure to be followed and the issue of truth itself.[12]

(1) First of all, we might usefully point out that *not every sentence* aims to be true and correspond to the facts. Descriptions can certainly fit or fail to fit the facts to which they are applied. But we would fall into the descriptive fallacy if we ignored the way in which expressions of faith like other sentences can include such forms as commands, wishes and even questions. When we utter these sentences, we do not say anything that can be called true or false.

Second, it could be helpful to recall the simple fact that the propositional formulations of faith do not as such coincide with the propositions in question. On the one hand, here as elsewhere we should reckon with the fact that different propositional formulas can express the same proposition: for example, "five plus five equals ten" and "5 + 5 = 10." On the other hand, the same propositional formulation could be used to express different propositions: for instance, "Outside the Church there is no salvation." At the very least what is meant by "outside" can be understood in different ways, and these various shades of meaning will alter the proposition being affirmed.

Third, we might discuss in detail the meaning of "truth" and "falsity," argue that as such truth belongs to the act of judgment (and not as such to propositional formulations), and go on to elaborate the reasons and criteria for calling judgments true or false. A true judgment of faith—despite its being only a fragmentary and provisional expression of the divine self-communication in Christ—would be one which here and now in *this* context and in answer to *this* question excludes the contradictory as false.

(2) All these approaches would be worth following up, but here I find it more useful to reflect briefly on the issue of truth at three levels: the levels of *being, knowledge* and *practice.*

Faith statements grapple with the challenge of expressing the *reality* or truth of the God who is revealed. Rather than thinking of matters impersonally, abstractly, and in general, believers find truth in this interpersonal relationship which they experience with the Triune God. Truth is the human face of God revealed in Jesus Christ. The permanence of truth is the permanent reality of the risen Lord as the way to the Father through the Holy Spirit. This truth of the Father, Son and Holy Spirit in themselves (*in se*), if disclosable and disclosed, is so far from being fully describable that it remains the ultimately mysterious reality which will always transcend all faith statements with the full range of their actual and possible meanings.

What do we expect to find and *know* when we read or hear inherited confessions of Christian faith? These statements, if received with sympathy, can set up the conditions for experiencing, understanding and seeing something of the ultimate truth about God, human beings and the world. The internal influence of the Holy Spirit can accompany this external word to activate our hearing and unveil the truth. In the past, under the impact of the same Holy Spirit, large and leading groups of our Christian predecessors chose to express their experience of God through various formulations of faith. These statements can light up matters for us and generate a situation in which once again God speaks to us, so that we are enabled to confess the truth and commit ourselves. Thus meaning and truth happens for us (*pro nobis*).

Finally, the truth mediated by statements of faith will be known by dwelling in it. When their truth *transforms praxis* and enriches the lives of believers, by leading them into deeper union with God and with one another, it vindicates itself through their experience. Thus the revealing and saving functions of these statements show up in practice. If they deal with revealed truth, they are also revealing truth and converting lives. What will be said later about the saving truth recorded and communicated by the inspired Scriptures applies, *mutatis mutandis,* to the transforming truth of traditional statements of faith coming from the post-apostolic Church. They call us to life and transform our lives.

Hence we should be slow in giving an unqualified "yes" to Schillebeeckx's claim: "A statement of faith does not become true because it is put into practice or untrue because it is not put into practice."[13] Surely we "keep the word of God" by practicing it? If a statement of (alleged) faith is *never* actually put into practice or at best does no more than awkwardly yield some kind of practice by a small group of believers, one could well wonder about its truth. Here, life and practice are at least a major measure of truth. This point will recur later when we examine the ways in which the Vincentian Canon and the "sense of the faithful" function to help our discernment of truly authentic traditions.

IV
THE AUTHORITY OF FAITH STATEMENTS

If this chapter on shared statements of Christian faith is not to remain patently incomplete, it should include something on the authority of such statements. "Authority" is an ambiguous word, all too easily associated with freedom being suppressed and not created. At least for Roman Catholics, Church authority suffered such a crisis of plausibility from the 1960's that it might seem better to drop the term altogether and simply speak of the functions, meaning and truth of faith statements. However, it still appears possible and in fact advisable to keep the term and try new—or rather renewed—approaches to our vision of what authority entails.[14]

1. Three Bases of Authority

Max Weber produced a classic analysis of *types of authority* based on the presumed sources of legitimacy, and this analysis can help us here. He associated authority with "the probability that a command with a given specific content will be obeyed by a given group of people."[15] Here we can extend this account and speak of "the probability that a faith statement with a given specific content will be found to be meaningful and true by a given group of Chrstians, and hence will be believed and put into practice by them." In other words, we should expect that a statement of faith coming from some authority in the community will function (descriptively and prescriptively) to shape and direct the confession and commitment of believers.

Weber identified three possible ways for legitimizing authority: it could have a *charismatic, traditional* or *rational* basis. The charismatic basis of legitimacy derives from such personal gifts as knowledge, leadership and holiness. This is the authority enjoyed by the scholar, the statesman and the saint. Traditional authority rests on a belief in "the sanctity of immemorial traditions and the legitimacy of the status of those exercising authority under them." Third, rational authority comes from "a belief in the 'legality' of patterns of normative rules and the right of those elevated to authority under such rules to issue commands."[16] This authority is usually associated with bureaucratic structures and with set procedures that are ordered toward definite objectives. Such authority is understood to be a function of an impersonal, legal order and not be vested in "sacred persons" as such. Weber, of course, proposed these three bases as "ideal types" which could be combined in various ways. Thus a Catholic might legitimize the authority of bishops for two reasons: the sanctity of their immemorial office (the traditional basis) and—on the grounds that "the alternative to an organized Church is a disorganized Church"—the need to run the Church in an orderly, effective manner (the rational basis).

Weber's analysis suggests the *personal, traditional* and *institutional* grounds which can legitimize faith statements and so support the antecedent probability that such statements will enjoy their expected results for the theory and practice of Christianity.

The special, personal experience of the earthly and risen Jesus made members of the apostolic community uniquely authoritative for later Christians. By testifying to that foundational experience and its various preached expressions, the New Testament with its many confessions of faith shared in that apostolic authority. Thus the authority vested in the first Christians, and especially in the core group of apostles, flowed over into their written records. In this derivative way the statements of the New Testament can continue to make demands on believers and be expected to have effects on their confession and commitment.

In the post-apostolic Church, personal gifts of holiness, knowledge and spiritual insight have repeatedly conferred on certain Christians the quality of being entitled to be heard, respected and followed when they formulate their faith. This is the authority enjoyed by the scholar, the prophet and—above all—the saint. Thus those who respond more fully to the call of the Spirit are singled out by the ARCIC in its 1976 Venice Statement on "Authority in the Church": "By the inner quality of their life they win a respect which allows them to speak in Christ's name with authority."[17] This kind of personal authority attaches to the testimony of men and women who have received particular gifts and especially to those who submit to Jesus Christ in a more generous way and live in greater fidelity to his revelation. When they express their faith, they know what they are talking about.[18]

Then the ordained ministry provides traditional and institutional grounds for certain believers like bishops exercising authority in teaching Christian faith as well as in other ways. It is obviously desirable that the *personal* authority of wisdom and holiness accompany such official, pastoral authority. If not, the *de iure* authority of the bishops will be lessened *de facto*. But as such their official authority derives from public ordination and appintment rather than from personal gifts.

To sum all this up: During nearly two thousand years of Christianity general councils, Popes, local conferences of bishops and a vast range of other groups and individuals have produced confessions of faith. In evaluating the authority of any such statements, we should first check their source. Does the authority in question rest on the apostolic function, personal gifts, ministerial ordination or some other charismatic, traditional or institutional basis?

2. Degrees of Authority

Not only the source but also the degree of authority enjoyed and in fact invoked should be recalled. The nature and extent of the legitimate expectation that certain individuals and groups will guide other Christians through their faith statements will vary enormously. A general council of the Church which aims to express matters of faith in solemn definitions obviously takes on a much higher degree of authority than a national conference of bishops. The faith statements of a Pope—specifically those invoking some degree of authority—can rightly be expected to have a more universal effect than the formulations of a leading theologian. There should be no need to pursue this point doggedly. The degree of legitimate expectations about the impact of faith statements will run all the way from the rather slight to the very strong.

Here one further point calls for attention. Nowadays even those who used to maximalize the degree of authority attaching to faith statements, particularly those coming from the Pope, have made their peace with the fact that the degree of authority possessed by some person or group is—to put it mildly—not necessarily the degree of authority actually invoked in support of a given statement. The Second Vatican Council, for example, had the authority *to define solemnly* matters of faith, but it did not in fact invoke such authority when issuing its documents. In general we should never presume a higher degree of authority than the one which is clearly claimed. The 1917 Code of Canon Law wisely took a cue from the First Vatican Council (DS 3011) when it insisted on such an approach to solemnly defined formulations of faith: "Nothing is to be understood to be dogmatically declared or defined unless this is manifestly so" (Canon 1323). In the case of lesser formulations of faith this canon would also encourage us not to allege degrees of authority higher than those which are clearly invoked.

3. The Object of Authoritative Statements

Further, one must not forget to note *the point at issue* in a given statement of faith. It could be something touching the heart of Christian experience and faith such as the universal value of Christ's saving death and resurrection. Or again it could be a statement on a current issue of justice and peace like the nuclear arms race. Such teaching can be extremely important for the whole world but *as such* cannot purport to be derived directly from God's self-communication in Christ. Bishops, popes and councils will deal with matters of revelation but they will also—as part of their pastoral responsibility—teach on topics which do not precisely involve and express revealed truth. In that case their statements can no longer properly be called "formulations of faith."

We can fire and fuse these reflections into three questions which might act as rules of thumb for interpreting the authority that belongs to formulations of Christian faith. First, *what basis* legitimizes the authority behind a given formulation? To put the same question another way: *Who* has produced or endorsed this statement and what legitimizes their authority? Are we dealing with something coming from the apostle Paul, a medieval Pope, a series of Church councils, a group of contemporary theologians, some Vatican congregation, a modern Pope supported by all the national conferences of bishops, and so forth? Second, *what degree of authority* is actually being exercised by the author or authors in making this statement? One council might simply teach in a general, pastoral way. Another council could put its full authority behind some formulation of faith. A solemn papal definition differs from an encyclical and even more from declarations of Vatican congregations precisely through the degree of authority being invoked. Third, *what was or is the point at issue* in the given statement of faith—a matter of revelation or some teaching which may apply or touch on matters of revelation but which cannot purport to be as such revealed truth?

4. Authority and Freedom

Whatever particular shape the authority of faith formulations takes, true authority—here as elsewhere—is never a force despotically imposed from outside so as to control and coerce beliefs and actions. Naked power can brutally have its own way in the public realm, but genuine authority will never bludgeon people into submission and is exercised only over those who voluntarily accept it. Those who are credited with such authority know that the internal influence of the Holy Spirit will accompany the external word—in this case some formulation of faith—and that this influence will enable the hearers to paraphrase the truth for themselves, join in the common confession of faith and reach a renewed commitment.

What Paul VI said in *Octogesima Adveniens* about truth fits very well the way in which the authoritative teaching of faith formulations should help believers to understand and accept this teaching: "It is only with the power of truth itself that the truth imposes itself, and it penetrates the human spirit with gentleness no less than force" (n. 25).

A comprehensive treatment of the authority of faith statements would discuss further material: for instance, the teaching and implications of documents from the Second Vatican Council like *Lumen Gentium* (for example, n. 25) and *Dignitatis Humanae*. However, such a fuller treatment belongs more to ecclesiology than to fundamental theology. What fundamental theology calls for rather is some attempt to show at least briefly how the theory and practice of authority which has just been outlined is truly rooted in the New Testament expression and interpretation of the divine self-communication in Christ. St Paul's Letter to the Galatians can be very instructive here.

5. The Letter to the Galatians

The authoritative tone of this letter is unmistakable, above all in the opening section where the apostle anathematizes those who would preach a Gospel different from the one he has received and passed on. Paul's forcefulness is understandable. He is dealing with an issue that lies at the heart of Christianity: the way sinful human beings are justified by and before God. Nevertheless, in presenting the truth once again to the Galatians, Paul uses a variety of arguments. He appeals as much to their experience as he does to his own apostolic authority. He argues from Sacred Scripture, as well as adducing the fact that the churches in Judea openly agree with his Gospel. He cites not only his confrontation with Peter, but also Peter's acceptance of his Gospel.

We can list some of the things which Paul does *not* do in Galatians:

• He does not appeal merely to some written source, as if to say, "We find this doctrine in the Scriptures or in the documents of some council and that's that."

• He is not content to affirm and impose the correct doctrine of justification simply on the basis of his own apostolic authority.

• Nor does Paul require his readers to abdicate their judgment in favor of some other institutional figure by declaring, for example, "You must believe the doctrine which Peter teaches as a mouthpiece of God."

• Nor does the apostle ask his readers to abdicate their judgment in favor of some institutional group, let us say, some board of church directors in Jerusalem.

What Paul does in his Letter to the Galatians is to formulate and witness to the truth of the Gospel. He expects that he will be heard and that his message will be accompanied by the working of the Holy Spirit in his audience. He commends this message to their free and intelligent conscience. Paul does not hesitate to present to the Galatians involved argumentation which he hopes will bring conviction. The Letter to the Galatians suggests then the following *guidelines* for the theory and practice of authoritative teaching in the Church.

(a) *Authority should commend itself.* It should be convincing, even as Paul sets out to be convincing in the arguments he puts before the Galatians. There is no room for abdication of thought nor for mere external agreement coupled with internal doubts and dissent. What is called for is a free acceptance of a message which is intelligently understood. We are worlds apart from the advice of a vicar-general who after the publication of *Humanae Vitae* in 1968 told the Catholic public: "When the Pope issues a decree, whatever we may believe in our hearts, outwardly we must accept." St. Paul could never endorse that sentiment. It is what the Galatians believe in their hearts that matters to him more than what they do or decline to do.

(b) Authoritative teaching must express and be seen to express *the common faith* of the Church. Even in Galatians where Paul shows more concern than anywhere else to maintain that he has received his apostolic authority directly from God, he nevertheless feels obliged to argue that in his teaching he enjoys a communion with the churches of Jerusalem and Judea.

(c) Paul's approach indicates that Church teaching should be drawn from and related to *the lived experience* of those to whom it is addressed. He writes: "Let me ask you only this: Did you receive the Spirit by the works of the law or by hearing with faith? Did you experience so many things in vain—if it really is in vain? Does he who supplies the Spirit to you and works miracles among you do so by works of the law, or by hearing with faith?" (3:2ff.).

(d) *Appeals to loyalty* and love have their place in the apostle's teaching. Paul reminds the Galatians of the friendly welcome they gave him when he first preached the Gospel among them on the occasion of an illness (4:14f.). At the same time, the letter illustrates the possibility of loyalty leading believers astray. Peter's action in separating himself at Antioch from the Gentile Christians brought moral pressure to bear on Barnabas and others. Out of loyalty to Peter, they acted in a way that was tantamount to formulating and proclaiming a false Gospel.

(e) In presenting the truth Paul acknowledges that *what he does* or rather has done proves as important as what he says. He recalls that he did not yield to some false brethren (who apparently wanted Titus circumcised) and that he opposed Peter's action at Antioch. Paul consistently recognizes that his life, no less than his proclamation, mediates God's self-revelation in Christ. Here the apostle's attitude does not encourage us to press *too far* the traditional distinction between teaching and action, between what people in authority say and what they do. In these terms the Holy Father is declared to be infallible in his most solemn acts of teaching, but not impeccable in his actions. But, as a matter of fact, actions can speak louder than words, and what a Pope does, particularly a Pope in a world of modern communications, can be as helpful (or harmful) for the preaching of the good news as what he says. This point emerges clearly from Paul's approach to the Galatians, as well as from common experience.

Finally, a cautionary footnote on St. Paul. At our peril we neglect the way in which the apostle was conditioned *both* through his historical, social and religious background *and* through his personal character. He was obviously a difficult, aggressive person who not only reacted vigorously, if not violently, againt opponents, but also managed to clash with many of his close associates (Mark, Barnabas, Peter and so forth). When we draw on Paul for help in interpreting the place of authority in faith formulations or further matters of Christian life, we need to recall the personal and social factors which colored what he wrote. To put it mildly, Paul did not offer some "pure" doctrine which came straight down from heaven.

EXCURSUS:
THE MAGISTERIUM

There is a clear danger of overloading this chapter with detail that belongs to ecclesiology rather than fundamental theology. However, by discussing the authority of faith statements I have in effect committed myself to expound something on the magisterium or teaching office of the Church.[19]

If all believers can teach others about their experience of the divine self-communication in Christ, only those who constitute the magisterium have the authority for doing so officially. This task of teaching with authority belongs both to the college of bishops and to individual bishops united in a hierarchical communion with the bishop of Rome. A number of headings can sort out and give shape to the main things which concern fundamental theology at this point.

1. The Magisterium and the Community

The divine self-communication comes to human beings who are essentially social, and hence it necessarily involves the community. In the language of the Second Vatican Council we have here "the word of God which is entrusted to the Church"—that is to say, to "the *entire* holy people" who are called to confess their faith and live by that word. Within the whole community those who make up the magisterium "serve" this word of God and "authentically interpret" it (*Dei Verbum,* n. 10), and they should have no other aim than that of helping this saving revelation reach every new generation.

But if the whole community is the prime recipient and visible carrier of the divine self-communication in Christ and if right from the origins of the Church Christians have trusted to the invisible guidance of the Holy Spirit in interpreting, expressing and remembering that definitive self-communication of God (Rom 8:14; Jn 14:26; 16:13; 1 Jn 2:27), how can we come to terms with the existence of a special board of official teachers within the community? Here, however, we should recognize a clear coherence between the situation of the apostles in the period of foundational revelation and that of the bishops in the period of dependent revelation—a coherence that lends credibility to the role of the magisterium. Just as an apostolic group was formed once and for all to witness to the resurrection, found the Church and be the original mediators of the definitive divine self-communication in Christ, so in the subsequent life of the post-apostolic Church those who make up the magisterium bear a special responsibility to preserve a proper continuity with the foundational revelation and apply that revelation to the new challenges which the on-going course of human history presents. This magisterium neither supplants the role of the Holy Spirit nor undercuts the proper priority of the whole community. Rather it serves the Church as a divinely chosen means of handing on the essential confession of faith, inasmuch as it activates or reactivates basic Christian experiences and beliefs among the faithful and leads them to a fuller Christian life. The existence of such a magisterium might in any case be expected if we acknowledge the intersubjective nature of truth. Truth, including revealed truth, is experienced by human beings in community. This makes it more plausible that the Church should be equipped with an institution (the magisterium) which functions to help people experience and abide in the truth of revelation.

We can put the relationship between the Church at large and the magisterium this way: As we saw earlier, believers not only confidently commit themselves to a personal relationship with Christ, but also confess the divine self-communication which they experience in him. They respond to that definitive revelation of God by expressing and formulating their experience of faith. In the first instance the members of the magisterium belong to that believing and confessing Church. But they also serve to express in a fully visible and authoritative way the common faith. Among the general body of believers the magisterium enjoys an obvious visibility and clarity when it formulates matters of faith.

2. The Magisterium and "Dogmas"[20]

Among the major means adopted by the magisterium for confessing Christ and communicating the faith have been those solemn acts of teaching that over the last century have been lumped together under the technical term of "dogma." In my work *The Case Against Dogma* I ended by arguing that for a variety of reasons this *term* should be dropped from our theological vocabulary. Many misinterpreted the book, some reviewers like Bishop B. C. Butler, Avery Dulles, Donald Keefe, Nicholas Lash and Michael Williams discussed the point at issue,[21] but theologians in general (and statements coming from the magisterium) continue to use the category "dogma." This language persists. Hence it seems reasonable to dedicate some space to clarifying what still remains current terminology.

After being refined and restricted in meaning, "dogma" has come to signify in the jargon of twentieth-century theology: (a) a divinely revealed truth, (b) proclaimed as such by the infallible teaching authority of the magisterium, and (c) hence binding now and forever on the faithful. This account calls for some comments.

(a) Only revealed truth which is seen to come from the climactic divine self-communication in Christ can become "dogma." That period of *foundational* revelation, the *constitutive* phase in which the Church came into being, ended with the apostolic age. *As such* there were no "dogmas" in the New Testament which recorded the original experience, faith and preaching of the apostolic Church. Starting from the Council of Nicaea (325), "dogmas" have emerged in the *interpretative* phase of *dependent* revelation—in that continuing history of a community which has fully come into existence and now looks back *both* to the climax of the divine self-communication in Christ's incarnation, life, death, resurrection and sending of the Holy Spirit *and* to those men and women who founded the Church.

(b) Then the members of the magisterium must authoritatively formulate something as revealed truth if it is to attain the status of "dogma." They may do this formally by defining the truth. Thus in an act of the "extraordinary" or "solemn" magisterium a Church council can solemnly proclaim that Christ "instituted" seven sacraments (the Council of Trent) or a Pope can define that the Virgin Mary through the anticipated merits of her Son was preserved free even from original sin (Pius IX). "Dogmas" may also be expressed in the ordinary, day-to-day teaching of bishops and Popes. Thus it has never been formally defined that Christ is universal Redeemer. This truth is classified as belonging materially to Catholic faith (*de fide catholica*) as a "non-defined dogma," but has never been formulated as an explicit "dogma" (*de fide definita*). Let me introduce a table to illustrate more fully the terminology which Catholic theologians have commonly used. The ordinary, universal magisterium is described as teaching "non-defined dogmas" when (a) the bishops throughout the world in union with the bishop of Rome, (b) representing the whole

Church and proclaiming the truth to the whole Church, (c) unanimously teach as such some revealed truth to be held now and forever. To quote the Second Vatican Council:

> The bishops . . . proclaim infallibly the doctrine of Christ on the following conditions: namely, when, even though dispersed throughout the world but preserving for all that among themselves and with Peter's successor the bond of communion, in their authoritative teaching concerning faith and morals, they are in agreement that a particular teaching is to be held definitively and absolutely (*Lumen Gentium,* n. 25).[22]

As regards the whole table, Catholic theology has recognized "dogmas" at the asterisked points.

3. The Magisterium and Theologians[23]

Let me conclude this excursus by looking at and defining briefly the relations between the magisterium, which as such has an *institutional* (traditional and rational in Weber's terms) basis for its authority, and (professional) theologians whose authority rests on the quality of their theological gifts (a *charismatic* basis in Weber's terms).

The magisterium and theologians share the same goal—that of serving the community in presenting clearly and fruitfully in every generation the good news which is the divine self-communication in Christ. Over and over again the history of Christianity illustrates the reciprocal relationship that has existed between the magisterium and theologians as they attempted to activate or reactivate the saving revelation of God in people's lives. Theologians have hammered out concepts, clarified questions and elaborated systematic ways of presenting the Christian confession of faith. This theological work has repeatedly fed into the teaching of councils, Popes and bishops. Thus Thomas Aquinas' teaching on such matters as the sacraments helped shape the formulations of the Council of Trent as well as some items in the constitution *Dei Filius* from the First Vatican Council (DS 3001, 3005). The Second Vatican Council drew heavily on theologians for all kinds of material—for instance, its use of the term "salvation history." In short, the language and teaching of councils and bishops does not drop from heaven, and at least to some extent it is true to say that the theology of one generation can become the magisterium's teaching in another generation (or even later in the same generation).

Then in the aftermath of councils and pieces of papal teaching—particularly when the magisterium has solemnly defined something—such official formulations of Christian faith can be legitimately expected to

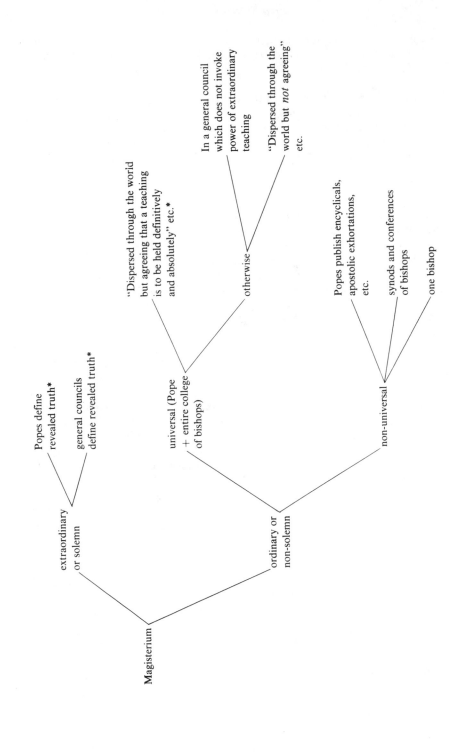

guide subsequent theological reflections. Thus the teaching of Chalcedon has rightly directed and affected Christological work for over fifteen hundred years. As it looks back on magisterial teaching and above all teaching of great importance—whether it is presented or evaluated as "defined dogma" or not—the magisterium has the right to interpret that teaching "authentically," whereas theologians come on the scene to interpret matters "scientifically." They should *both* investigate the historical origins of magisterial teaching (for example, the documents from some Church council) *and* then help to make such teaching "living and fruitful" (*Mysterium Ecclesiae*) by explaining it, paraphrasing it and finding fresh and suitable formulations to re-express it.

This excursus on the magisterium could have come at the very end of the book—after the treatment of tradition and Scripture. Such a sequence would have followed precisely the order indicated by *Dei Verbum:* "In the supremely wise arrangement of God, sacred tradition, Sacred Scripture and the magisterium of the Church are so connected and associated that one of them cannot stand without the others" (n. 10). The magisterium looks to tradition and Scripture as the source from which it draws the revealed truth which should fuel Christian faith. We can now move on to consider the community tradition and inspired Scripture which have recorded, transmitted and interpreted the human experience of that divine self-communication which climaxed in Christ.

VII. TRADITION: THE ECUMENICAL CONVERGENCE AND COMMON CHALLENGE

Tradition is a mystery which cannot be simply resolved. It can, however, be elucidated, if it is studied not only as a theological theorem but also as a religious phenomenon.

Robert McNally

Tradition is the aggregate of customs, beliefs and practices that give continuity to a culture, civilization, or social group and thus shape its views.

Encyclopaedia Britannica

There are at least two compelling reasons for this book dealing with tradition. The first is anthropological, the second is theological. The theological challenge of tradition presupposes a human reality—which once again illustrates in a rough kind of way the truth of the old dictum about "grace building on nature (gratia extollit, perficit, non destruit naturam)." Inasmuch as the experience of the divine self-communication in Christ is a human and *historical* phenomenon, it involves tradition. Inasmuch as this experience concerns a *definitive,* divine self-communication, it raises the question: How is this experience re-enacted over successive generations without losing its proper identity? We can begin with these two themes, and then go on to trace the ecumenical convergence which allows Christians to face the common challenge of "finding the Tradition within the traditions."

1. The Human Reality of Tradition

People sometimes attach the label "traditional" to those extreme conservatives who crave the past, resent the present and dread the future.

In that sense the "traditional" person is the *laudator temporis acti* who idealizes past history and old experiences in an excessive and unrealistic way. However, this is a partial use of the term which could lead us to overlook the fact that tradition belongs essentially to the social and historical existence of all human beings.[1]

Human life is simply unthinkable without the element of tradition. Hence it is clear that Robert McNally did not go far enough when he observed: "Tradition . . . can . . . be elucidated, if it is studied not only as a theological theorem but also as a religious phenomenon."[2] Over and above being a religious phenomenon, tradition shapes the whole cultural existence of men and women. In fact at this level "tradition" is almost synonymous with a society's whole way of life or, in a word, with its culture. Let us briefly recall then how tradition functions as a human reality to secure a society's continuity, identity and unity.

Tradition fashions *the bond between successive generations* in a society. We receive from the past our language, laws, symbols and all those ideas and "feelings" which are generally accepted unquestioningly and provide India, Italy, Madagascar or any other society with its characteristic cultural values. Even if members of a given society rarely stop to formulate and reflect on what they have taken over, they remain radically indebted to the past for the inherited values and expectations which give life its meaning and provide ideals to be striven for. Thus one generation passes on to another norms, attitudes and behavior patterns by which society has hitherto functioned and now seeks to perpetuate itself. Of course, the newcomers may challenge, reject and modify traditions which they receive, but they can never do so totally. Any such *complete* break with the past—*du passé faisons la table rase*—is never a genuine option. At least initially these newcomers to an existing society are taught to live by the existing ways. Otherwise they would be incapable of adjusting, altering and rebelling against what the previous generation has handed on to them.

In 1968 the North Atlantic countries witnessed a massive rejection of tradition, especially among the student population. But then the 1970's saw many young people disillusioned with change and revolution. At the end of the decade large segments of the Moslem world marked the fourteenth centennial of the founding of Islam by intensely expressing their revulsion against the loss or threatened loss of traditional values. The pendulum swings forward and backward. But neither total revolution nor rigid tradition will ever finally dislodge the other. Permanence and a hunger for permanence are as essential a feature of human experience as change and a yearning for change.

Back in Chapter II, when dealing with "the experience itself," I drew attention to the way in which experience goes beyond our expectations. It entails novelty. The new comes in on top of the old. But for this to be so the old must be there. Even in the most unexpected and novel experiences that happen to an individual or a group, some permanent "traditional" substratum is inevitably preserved—no matter how many factors are new. Thus change and tradition, so far from being mutually exclusive, stand in function of each other.

Besides effecting continuity within the flow of history, an inherited tradition and its related culture *identify* us here and now at our deepest levels. Our traditional values and conventions help establish our cultural identity as Canadians, Indonesians, Scots or whatever, and thus effectively *unite* our societies. In short, tradition works as the principle of continuity, identity and unity in any human society—between generations and within a given generation.

It is clear from all this that tradition transcends not only individuals but also the present history of a group. It covers the collective experience of a group here and now, as well as all those expressions of experience which one generation transmits to another. What has been said here forms then a gloss on the treatment offered in Chapter II on the collective subject of experience. In receiving, changing and handing on its tradition, a social group acts as the collective subject, interpreter and administrator of its tradition. This collective subject experiences and hands on something which is more than the mere sum of individual experiences and their expression—namely, its cumulative experience.

When we move now to discuss Christian tradition, it would be false to act as if it simply conformed to the clear and typical trajectory of tradition in "ordinary" human affairs. Christians look back through their history and tradition to a definitive and *absolute point of reference,* an unsurpassable climax in the first century of our era. Admittedly other groups and societies may cherish the memory of some foundational event like their war of independence, the landing of some pilgrim fathers, or a glorious revolution which they believe to have transformed the subsequent course of their history. In ways that bear some analogy to the Christian model, people can cherish the spirit of their national tradition and seek to renew themselves through the records and traditions that derive from events which brought their country into existence. But doubts will press up whenever they credit any foundational episode with an absolute, unsurpassable value. No nation has security of tenure. It could go out of existence, or it may in some future time be dramatically torn apart and recreated through events which will provide a radically new point of departure. Christians, however, believe the coming of Jesus Christ to be the definitive climax of the divine self-communication, trust that the Church which he founded will not disappear in the course of history, and—as we will see—acknowledge the Holy Spirit as the invisible bearer of their essential tradition.

Nevertheless, despite these differences, we would ignore at our peril the realities of normal human tradition. It is in and through those realities that Christian tradition operates in ways that recall the incarnation itself. Of course, pressing the parallel could lead us astray. But ignoring it would be equally wrong. The divine reality involved in handing on and re-enacting God's saving self-revelation, as it were, takes flesh in various traditional customs, beliefs and practices which provide human beings with their social continuity, identity and unity. If Christian tradition is "truly human" as well as "truly divine," we must attend to the first item and do so not least because, as we shall see in the next chapter, human weakness can let inauthenticity creep into various traditions.

To sum up: When the divine self-communication reaches men and women, this experience happens to them as traditional beings. That revealing and saving self-communication of the Triune God does not do away with the essential structures of human reality but occurs within the whole historical, social *and traditional* context of earthly life. Thus it becomes imperative to study the place of tradition when believers interpret and express for subsequent generations their experience of God.

2. The Theological Issue

From a theological point of view the key issue of tradition can be presented this way: In the history of Israel and then definitively in the life, death and resurrection of Jesus Christ the saving revelation of God took place. This period of *foundational* revelation ended with the apostolic age and gave way to the era of *dependent* revelation in which Christian believers now live. God's last word had been uttered, the Church was founded, and the writing of the inspired Scriptures (which recorded the foundational experiences and interpretations of the divine self-communication) likewise came to a close.

That all leaves us with two basic questions. (a) How can we be sure and ensure that the original, foundational revelation remains living and effective in the present Church? To put matters more precisely: In the life of Christianity how does one generation know that, as it expresses and transmits to another what it has experienced of the divine self-communication, there will be real continuity between the foundational revelation which occurred then and the dependent revelation which takes place now? How does it know that there will be no loss of essential identity in re-enacting the basic experience of God's self-communication in Christ? (b) What respective roles do tradition and the Scriptures play in transmitting and actualizing the experience of that divine self-communication? This question logically follows from the fact that in Christianity the traditionary process is carried on by a group which has inherited inspired writings from the founding period of the Church.

Question (a) will be handled in the next chapter. Question (b) was the troubling and elusive question which the Protestant Reformers and the Council of Trent handled and bequeathed to posterity. To that we can now turn.

As regards the whole sixteenth-century controversy on tradition and Scripture I do not plan to burden the reader with a heavy amount of historical and theological information.[3] A summary account will suffice to provide the necessary background for contemporary issues.

To begin with, in its decree of April 8, 1546 (DS 1501–08) the Council of Trent did not intend to give a complete exposé on tradition but wished to oppose the "Scripture alone" (sola Scriptura) principle of the Reformers. After acknowledging "the Gospel" (which approximates to what this book calls foundational revelation) to be "the source of all living truth and all regulation of customary observances" (fontem omnis et salutaris veritatis et morum disciplinae), it pointed to the written books and un-written (apostolic) traditions as "containing" this truth and regulation ("hanc veritatem et disciplinam contineri in libris scriptis et sine scripto traditionibus"). Over against any attempt to make the Bible the sole means of revelation and guide to faith, Trent maintained that the Church's tra-dition also preserved and disclosed "the Gospel." We can expect to find revelation expressed, recorded and actualized through various traditions, as well as through the inspired Scriptures.

But what did Protestants intend by *sola Scriptura*? The explosion of publications which followed the invention of printing aided and abetted the humanist renaissance, which numbered many Reformers among its leaders. Excitement over the Scriptures and their message of forgiveness, grace and freedom joined forces with a vigorous reaction against both decadent traditions and various commandments of the Church that bound under serious sin. Many of the Reformers, when they rediscovered central themes of the New Testament, turned against such human enactments as the laws of fasting, the rule of annual confession, the practice of in-dulgences and the obligations of celibacy for priests and religious. *Sola Scriptura* first emerged as a battle cry in the call to reform the Catholic Church, even if it rapidly became the decisive norm in the doctrinal dis-putes between Luther, Zwingli and other Reformers.

The main thrust of the principle could be put as follows: Within the limits of the biblical text the Holy Spirit actively expresses the saving truth of revelation and brings into play the living reality of Jesus Christ. This activity which authentically brings to the Christian the presence of the Lord remains restricted to the interpretation of the scriptural text. Hence the Bible alone takes on the role of being the exclusive rule of faith. No other authority really counts. Hence the 1963 Faith and Order conference summed up the scope of *sola Scriptura* this way: "The Prot-estant position has been an appeal to Holy Scripture alone, as the infallible and sufficient authority in all matters pertaining to salvation, to which all human traditions should be subjected."[4]

The theme of authority should make it clear what lay at the root of the controversy over tradition and Scripture: divergent views of the Church. In general—and I recognize that this is a massive and risky generalization—Protestants differed from Catholics in separating the activity of Christ's Spirit from the visible, historical community with its inherited traditions and authoritative magisterium. In the short or the long run this rejection of the magisterium *either* meant an exclusive autonomy was given to the Scriptures (to be interpreted through private enlightenment coming from the Holy Spirit or—and this came later—in dependence on the latest, shifting results of biblical research), *or* else reason took full charge, as was the case with the typical religious stance of the Enlightenment. Over against and such a Protestant trend, Catholics believed that Christ's Spirit both supported the wider community with its traditions and guaranteed those empowered as members of the magisterium to teach authoritatively, as well as to guide and sanctify other believers. In other words, the Holy Spirit's active presence was acknowledged to extend beyond the situation of individual believers reading the Scriptures, preachers expounding the Scriptures and ministers using the Scriptures in sacramental actions.

Apart from the basic divergence over ecclesiology, Catholics and other Christians (Anglicans and Orthodox) have raised various objections to the *sola Scriptura* view that the Bible by itself can and should determine faith and practice for Christians. First, it is a trite truth to remark that the Bible itself nowhere claims to "contain" all revelation or to be—independently of tradition—the exclusive norm of faith. Moreover, as the form-critical method has demonstrated with relentless thoroughness for both the Old and the New Testament, the Bible is through and through the product of the community's traditionary processes. It is nothing more nor less than the literary product of the Hebrew and apostolic traditions, and without them it would never have come into existence. Hence if the community's tradition actively led to the formation of the Scriptures, one can rightly expect the same tradition to remain active in interpreting, applying and living out the Scriptures, in bringing about the experience of (dependent) revelation, and in guiding the response of faith. After all, the Bible nowhere declares its autonomy, as if it had supplanted tradition, the very force which brought it into existence, and had become the exclusive role of faith, once the apostolic generation had died out. It seems thoroughly reasonable to argue that those who separate the Bible from tradition in fact diminish its value and impact by taking it out of its natural setting.

Besides, it took (post-apostolic) tradition to recognize *these* Scriptures as inspired and exclude other books from the biblical list or canon. In that sense it needed tradition to clarify just where the inspired and authoritative Scriptures were to be found. At the same time, however, Karl Rahner rightly remarks that the recognition of the extent of the canon is a special affair which does not exemplify the general relationship between tradition and Scripture.[5] That general relationship is seen at two different points—when the Bible first formed (through the Israelite and apostolic traditions) and when it was later interpreted by post-apostolic tradition.

Second, the overwhelming majority of Protestant Reformers never in fact based their belief and practice solely on the Scriptures. They retained, for instance, the traditional belief in the Blessed Trinity, even though—as I noted in Chapter III—a clear distinction between the risen Christ and the Holy Spirit and, in general, a properly articulated doctrine of the Trinity remained to be worked out through the early Church councils. Another example: Most Protestants did not appeal to the *sola Scriptura* principle and abandon infant baptism, a practice which can hardly claim anything like an explicit and compelling warrant in the New Testament text by itself.

This whole problem of basing belief and practice on the Scriptures opened up even more alarmingly as modern historical exegesis emerged in the aftermath of the Reformation and the Enlightenment. The Fathers of the Church and then the theologians of the Middle Ages found a generous range of meanings in the Bible. Beyond the literal meaning (that is, the meaning which the author intended to convey), they recognized three further "spiritual" senses of the Scriptures: the allegorical, tropological and anagogical meanings.[6] On that basis they could have no difficulty whatsoever in accepting that the Scriptures "contained" all revelation and hence were "materially sufficient" in communicating revelation, even if the Bible was not "formally sufficient" inasmuch as it needed the interpreting help of tradition. In line with this approach to exegesis the Middle Ages understood theology as "the science of the Scriptures" and theologians as "the masters of the sacred page (magistri sacrae paginae)." But once a strict historical exegesis began to confine the sense of Scriptures to their literal meaning, it became much more problematic for Protestants to support their Christian faith and practice simply and solely on the basis of the Scriptures.[7] In a later chapter we return to the issue of scriptural meaning and interpretation.

Third, inevitably Catholic critics have made much of the fact that the Bible has sometimes brought as much division as unity. If the objective meaning of the biblical texts emerged with the simple clarity of basic mathematics, the Scriptures might have brought about concord in interpreting and expressing the Christian experience of the divine self-communication. But, as I argued in the previous chapter, we both discover *and create* meaning when we read traditional Christian statements of faith. The point applies also to the Bible. Not only do the public contexts change but also individuals bring their deep questions, previous experiences, inherited assumptions, actual commitments and whole personal history to the reading of the scriptural texts. With an awful inevitableness Christians have moved beyond legitimate personal paraphrasing to "find" mutually exclusive meanings in their common Bible and even in the same passages of the Scriptures. Right from the early centuries of Christianity, protagonists of divisions and heresies like Arianism have normally attempted to support their interpretations of (foundational) revelation by appealing to the Scriptures. Here the verdict of history is sharp and suggestive. The principle of *sola Scriptura,* if taken strictly, could never really promise to bring agreement about the right way to interpret, express and live out the experience of the divine self-communication in Christ.

Fourth, it is obviously too much to ask the Scriptures by themselves to provide answers, especially full and universally convincing ones, to the challenge: How should we interpret and express—and that means reinterpret and re-express—the foundational experience of God's self-communication in the face of new questions, unexpected problems, and the whole medley of fresh experiences which make up the total complex of human history? More briefly, how can the Bible by itself respond to issues which arise only in the course of human history? For instance, Greek philosophy raised questions about the "person" and "nature(s)" of Christ which the New Testament could not fairly be expected to answer clearly. The authors of the New Testament and the traditions they drew on did not face such questions and hence could hardly be expected by themselves to provide the appropriate answers. And yet these questions touched something utterly basic about the Christian experience: the true and right ways of discerning, interpreting and expressing what or rather whom the disciples had experienced in the life, death and resurrection of Jesus Christ and the coming of the Holy Spirit. The questions were crucial, but the New Testament by itself could not simply provide the answers.

Thus far I have been rehearsing some of the main difficulties which Catholic theology has detected in the *sola Scriptura* principle. But the problems were not all on "the other side." In its brief rejection of *sola Scriptura* Trent, as we have seen, spoke of "all saving truth and all regulation of customary observances" being "contained" in tradition and Scripture. So long as post-Tridentine Catholic theology understood revelation as God manifesting certain (otherwise undisclosed) truths, it remained comfortable with such language. It was concerned to identify the "source" where various revealed truths were to be found and from such a "quantitative" point of view could raise the question: Is the Bible alone "materially sufficient"? That is to say, does it "contain" all the truths of revelation or are some of them (for instance, the immaculate conception and the assumption of the Blessed Virgin Mary) "contained" only in tradition?

In juxtaposing tradition and Scripture in this material way, this "quantitative" approach in effect degraded tradition. It became a mere vehicle for transporting a revealed content, and precisely as such turned into something extrinsic to revelation. The traditionary process, understood in this way, could never prove revealing but became a task for the memory. After the apostolic generation (which received all the truths of revelation but did not record all of them in the inspired Scriptures) had disappeared, later Christians had the duty of preserving through tradition the fullness of that revelation to the apostles. Despite the threatening passage of time, faithful tradition as well as the survival of the Bible enabled the Church to preserve all the truths revealed at the foundation of Christianity.

Furthermore, post-Tridentine Catholic theology notoriously read Trent's decree as if it were teaching two "materially" separate and equally valid "sources" of revelation, one being tradition and the other Scripture. J. H. Geiselmann, even if some details of his case had to be corrected, firmly established the point.[8] The "two source" theory of revelation could not claim to be supported by Trent's teaching, which in any case reserved the term "source" exclusively for "the Gospel," or the *one* message of salvation communicated by Christ.

I hope this does not parody what a "propositional" view of revelation entailed for the typical Catholic version of the tradition-Scripture issue. Once the shift came to the interpersonal or dialogue model of revelation (see Chapter III), the whole discussion got altered. Whether in the foundational or in the dependent stage, revelation primarily means a gracious call to enter by faith here and now into the mystery of a relationship with the Triune God. This presence of saving revelation comes about when human beings are addressed through hearing sermons, reading the Scriptures, receiving the sacraments, facing various challenges in their daily lives and meeting other experiences. Seen as this kind of personal event, revelation is something which happens and is not, properly speaking, "contained" in a book (the Bible) or in traditions which believers inherit from previous generations of Christians. If revelation consisted primarily in a body of truths, we could remain at ease with the old terminology. But since revelation is the living reality of a personal meeting, it is not happily described as being "contained" in anything, whether it be Scripture or tradition.

3. A Catholic Position

Something essential would be missing from this summary account of the Reformation controversy and its aftermath if I failed to mention the recent re-evaluation of tradition which has come from some Protestant theological and philosophical circles. Gerhard Ebeling, for example, maintains that the reflection on proclamation (which he considers to be theology's proper task) should also be concerned with the "proclamation which has already taken place," and thus he can write: "The task which theology is given to do is identical with the gift it receives from tradition." Hence "the task of handing on this tradition . . . is clearly constitutive for theology."[9] It may seem astounding that a theologian who is so consciously loyal to the Reformation as Ebeling could approach theology in the spirit of "traditio quaerens intellectum" (tradition seeking understanding). The change that we see here is at least partly due to Hans Georg Gadamer's contribution to hermeneutics. This Protestant philosopher incorporates tradition into interpretation and explains it not as an obstacle but as the necessary context for the recovery of meaning.[10] And then more than any other event the 1963 Faith and Order meeting revealed a great and deep shift in Protestant attitudes to tradition. We shall return to that shortly.

But before recounting some details of the emerging consensus, it could help to outline what as a Roman Catholic theologian I take to be a workable understanding of *the relationship between revelation, tradition and Scripture.*

(a) The apostles and those associated with them experienced the climax of foundational revelation and faithfully responded by interpreting and expressing this experience through the apostolic preaching. In and through this preaching, the conferral of baptism and the celebration of the Eucharist, they fully founded the Church.

(b) The apostolic age brought not only the founding of the Church and the last constitutive phase of the special history of revelation and salvation, but also the composition of the inspired books of the New Testament. Under the guidance of the Holy Spirit these books (which drew on personal memories as well as on oral and written traditions) fixed in writing for all time the apostolic preaching as the normative response to the definitive revelation of God in Christ.

Incidentally, I am not claiming here that the sacred writers were necessarily aware of doing all that. The results of their activity may not simply be measured by their conscious intentions. I shall return later to this issue.

(c) The books of the New Testament—together with the inspired writings of the Old Testament—do *not* as such coincide with revelation. The difference between revelation and Scripture is the difference between *a reality* and *a record.* We cannot simply identify revelation with the Bible, even if, as we shall see in a later chapter, we rightly speak of these Scriptures as "the word of God." In a normative way the Scriptures record the human experience of foundational revelation, as well as the ways in which men and women responded to, interpreted, expressed and remembered that experience. Thus this scriptural witness remains distinct from the experience of revelation itself, just as a written record differs from a lived reality.

Hence it is clear how foundational revelation comes *before* the Scriptures. Dependent revelation comes *after* the writing of those Scriptures ended. Hearing, reading and praying out of the Scriptures can bring about now the living experience of (dependent) divine revelation. In that case the Scriptures help to initiate and to interpret what believers experience today of the divine self-communication. Yet once again in this era of dependent revelation the Scriptures differ from revelation itself in the way that an effective and "inspiring" record differs from the lived event of dialogue with God.

(d) Similarly, tradition never literally coincides with revelation. As such, tradition cannot precisely "hand on" the experience of revelation. It can prove revealing in the sense of recalling revelation, pointing to it, offering means to experience it, and in general interpreting, expressing and remembering revelation. What tradition properly speaking communicates is an account and appreciation of revelation which can serve to instigate and interpret for others the experience of the divine self-communication. Thus revelation differs from tradition as a lived experience is to be distinguished from the community interpretation and expression which get transmitted through history. In short, we cannot simply identify either tradition or even Scripture as such with the experience of God's revealing and saving presence.

Once again, however, let me refer back to Chapter III and what I wrote there about the link between the interpersonal and the propositional models of revelation. While revelation should be primarily understood as the experienced event of the divine self-communication, nevertheless this event communicates true knowledge about God and the divine designs for human beings. In other words there is (secondarily) a propositional content to revelation. Hence in this sense tradition does hand on revealed truths, even if it cannot precisely as such hand on the experience of revelation itself.

(e) How then should the *post*-apostolic tradition of the Church in its "interpretative" phase be understood, and how does it "retrospectively" relate to the apostolic Scriptures? First of all, it is high time to distinguish between the *active process* of tradition *(actus tradendi)* and the *object* or content of tradition *(traditum)*. These two "moments" need to be distinguished, even if they cannot be separated. A traditionary process by definition involves handing on something.

At the *visible* level the entire people of God are engaged in the *process* of transmitting tradition and bringing about for others the experience of the divine self-communication. And they do so by using the Scriptures, celebrating the Eucharist, administering and receiving the sacraments, preaching, composing sacred music, writing catechisms, teaching catechetics and in all the other indefinitely many ways through which they express to and for others their Christian experience and faith. Seen as such an active process, the tradition of the post-apostolic Church includes but obviously goes well beyond the Scriptures. Handing on and interpreting the Scriptures is only one major part of this traditionary activity.

In this *active process* there exists a mutual priority between tradition and the Scriptures. On the one hand, authentic tradition seeks to remain faithful to the normative record of Christian origins and identity which it finds in the inspired Scriptures. On the other hand, fresh challenges and a changing context require tradition to do what the Scriptures cannot do for themselves. It must interpret and apply them so that they can take effect by becoming the revealing word of God to new readers and hearers today. In this way tradition (and the Christian life to which it gives shape and force) not only forms an extended commentary on the Scriptures but also allows them to come into their own and bring Christ to people.

In the traditionary process the members of the magisterium (the bishops and the Pope) have a special but not an exclusive role as "bearers" of tradition and (subordinate) mediators effecting the lived event of revelation. Tradition as an action is thus tied in a special way to the bishops, inasmuch as they function as successors to the apostles. In the excursus to the last chapter I pointed to the way in which the members of the magisterium enjoy a particular visibility and clarity among the general body of believers when they formulate matters of faith. Even more generally in their role as carriers of tradition, they are clearly visible and identifiable when they transmit matters of faith and Christian practice.

The "object" (*traditum*) of the traditionary process consists at the visible level of all the things, activities and memories that make up the total reality of the Church. In this sense tradition entails the whole aggregate of customs, beliefs and practices which give Christians their continuity, identity and unity. Looked at in this total way, tradition as an "object" includes the Bible (one of the major items to be handed on from generation to generation), but goes beyond it. The Church as a whole clearly transmits more than just copies of the Scriptures.

Can the magisterium affect the object of the traditionary process? Clearly it can and does. On the one hand, the magisterium both formulates statements of faith and takes practical decisions which affect the life of the Church. And it does this in the light of Scripture and tradition. But, on the other hand, these decrees and decisions then become elements in the tradition to be transmitted to the next generation of believers. Hence, although we cannot simply identify the teaching and general activity of those who make up the magisterium with the object of tradition, nevertheless the exercise of the magisterium does influence and modify what is handed down.

And, of course, in any generation the whole people of God will not transmit all that they received *exactly* as it was received. Language shifts occur, the flux of experience calls forth fresh interpretations and expressions, and the emerging signs of the times offer their special messages to those who accept in faith the divine self-communication. Certainly an essential continuity is maintained, and that happens not simply because one generation hands on to the next the unchanged text of the Bible. The dependent revelation which is experienced now remains essentially continuous with the original, foundational revelation which the apostles received in faith. All the same, the whole Church, no less than the members of the magisterium, clearly modifies to some degree that aggregate of beliefs, customs and practices (tradition as "object") which gets transmitted from one generation of believers to another.

To draw this together: Understood *either* as the active process *or* as the object handed on, tradition includes Scripture rather than simply standing alongside it. In both senses tradition is much more extensive than Scripture.

4. The Ecumenical Convergence

The 1963 conference of Faith and Order revealed several striking lines of convergence with the Catholic teaching and reflection on tradition which were to be incorporated in a document which the Second Vatican Council eventually promulgated in 1965, *Dei Verbum*. The now classic work of Yves Congar, *Tradition and Traditions,* which originally appeared in two volumes,[11] provided much of the theological justification for the statements endorsed both in Montreal and Rome. Let me sketch then some lines of ecumenical convergence which particularly concern the scope of this book.

(a) The *model of revelation* as a divine self-revelation which calls human beings to enter a communion of life and love with the Triune God was decisive for the Montreal report, Congar and *Dei Verbum*. As all agreed that revelation is primarily a personal dialogue or encounter rather than the communication of a body of truths, the heat was taken out of any "quantitative" debates about some revealed truths being "contained" in Scripture and others being possibly "contained" only in tradition. Thus

Dei Verbum took up the theme of tradition only after it had clearly laid out in the first chapter its teaching on God's *self*-revelation.[12]

(b) Both the Montreal report and *Dei Verbum* adopted "total" views of Tradition as that *whole living heritage* and entire good news which forms the "object" of the traditionary process. (From this point on let me talk of "the Tradition" or *Traditum* [with a capital T] when I use the word in this sense.) Thus *Dei Verbum* spoke in the following terms:

> What was handed on by the apostles comprises *everything* that serves to make the people of God live their lives in holiness and increase their faith. In this way the Church, in its doctrine, life and worship, perpetuates and transmits to every generation *all* that it itself is, *all* that it believes (n. 8).[13]

The Montreal report likewise described Tradition as "the Gospel itself, transmitted from generation to generation in and by the Church."[14]

The Montreal report leaned toward interpreting the essential *Traditum* as "Christ himself present in the life of the Church."[15] It preferred to move beyond the *visible,* human realities which make up the total Christian life of faith and emphasize the (invisible) truth and reality of the risen Christ divinely present among us. The following statement demonstrated this move from (public) human faith to (invisible) divine presence as constituting the heart of *the Traditum:*

> What is transmitted in the process of tradition is the Christian faith, not only as a sum of tenets, but as a living reality transmitted through the operation of the Holy Spirit. We can speak of the Christian Tradition (with a capital T), whose content is God's revelation and self-giving in Christ, present in the life of the Church.[16]

Hence the report could rightly remark: "The Tradition of the Church is not an object which we possess, but a reality by which we are possessed."[17]

Understood in this way, the Tradition comes to more than just the visible sum of beliefs and practices which Christians hand on. It is the saving presence of Christ engaged in a process of self-transmission through his Holy Spirit in the continuing life of the Church.

(c) That brings us to face a further item in the converging lines of agreement: *the invisible role of the Holy Spirit.* If the people of God are the visible bearers of Tradition, *traditio* as a traditionary action takes place "through the power of the Holy Spirit."[18] Ultimately, as Congar insisted, Christ's Spirit is responsible for maintaining the integrity of the Tradition and thus guaranteeing the Church's essential fidelity to the original experience of the divine self-communication in Christ.[19] *Dei Verbum* introduced what amounted to the same point: "The Holy Spirit, through whom the living voice of the Gospel rings out in the Church—and through it in the world—leads believers to the full truth, and makes the word of Christ dwell in them in all its richness" (n. 8).[20]

(d) Under (b) I remarked on the total view of the Tradition or *Traditum* which both *Dei Verbum* and the Montreal report supported. This *one Tradition,* however, is expressed through *many traditions* or *tradita.* The Montreal report illustrated how this expression in particular traditions takes place at the levels of liturgy, doctrine and life:

> Tradition taken in this sense is actualized in the preaching of the word, in the administration of the sacraments and worship, in Christian teaching and theology, and in mission and witness to Christ by the lives of the members of the Church.[21]

In this terminology the specific traditions become "the expressions and manifestations in diverse historical forms of the one truth and reality which is Christ."[22] Even if it spoke of an "entire heritage" rather than the Tradition, the Second Vatican Council's Decree on Ecumenism, *Unitatis Redintegratio,* similarly suggested how the one *Traditum* gets expressed in the many *tradita:* "This entire heritage of spirituality and liturgy, of discipline and theology, in the various traditions, belongs to the full catholic and apostolic character of the Church" (n. 17).[23]

(e) This actualizing and expressing of the one Tradition in the many traditions entails not only a rich diversity but also a key problem. Granted that we never find the Tradition "neat" but always embodied in various traditions, do all those particular traditions always actualize authentically the essential *Traditum?* The Montreal report put the issue this way:

> Do all traditions which claim to be Christian contain the Tradition? How can we distinguish between traditions embodying the true Tradition and merely human tradition? Where do we find the genuine Tradition, and where impoverished tradition or even distortion of tradition?[24]

A year later at the third session of the Second Vatican Council Cardinal Meyer of Chicago raised what was essentially the same problem in a debate on the text which was to become *Dei Verbum.* He pointed to the "limits" and "defects" which show up repeatedly in the history of the Church and its traditions. He offered some examples: the long neglect of the doctrine of the resurrection, an exaggerated casuistry in moral theology, a non-liturgical piety and the neglect of the Bible. He asked that the text of *Dei Verbum* should admit the existence of such defects and point to the Scriptures as the norm which always helps the Church to correct and perfect its life.[25] In fact Cardinal Meyer's suggested addition was not adopted. But *Dei Verbum* did insist that the Scriptures should "constantly rejuvenate" theology and the life of the Church (n. 24).[26]

(f) *Dei Verbum*, however, also alerted its readers to the difficulty of using the inspired Scriptures as the only source of certainty in assenting to given truths, or—to transpose the point into the precise terms of our problem—as the sole means for confidently establishing where the true Tradition is to be found among the diverse traditions. In what has to be the understatement of the whole document, *Dei Verbum* declared: "The Church does not draw its certainty about all revealed truths from the holy Scriptures alone" (n. 9).[27]

The Montreal report put its finger squarely on the difficulty:

> Loyalty to our confessional understanding of Holy Scripture produces both convergence and divergence in the interpretation of Scripture. . . . How can we overcome the situation in which we all read Scripture in the light of our own traditions?[28]

In other words, inherited traditions and all their other presuppositions inevitably cause Christians to *create* meaning, as well as discover it, when they read and interpret the Bible. The quality of their faith and practice will always determine at least to some extent how they interpret the biblical texts. Hence it is neither feasible nor possible to use the Scriptures as the *sole* criterion for sorting out defective and authentic traditions so as to find the Tradition within the traditions. What other possible criteria can support the Scriptures in this task of discernment and interpretation? To that question we turn in the next chapter.

VIII. FINDING THE TRADITION WITHIN THE TRADITIONS

> *The appalling possibility that Kierkegaard insisted we consider is that God's teaching might not agree completely with the predilections and the conscience of the present age.*
>
> Walter Kaufmann

> *We live to advance, appreciating at the same time whatever the past has to offer us in the line of experience. But we must move ever further onward along the road which our Lord has opened up before us. The Christian life is not a collection of ancient customs.*
>
> Pope John XXIII

In a rich variety of ways the Christian community expresses, remembers, records and passes on the collective experience which has been lived through and accumulated in the history of this religious group. One generation of believers transmits to another all its Scriptures, doctrines, liturgical practices, ethical norms and ideals, actual patterns of behavior, methods of organization—in short, the whole *Tradition* (or *Traditum*) that visibly makes up the Church's entire existence at the levels of "teaching, life and worship."[1]

On the one hand, the Tradition (with a capital T) needs the particular traditions if it is to be preserved and disclosed. But, on the other hand, not all these traditions (*tradita*) prove of equal value in genuinely expressing and actualizing the foundational revelation. In the Church's traditions decline and corruption show up, as well as progress. Some *tradita* may turn out to be mere "traditions of men" (Mk 7:8) which distort or misrepresent the true Tradition, that continuing presence of Christ through his Spirit in the life of the Church. Or else language shifts and other cultural changes may have made some traditions unworkable or unintelligible. In any case all particular traditions must be appropriated, checked, translated and renewed in every generation of Christianity.

We can approach the question as follows. When our inherited traditions intersect with our present experiences, two things happen. The various doctrinal, liturgical and moral traditions will help us to discern and interpret what we experience. At the same time our new experiences may call into question and challenge some old traditions concerned with Christian belief, worship and way of life. For instance, a gap may open up between the language of contemporary culture and that of traditional teaching. This kind of tension may be ignored or suppressed, but the price of artificially maintaining old traditions will be a loss of genuine Christian living. Yet sooner or later fresh experiences will always bring home new perspectives on some inherited attitudes and practices. Thus the ecumenical, feminist and charismatic movements, the arms race, widespread injustice and hunger, and other elements in the Church's total environment in their different ways raise the questions: Where have Christian traditions remained faithful to the foundational revelation and where have they obscured it? What new practices and expressions of faith should be incorporated into official Christianity?

How then can the present generation of believers go about discerning and interpreting both the great mass of traditions it has received from the past and those new practices and expressions of faith which are always springing up, at least here and there, among believers? Are there criteria to help us truly identify, faithfully preserve and effectively translate into present terms what the Roman Canon describes as "the Catholic faith that comes to us from the apostles," what the Council of Trent calls "the purity of the Gospel" (DS 1501), or what the 1963 meeting of the Faith and Order Commission names as *the* Tradition within the traditions? In equivalent terms, this finding the Tradition within the traditions is the task of allowing revelation and salvation to be more effectively actualized at each stage in the Church's changing history. Or in other terms this is the theme of the "Ecclesia semper reformanda," that obligation to reform the Church constantly which the Second Vatican Council's Decree on Ecumenism heavily stressed.[2]

I understand Karl Barth's warnings about tradition to amount to the same thing. He remarks on the fact that the New Testament uses *paradidonai* (and *paradosis*) both of Judas handing Jesus *over* (Mk 14:10; 1 Cor 11:23) and of Christians handing *down* their tradition (1 Cor 15:3; 2 Thess 2:15). Christians must hand down their message, but in doing so they may, like Judas, betray their Master. Just as the historical Jesus surrendered himself into the hands of men, so the risen Christ has become the "object" to be transmitted and can be misrepresented by particular traditions.[3]

In the whole discerning process it would be absurd to expect that the Gospel, the Tradition, or—to put it in equivalent terms—the truth and saving reality of Jesus Christ could be experienced "neat." The (one) Tradition can be found only in and through the (many) traditions. The Gospel, transmitted in and by the Church, never exists in some abstract, ideal state, but only as actualized and interpreted through "the preaching of the word, in the administration of the sacraments and worship, in Christian teaching and theology, and in mission and witness to Christ by the lives of the members of the Church."[4] What criteria are available to recognize and faithfully conform oneself to the Tradition within the traditions? *The* Tradition must never be betrayed, but the traditions—which run all the way from the preservation of relics, the practice of indulgences and the Latin Mass through methods for appointing bishops to current formulations of doctrine—undergo and should undergo change. We must uphold *tota Traditio* but it would be both a betrayal of Christianity and an impossible task to maintain at all costs *omnes traditiones.* However, what principles are available to guide our discernment, interpretation and innovations?

1. The Magisterium

In the Church's magisterium Catholics enjoy a clear and visible criterion for maintaining a creative fidelity, as they receive what previous generations have passed on and attempt to discern what the Spirit could be saying to the churches now. The magisterium will guide the Catholic believer's choices in that permanent dialogue between inherited traditions and new experiences.

Nevertheless, this criterion does not suffice by itself. On given issues the magisterium may never pronounce or only speak after many years have elapsed. In the meantime, however, believers will have to respond and react to the question: Does this or that tradition misrepresent or deviate from the foundational revelation? Further, the magisterium is a proximate criterion which points beyond itself. Then the Pope and bishops in their magisterial role do not constitute an ultimate criterion but are bound to adhere and submit to Christ's saving revelation.[5] On this point the Second Vatican Council's Constitution on Divine Revelation has been quoted a thousand times but one more time will not hurt:

The task of giving an authentic interpretation of the word of God, whether in its written form or in the form of Tradition, has been entrusted to the living teaching office of the Church alone. . . . Yet this magisterium is not superior to the word of God, but is its servant.[6]

2. Universality, Antiquity and Consent

The Canon of Vincent of Lerins offers a further criterion for assessing traditions: "That which has been believed everywhere, always and by everyone—this is truly and properly Catholic."[7] In their own fashion others have articulated part or all of this criterion. Thus St. Augustine wrote: "Securus iudicat orbis terrarum" (The whole world judges securely).[8] But Vincent of Lerins' statement has become the classical one. Let me here indicate rapidly some necessary qualifications and limitations.

There is no escaping the fact that the Vincentian Canon is to a degree a Christianized version of the ancient argument from universality, antiquity and consent: What has been everywhere believed by everyone from time immemorial must be true. Or to put it another way: What was universally believed by everyone at the beginning was the pure, unadulterated truth. Errors came later. Hence we should presume that ancient traditions which were universally and commonly believed carry the truth and that novelties involve falsehood.

To identify the Vincentian Canon as a Christianized version of a classical principle is not *eo ipso* to allege that the Canon is automatically and totally wrong. After all the Greek and Latin thinkers could have some truth on their side. But one should not overlook a very similar appeal to universality, antiquity and consent in writers like Cicero. Precisely on that basis he argued for the existence of the gods and the reality of prescience and foretelling.[9] However, we would get things wrong if we overlooked a point made in the excursus on philosophy and theology. To a lesser or greater extent, Christian theology will *always* modify ideas which it takes over from philosophy and other sources. Philosophical concepts and principles (such as the criterion of universality, antiquity and consent) cannot be expected to move without change into the theological framework.

What then should be said of the Vincentian Canon? Essentially it appeals to a process of historical verification in support of whatever traditional beliefs and practices are being questioned. To retain some theological validity, however, the Canon requires a number of modifications.

(a) First of all, the Canon needs to be qualified as follows: "What has been believed everywhere, always and by everyone *precisely as part of the saving Gospel of Christ*—this is truly and properly Catholic." Notoriously Christians have for centuries shared with others false beliefs about the nature of the universe, human procreation and the activities of witches, as well as accepting with their contemporaries such immoral practices as slavery. In the face of such obvious and persistent difficulties from Christian history, we should introduce some such qualification and give the Vincentian Canon a chance.

(b) Further, it is clear that very few traditional beliefs and practices could literally verify the Canon. No one has ever established that some traditional doctrine has been *quite literally and explicitly believed, always, everywhere and by everyone.* It is hard to imagine how this could ever be established. Taking the Vincentian Canon slightly less literally but still pretty rigidly, we could perhaps demonstrate a clear antiquity, universality and general consent for such an utterly basic belief like Christ being Savior of mankind. For other such doctrines and practices as the real presence in the Eucharist, original sin, the existence of purgatory and the validity of prayers for the dead, we would have very considerable difficulties in showing anything like an explicit acceptance "always, everywhere and by everyone."

We could help matters by adding a qualification: "What has been believed *at least implicitly. . . .* " That addition would give the historian more hope of demonstrating that at least a few traditions were latently and implicitly held "always, everywhere and by everyone."

We could add another qualification: "What has been believed at least implicitly always, everywhere and by everyone—*at least that* is truly and properly Catholic." In other words, we could use the Vincentian Canon as an inclusive, rather than an exclusive, criterion. It would *not,* therefore, exclude some traditional beliefs which *as a matter of fact* could have been held implicitly "always, everywhere and by everyone," but which we *cannot historically prove* to have been so held.

(c) Even after we have added these different qualifications to the Canon, several questions press themselves on our attention. Who, for instance, is to count as "everyone"—only those who *on other grounds* we hold to be orthodox believers, or all practicing Christians? Difficulties over traditions arise precisely when everyone did not and does not agree. If we look back to the Christological controversies of the early centuries we can only wonder what the results would have been had the Vincentian Canon been strictly applied. At their height the Arian party could well have successfully employed such a principle against Athanasius and his followers, who—as John Henry Newman insisted—appeared to be innovating radicals fighting for a strange terminology against the proper traditionalists. In later centuries the prophetic few who campaigned for such reforms as the abolition of slavery would hardly have helped their cause by appealing to "what has been believed and practiced always, everywhere and by everyone." In short, counting noses might not determine too readily the status of inherited traditions. Even in the milder form of moral unanimity the Vincentian Canon does not easily fit the cases in which prophetic minorities in the Church have challenged certain traditional attitudes and practices and eventually, but only eventually, have been proved right in their discernment of the Gospel demands. As Newman remarked, "The number of persons holding an idea is no warrant for its objective character, else the many never could be wrong."[10] From time to time "the many" have turned out to be wrong in the traditions they have received and handed on—at the level of belief, worship and patterns of behavior.

Frequently "everyone" has been taken in a somewhat restricted way to denote the consent of the Fathers of the Church. Thus some traditional beliefs and practices have been justified by appealing to "the teaching of the holy Fathers," their "ancient tradition," and their "unanimous consent."[11] Whatever the value of such general appeals, Newman and others have pointed out how difficult it is to claim for any specific doctrine whatsoever that *all* the Fathers of the Church *explicitly* and *directly* teach it.

(d) If consent ("everyone") raises problems for the Vincentian Canon, so too do antiquity ("always") and universality ("everywhere"). In assessing inherited traditions what should we accept as counting for "always" and "everywhere"? Will relative antiquity count as "always" or must the tradition in question necessarily go back to the very origins of Christianity? What constitutes the geography of orthodox faith implied by "everywhere"? Newman summed up the problem this way:

What is meant by being "taught *always*"? Does it mean in every century, or every year, or every month? Does *"everywhere"* mean in every country, or in every diocese? And does "the consent of Fathers" require us to produce the testimony of every one of them? How many Fathers, how many places, how many instances constitute a fulfillment of the test proposed?[12]

(e) Obviously we could end up establishing *only part* of "the test proposed." Thus we might establish antiquity without universality and consent. Something was believed always but not everywhere and by everyone. Or we might prove universality without antiquity and consent. Something has been believed everywhere but not always and by everyone. Or again we might demonstrate a general consent (either now or in the recent past) but have to admit that we cannot do the same for antiquity and universality. Something is now believed by everyone but this has not always and everywhere been the case.

In brief, the three elements that make up the Canon are not only distinguishable but also separable, as Vincent of Lerins himself realized. On the one hand, he knew that Arianism had spread very widely and so he could only invoke antiquity ("always") but not universality ("everywhere") against that heresy.[13] On the other hand, Donatism may have won a broad following in Christian Africa but it remained geographically confined. Hence Vincent appealed to universality ("everywhere") but not consent ("everyone") against the Donatists.[14]

(f) So far this discussion of the Vincentian Canon has had the effect of filling it out into a larger and more flexible shape: "That which has been believed—at least implicitly—always, everywhere and by everyone precisely as part of Christ's saving Gospel—at least *that* is truly and properly Catholic." Yet even in this larger shape, it may not function too well as a total entity and, as we have just seen, the separable elements of "always, everywhere and by everyone" may have to set up on their own or as pairs rather than as a triad.

If then the Vincentian Canon requires so many qualifications and adjustments to avoid being patently useless and false, is it any real help? Newman did not think so. The Canon, he concluded, hardly yields "any satisfactory result. The solution it offers is as difficult as the original problem."[15] Yet I wonder whether the Canon has worn so badly that it is no longer workable.

Ultimately, it seems to me, the Vincentian Canon classically recalls that intersubjective nature of inherited Christian truth and life which must play an essential part in any discernment of traditions. Such discernment takes place in a Church community bonded together by a complex history of belief and practice. Any judgments and decisions about inherited traditions must be seriously checked against the collective experience of earlier Christians. Certain movements and trajectories can suggest ways in which the enduring presence of Christ's Spirit has shaped different Christian traditions and so preserved *the* Tradition. Even if it does not explicitly invoke the Holy Spirit, the Vincentian Canon reminds us that we must search for signs of the Spirit's enduring guidance in *past* generations of Christians. God is faithful. We can expect that we will find help by examining the ways our Christian predecessors experienced and expressed God's revelation and grace.

A few remarks about this scrutiny of the past. First, if something has been accepted, believed and practiced "never, nowhere and by no one," that should give us pause in our endorsement of some current traditions. Then too in searching for a usable past, we need to be on our guard against simply looking for what we want to find, tracking down traditions to support judgments we have already discretely made, and hence being committed to accept lesser hints rather than follow the general weight of testimony. Newman articulates this warning, albeit with a somewhat different purpose: "And do not the same ancient Fathers bear witness to another doctrine, which you disown? Are you not like a hypocrite, listening to them when you will, and deaf when you will not? . . . You accept the lesser evidence, you reject the greater."[16] Third, one would risk turning into an incautious *laudator temporis acti* who blandly idealizes the past if one ignored the fact that every tradition is historically conditioned, even those at the very origins of Christianity. For instance, was the "loyal" attitude of the first Christians toward the Romans (reflected in Luke/Acts, 1 Peter, Romans 13 and elsewhere in the New Testament) a normative, intrinsic consequence of their experience of Jesus or simply a prudent stance dictated by the circumstances?

Granted all these cautionary remarks, the traditions of the Christian past, despite all the sinful corruptions, will, nevertheless, disclose the living presence of *the* Tradition, the unfailing influence of Christ's Spirit and not just "the dust and debris of two thousand years."[17] As we seek help in discerning particular issues in our present traditions and experiences, we may find only thin trajectories, small hints and minor signs in the past. But some usable traditions will be there to challenge and illuminate us. For example, present experience of the women's movement in the Church—or would it be more accurate to say "women's movements"?—has prompted some to turn back to Julian of Norwich, St. Anselm of Canterbury, Isaiah and others for their use of feminine imagery in speaking of God and/or Jesus. Here and elsewhere, the records of past Christian experience will help us to discern and interpret the present.

To conclude this treatment of the Vincentian Canon, it could ultimately be rephrased this way:

> What we can discover to have been believed and practiced *at least* sometimes, in some places and by some Christians as part of the good news and which promises once again to be *life-giving*—that can truly and properly direct our discernment of present traditions and experiences.

"Life" in the mere sense of quantitative success is no necessary guide to truth, as Newman warned: "Life is no criterion of truth, for unreal, but plausible or isolated, ideas may powerfully affect multitudes."[18] However, what has once given and now promises again to give and enhance genuine life in Christ can be safely followed. Thus the Vincentian Canon, if it encourages an interest in earlier Christian experience, it does this in order to find and accept life-giving sources and not simply to augment "objective" historical knowledge.

3. The "Sensus Fidelium"

Where the Vincentian Canon focuses on the *past*, the *sensus fidelium* looks to the *present* sensitivity found in the whole body of believers. Here and now the Holy Spirit guides their instinctive discernment and judgment in matters of faith. As constituting the body of Christ they enjoy an "intimate sense" of the "spiritual realities which they experience."[19] This *sensus fidelium* is based on nothing more nor less than the Johannine understanding of the Holy Spirit as communicating to the body of believers that truth which is Christ himself.[20] By shaping and guiding the corporate mind of the Church, the Holy Spirit provides a further criterion for testing and scrutinizing inherited traditions.

Inasmuch as the *sensus fidelium* involves the Spirit, it can seem obscurely dangerous to some people. By appealing to something invisible, does this criterion provide a warrant for intolerable excesses of all kinds? However, in the long run or even in the short run two safeguards are available. Do we see that a given discernment of inherited traditions which primarily appeals to the Holy Spirit in fact brings a union of minds and hearts and other visible fruits of the Spirit (Gal 5:22f.)? By its fruits we can know the presence of a true *sensus fidelium*.

Second, this criterion must ultimately look to the Spirit's impact on the *collective* mind of the *whole* Church. It does not justify the aberrations of small groups, nor does it support a discernment which makes little attempt to reflect on world Christianity and takes the traditions of one continent or even one country as decisive. Of course, there are immense difficulties here. How do we establish the *sensus fidelium* of Christians or even simply of Roman Catholics who across the world exhibit many cultural diversities and divisions? Nevertheless, this third criterion rightly directs us to examine the faith and practice of the *whole* Church—"from the bishops to the last of the faithful."[21]

At times, however, we may want a unified *sensus fidelium* which we cannot get. Just as in the past, so now difficulties will flare up precisely when the whole Church does not appear to judge matters of faith in the same way. In this century the discernment of small groups eventually led the majority to find richer peace, joy and life through the liturgical and ecumenical movements. We can readily agree that those groups of pioneers who brought the Church at large to a greater sensitivity in fact constituted genuine prophetic minorities. They first articulated what others later recognized as an authentic *sensus fidelium*. But can we discern and interpret other innovating groups who today challenge various inherited attitudes and practices? They do not represent the general consensus, and yet some of them *may* well turn out to be prophetic minorities who do experience in a special way the guidance of the Holy Spirit, express a genuine *sensus fidelium* and are called to prompt others into a more Christian discernment about the life of faith.

Once again we have no other means for assessing whether such innovating groups genuinely do express a true *sensus fidelium* than by (a) checking the visible fruits of the Spirit, and (b) analyzing them in the light of the other seven criteria discussed in this chapter.

4. Continuity

Right from the early centuries of Christianity continuity has proved a constant concern. At times true continuity with the apostolic Church was misunderstood as immobility by those who identified all change with heresy. They supposed that the "content" of Christian revelation had been clearly and comprehensively defined at the outset. Hence they believed it possible to maintain a complete, transhistorical continuity with what came to the apostles from Christ. But this was to identify continuity with immutability in a way that was incompatible both with the role of the Holy Spirit (Jn 16:13) and the ordinary dynamics of human history.

In its turn the modern magisterium has often been parodied for its constant recourse to continuity as a criterion for judgment. Wits have suggested a whole range of pronouncements which, even if they entail a change in policy, will, nevertheless, begin: "As the Church has constantly taught and practiced. . . . " However, this criterion, to which the magisterium gives an instinctive preference and which goes back in various guises to the origins of Christianity, houses no wishful assumption but a sound (formal) principle for evaluating traditions and introducing changes.

Jesus spoke of acting "like a householder who can produce from his store both the old and the new" (Mt 13:52). Changes in contemporary experiences, questions, interests and language can demand that certain Christian traditions be revived, modified or dropped, but without losing continuity with the essential message inherited from the past. Continuity does not in fact mean immobility, "the dead hand of tradition," and a rigidity which upholds the letter at the expense of the spirit. At the same time, however, there will inevitably be some tension between the demands of continuity and those of innovation. Since tradition works as a principle of continuity, identity and unity within any human society, inevitably some people will always fear that the questioning of particular traditions can only bring discontinuity, loss of identity and disunity.

Two questions must be responsibly answered: Faced with possible changes in these or those traditions, what do we judge will count as real continuity in the essential *Traditum?* What will prove faithful innovations that truly embody a *fidélité créatrice* (Gabriel Marcel)? There is no easy way of clearly and fully predicting in advance the precise ways in which authentic identity should be preserved and real continuity maintained in and through historical changes.

We could, for example, spot the false or merely apparent continuity involved in artificially retaining traditions which have become petrified and even oppressive. Or we could note how certain traditional concepts drawn from earlier experiences fail to fit present experiences. But in both cases we would need to establish what such a "fit" entails and what counts for petrifaction and oppression. In any case, as we saw in the last chapter, total discontinuity is simply inconceivable and impossible. There will always be continuity of some kind. The question comes to this: What counts as authentic continuity?

We might want to describe proper continuity as a homogeneous development as opposed to a heterogeneous development that introduces alien and unfaithful innovations. But this terminology simply shifts the question slightly to leave us with what is the same issue: What will count as homogeneous as opposed to heterogeneous development?

Some versions of this criterion for evaluating traditions lean more toward the preservation of what is already there—for example, the admonition of Pope Stephen I: "Nihil innovetur nisi quod traditum est" (Let there be no innovations except on the basis of what has been handed down) (DS 110). Other versions like the analogy of organic growth used by Newman among others highlight progress and change. But in both cases the key appeal is to a continuity which—through all the changes in particular traditions—preserves the essential identity in the Church, guided yesterday, today and forever by the Holy Spirit.

Seen this way the criterion of continuity does not prove really distinct in any serious sense from the second and third criteria. The Vincentian Canon and the *sensus fidelium* appeal respectively to that past and present guidance of Christ's Spirit which ensures an essential continuity in the truth. Beyond that visible continuity of the Church with itself there lies that living continuity of Christ with himself, maintaining through the Holy Spirit his people's essential fidelity to the revealing and saving divine self-communication.

5. Creed as Criterion

From the early centuries of Christianity the Apostles' Creed, the Nicene Creed and other brief summaries of faith have supplied a workable means for testing inherited traditions, assessing experiences and judging proposed innovations—specifically, at the level of *doctrinal* traditions. The confession of the key articles of belief helped to ensure an essential continuity in the Church's life of faith. In every age attention to the creeds will disclose the relativity and contingency of some doctrinal features of contemporary Christianity. In fact, there are few more effective ways of combating the persistent temptation to absolutize a whole range of particular doctrinal traditions which we receive from previous generations of believers than to lay them alongside some classical creed.

It was to "the essential elements and vital substance of the Gospel message" communicated by the Creed that the 1977 synod of bishops in Rome pointed in their closing message. The synod found in the Creed "the basic nucleus" which should guide catechetics (n. 8) and — one might add — the evaluation of inherited doctrines, formulations and attitudes in the area of traditional beliefs.

6. Apostolicity

Although as such it is not of apostolic origin, the Apostles' Creed refers us, of course, to those first Christians who experienced the life, death and resurrection of Jesus in a peculiarly direct way, witnessed to that experience, and under the guidance of the Holy Spirit set the Church going. The apostolic experience, faith and proclamation remain uniquely normative because of the special connection with Jesus Christ enjoyed by Peter, Paul and their colleagues. This norm of judgment found its classical champion in St. Irenaeus.

At one level this criterion of apostolicity relates back to the first, inasmuch as it indicates the basis for the magisterium's *authority*. The bishops enjoy a special share in apostolic authority, since they inherit— within the historical continuity of the Church's life—a particular responsibility for the apostolic mission and hence a particular responsibility to scrutinize, preserve and modify Christian traditions, be they doctrinal, liturgical or moral.

Looked at in a slightly different way, apostolicity coincides with the fourth criterion. Apostolicity expresses the *visible continuity* of the Church with its origins. By providing such continuity, the legitimate apostolic succession of bishops guarantees authenticity in the essential Tradition of the Church.

As regards the *information* it provides, the criterion of apostolicity reduces to the next criterion, the Bible. First, the Jewish Scriptures provided the biblical mirror in and through which the apostolic community interpreted their experience of Jesus and confessed him as the Christ of God. Then they recorded that experience and the faith it initiated in the writings which eventually came together to form the New Testament. Thus "the faith that comes to us from the apostles" comes to us through a scriptural record. The Bible—and, in particular, the New Testament— attests and makes present for us the experience, faith and preaching of the apostolic Church. As the voice of that Church, the Scriptures are the sign and guarantee of the apostolicity of the Tradition and some traditions. In certain theological circles it has been conventional to refer to the Bible as "The Book of the Church." It might be more accurate to call it "The Book of the Apostolic Church," that book through which the apostolic teaching becomes available to us.

Here I find Congar's position helpful. To begin with, he dissociates himself from various attempts to postulate the existence of an esoteric oral tradition from the apostles. He insists clearly on the public role of the apostolic Scriptures: "The apostolic writings are an indispensable reference, in fact, for testing in critical fashion the purity of the apostolic heritage." At the same time, he calls it a "stubborn and exclusive attitude" to hold that "throughout its history, at present and in the future, the apostolic Scriptures are the *sole* means the Church has received and still receives the apostles' teaching." Obviously tradition *as a process* remains a vehicle for transmitting apostolic teaching among other things.

What of particular traditions or *tradita?* Congar would not accept that among the *tradita* which tradition as a process preserves and transmits are some parts of the apostolic teaching which are not also, at least in some way, supported by Scripture. Certainly he admits that in the early years of Christianity some traditions which were not recorded in the New Testament could continue to transmit apostolic teaching. He rightly points this out: "If apostolic doctrine was able to exist in the Church, in the apostolic period, without writings, it could continue to do so." But then he notes the obvious difficulty for those who maintain that apostolic teaching has been transmitted apart from the Scriptures: "The only serious objection to be made here is that with the increase of intermediaries, the difficulties of faithful transmission would also be on the increase."[22]

In fact this problem must be taken further. "With the increase of intermediaries" *and* the long lapse of time, it has become extremely difficult, if not impossible, to distinguish between (a) genuine apostolic teaching that has reached us without being recorded in the New Testament, and (b) true doctrines and valid practices which have emerged and/or been preserved over the centuries when the Church reflected on, interpreted and applied the Scriptures—especially in the context of traditional liturgical practices. Thus under the guidance of the Holy Spirit the Church followed biblical hints and indications in believing in Our Lady's assumption or maintaining the practice of infant baptism. Congar certainly allows for this kind of guidance by the Spirit in the living interpretation of the Scriptures. That being so, it appears reasonable to account for all such authentic beliefs and practices which we do not find explicitly in the Bible but which emerged later in the Church's history as coming about through process (b), and not take them to be examples of (a), apostolic doctrine which has truly come down to us but neither through the New Testament record nor through reflection on that text.

What is at stake here is not the *sola Scriptura* principle. Far from embodying that principle, process (b) allows for the proper role of tradition in interpreting and applying the Scriptures. The point at issue concerns the possibility of the apostolic generation providing us with information *but not* via the inspired Scriptures. Given the organic life of the Church in which Scriptures and the whole traditionary process (above all, the liturgy) function together as a living unity, it seems highly implausible to hold for some apostolic teaching mediated to us neither through the New Testament nor through the traditional interpretation of the Scriptures but somehow reaching us on its own. The deep unity which *Dei Verbum* acknowledges to exist between "sacred tradition and Sacred Scripture" makes it hard to to imagine how process (a) could take place.[23]

To sum up: It seems to me that apostolicity, even more than any other criteria for discerning and interpreting the Church's traditions, lacks an independent force of its own. It can be either reduced to the first criterion (the magisterium), to the fourth (continuity), or to the seventh (the apostolic Scriptures). The bishops succeed to apostolic authority, and express the visible continuity of the Church with its origins, but have no extra information derived from the apostles which might go beyond the inspired record available to all believers.

7. The Scriptures

Both in its explicit teaching[24] and in its actual practice the Second Vatican Council appealed to the Scriptures as decisively important in guiding the belief and life of the faithful. Whether in testing established traditions, interpreting experiences, and judging proposed innovations or other Christian activities, the Bible is vital. Concrete traditions constantly change, but as the unchanging text the Bible remains a fixed point of reference. Since it normatively records the foundations of Christian faith in the experience and testimony of Israel and the apostolic Church, the Bible provides Christians with a mirror and test of their self-identity. Being true to the Scriptures means being true to their original identity. Christian life and practice should base itself on those Scriptures. That public and permanent record of Christian origins stands above all the criteria already mentioned, inasmuch as through inspiration it is formally the word of God.[25]

But to introduce the Scriptures as a supreme criterion for assessing traditions is to let loose at once a swarm of questions which the previous chapter already touched on. As the Bible does not interpret itself, how do we know that our appeal to scriptural texts is being truly guided by the Holy Spirit and is not just another tedious example of arbitrary exegesis or of an historical approach which respects the letter but misses the spirit? More and more—not only among Roman Catholics, Anglicans and the Orthodox but also among Protestants—the conviction has developed that the lived transmission of the Church's faith provides an indispensable commentary on the Scriptures. In other words, the interpretation of the Bible must take place in a traditional context. But in practice how will this help to evaluate the baptism of infants, the non-ordination of women, forms of papal government, developments in canon law and other particular traditions? However, a thousand difficulties should not make a doubt. No matter what precise approach we adopt to biblical interpretation, the Scriptures must remain decisive for Christian decision-making. At the end of this book I wish to suggest some guidelines for biblical interpretation.

8. The Risen Lord

Hugh of St. Victor pointed to the deepest unity of the Scriptures when he wrote: "Omnis Scriptura unus liber est, et ille unus liber Christus est" (The whole of Scripture is one book, and that one book is Christ).[26] Not only the Bible but also all the other criteria we have discussed should ultimately bring us to the crucified and risen Christ who remains living and present to communicate his truth and grace.

Any indications to the contrary notwithstanding, the magisterium is in the business of serving and proclaiming Christ (criterion 1). The faith and life of past and present Christians have centered on Christ, whose death they proclaim until he comes (1 Cor 12:26). The Holy Spirit who has directed them and continues to direct them does nothing else than bring them to praise the glorified Son of God (1 Cor 12:3) (criteria 2 and 3). Ultimately Christian continuity derives from Jesus Christ, "the same yesterday and today and forever" (Heb 13:8) (criterion 4). Any creed of the Church turns on the mystery of Christ, the center of salvation history (criterion 5). The unique experience and role of the apostles derived from the unique and definitive nature of God's self-communication in Christ's incarnation, life, death, resurrection and sending of the Holy Spirit (criterion 6). The Scriptures find their final and proper focus in the Word made flesh (criterion 7).

In their special way St. Paul's two letters to the Corinthians encourage us to make an explicitly Christological criterion *the* key to the discernment and interpretation of traditions. At our peril we let Christ get shaded and even lost in our Christian decision-making, at whatever level. The apostle points toward the Eucharist where we find the *Traditum* par excellence: the crucified and risen Christ handed over for us (1 Cor 11:23). In 2 Corinthians Paul reflects on his "weaknesses"—what we could call his sufferings or vulnerability (4:8ff.; 6:4ff.; 11:23ff.; 12:10). Through the painful weakness of his ministry the apostle sees himself conformed to Christ and recognizes the ultimate touchstone in the principle of "power made perfect in weakness" (12:9). To put all that in the perspective of this chapter, we can devise no more Christian way of reflecting on both our inherited traditions and new developments than by asking two questions: Do these traditions and/or these proposed innovations help us to celebrate better the Eucharist and thus proclaim more powerfully the death of the Lord until he comes (1 Cor 11:26)? What judgments and decisions about our established traditions will conform us more clearly to the mystery of Christ, who "was crucified in weakness, but lives by the power of God" (2 Cor 13:4)?

In a sense the Christological criterion does nothing else than apply to the particular issue of this chapter what *Dei Verbum* (n. 4) states in general about revelation. The Second Vatican Council there presents the crucifixion, resurrection and sending of the Holy Spirit as *the primary sign* of God's complete and perfected revelation. If the crucified and risen Christ serves as the primary sign of revelation, he should also be the primary criterion for testing the Church's traditions which seek to express and re-enact that revelation. In both cases the final authority must be personal, the divine self-communication in Christ, and not some abstract principle like continuity or apostolicity.

The Christological criterion extends beyond the living presence of the risen Christ here and now, and that in two ways—both back to the ministry of Jesus and forward to the coming fullness of the kingdom (1 Cor 15:23–28). First, the historical Jesus of the Synoptic Gospels was truly incarnated in his own culture; he radically reassessed the religious traditions of late Judaism, and through his selfless service of others, unswerving devotion to his Father's will and in other ways he exemplified for us primordial attitudes of permanent value. Living as he did before the Christian Church came into existence at Easter and Pentecost, Jesus was the perfect Critic, the great Outsider or Forerunner whose words and actions continue *both* to call into question particular Church traditions which obscure the essential experience of God's self-communication to human beings, *and* to encourage new developments which can more clearly re-express that experience for the present generation. As a matter of fact the history of Christianity shows how few methods can have greater power to create true sensitivity toward traditional beliefs and practices in the Church than regular meditation on episodes from the ministry of Jesus.

Second, the risen Lord points us forward to "the end when he delivers the kingdom to God the Father . . . that God may be everything to everyone" (1 Cor 15:24, 28). That coming divine rule, the "ever-greater" *eschaton,* dramatically reveals the provisional nature of even those traditions in the Church which—seemingly in the best possible way—express through teaching, life and worship what the experience of God's self-communication in Christ entails.

Reading over this chapter, I realize two things. First, I might have added endless references to the immense theological literature that attaches to each of the criteria. But by overloading the text with detail I could have distracted the reader from the main, and, it seems, the original point of the chapter: a statement of *all* the criteria for interpreting our inherited traditions, both in themselves and in their convergence toward the ultimate criterion, Christ himself. Second, the search for *the* Tradition within the traditions, the "purity of the Gospel," or call it what you will, is finally—as William Reiser pointed out to me—another version of the classic quest for the essence of Christianity.[27] Like that quest the search for *the* Tradition finds its ultimate goal in the person of Jesus Christ risen from the dead.

To conclude: The future of the Church can only be guessed at, not foretold. What Christian faith holds for certain, however, is that as long as the world survives the Church will too. But if the Church is going to face satisfactorily the challenges posed by the forces that currently move and change the world, both fidelity and freedom are needed. If "the purity of the Gospel" inherited from the apostolic Church is to be fully effective, the various traditions through which the experience of foundational revelation has been expressed must be interpreted, translated, modified, or renewed. Some of those traditions may prove to be mere traditions of men (Mk 7:8) which should be dropped. For this process of discernment Christian faith suggests a number of criteria which finally converge toward one point—not toward the claims of efficiency, the voice of democracy, or any other immediately attractive principle, but toward the crucified and risen Lord. The ultimate question must be: in the face of these or those particular traditions and fresh developments, what does obedience to the crucified and risen Jesus demand of us? Every faithful response here carries with it an enhanced life in him who came to bring us life and bring it in abundance.

IX. THE INSPIRED EXPRESSION OF FOUNDATIONAL REVELATION

> *Revelation affects the materials out of which the literary work is formed, while inspiration affects rather the literary process which brings the work into existence.*
>
> Luis Alonso-Schökel

> *Coleridge defined the inspiration of the Bible in terms of its power to "find" man, as no other book "finds" him. . . . It is this self-authenticating power of the written word without the aid of any human intermediary that lies at the heart of the conviction of the Church that the Bible is the word of God.*
>
> Stephen Neill

Those people who experienced the gratuitous self-communication of God which climaxed in the coming of Jesus Christ were not only linguistic and traditional beings (*homo loquens et traditionalis*) but at a certain stage in their history had also become writers (*homo scribens*). Hence it is no surprise that, drawn together in the Jewish community and then in the Christian Church, they should have written down what they could discern, interpret, express and remember from their experiences of God's presence and activity.

Back in Chapter II we saw how experience neither fully happens nor enjoys real meaning unless and until it is expressed—by being conceptualized, spoken of, written down, enacted, re-enacted and so forth.

Such expression, be it in word and/or deed, is no optional extra but belongs integrally to experience itself and in fact partly determines it.

Thus those who received the divine self-communication in that special history of revelation and salvation which ran through the Old Testament period and climaxed with the foundation of Christianity expressed, symbolized and acted out their experiences in a rich variety of ways. They used the community credos to tell in summary form of Yahweh's deeds for his people, they built the temple at Jerusalem, they performed acts of worship, they put together the inspired writings and so on. Some of these expressions, such as a specific pilgrimage to Jerusalem or a particular celebration of the Eucharist by an early Christian community, were fleeting actions that precisely as such came and went. Other forms of expression like the construction of a building or the preservation of Jesus' shroud resulted in some physical object remaining present in our world—either at a fixed place (like the foundations of the temple in Jerusalem or some piece of art on the walls of the earliest Roman catacombs), or as a movable object (like the shroud of Turin). In these cases the *original* thing continues to enjoy a physical presence that cannot as such be reproduced. Finally, the *literary* expression of the Jewish-Christian experiences produced papyri rolls, codices and so forth that could be reproduced at will and become widely accessible. In the case of such written results of religious experience the original work of the author or authors in question did not and does not (necessarily) possess the kind of importance that belongs, let us say, to an original fresco, building or shroud.

It is with the inspired, literary expression of the foundational experiences of those men and women who first constituted the Jewish people and then brought the Christian community into existence that these final chapters are concerned.

Further, we aim here to elucidate what writing *and then* reading these records of the foundational Jewish-Christian experience involve. For, if these documents organized and expressed in writing the original experiences of those who belonged to the constitutive period of the Jewish-Christian religion, they were also to generate (dependent) experiences of God in people who later heard and read them. By witnessing to collective experiences of saving revelation and the new self-identity which those experiences evoked, the Bible offered and offers subsequent generations the possibility of sharing those experiences and accepting that new identity. In this sense the Scriptures are both the effect and the cause of the divine self-revelation. The record of what was experienced *then* helps to instigate and interpret the experience of the divine self-communication *now*. Retrospectively the Scriptures record various experiences and realities. Prospectively these writings can prompt religious experience in their later readers. But this is to anticipate what is to follow.

I

PRELIMINARIES

In the first instance, we need to clarify the conceptuality, raise some major questions, and make some initial moves toward describing and explaining the Scriptures. On the side of the writers, there is the inspiration and truth of the Scriptures. On the side of the readers, terms like "canon" and "hermeneutics" should be at least provisionally accounted for.

(1) *Inspiration*[1] must not be identified with revelation, nor should the experience of inspiration be identified with the experience of revelation. The revealing and saving self-communication of the Triune God goes far beyond any divinely given impulse to write. The gift or charism of (biblical) inspiration is *only one* (major) instance of a special divine presence and activity aimed at manifesting and communicating God's saving love to human beings. It is to be seen within a broader and more fundamental context.

At the origins of Israel's history men and women experienced God's self-communication within the special history of revelation and salvation *before* any inspired Scriptures were written. Then the *content* of the Jewish (and later the Christian) Scriptures cannot simply be identified as revelation. These Scriptures record a wide range of realities which include not only the preaching of Jesus and the prophets and some immediate human responses to such revelatory experiences, but also things like the laws of Leviticus and the reflections of wisdom literature. If these laws and reflections express somehow the experience of God's saving presence, they do this only at a certain distance. In general the Scriptures record the human experience of the divine self-communication, but many particular passages and even books of the Bible do so in ways that remain somewhat remote from the immediacy of that experience. Further, *after* the Sacred Scriptures were all composed—that is to say, in the post-apostolic period of dependent revelation—revelation and salvation could and can be communicated not only through the medium of these writings but also in a host of other ways like the liturgy, the impact of other persons, the signs of the times and so forth.

If the *special* history of revelation forces us to differentiate between revelation and (biblical) inspiration, even more so does the *general* history of revelation. Outside the Jewish-Christian religion millions of men and women have experienced the divine self-communication without ever hearing or reading the inspired books of the Bible. In their case revelation can take place without the least contact with the results of biblical inspiration.

To insist further should be unnecessary. Revelation and salvation cannot be restricted to or identified with the inspired Scriptures without making a pack of impossible difficulties.

What then is the relationship between revelation/salvation and the inspiration of the Scriptures? In a preliminary fashion we could speak here of the difference between (a) the divine self-communication which indefinitely many people experience in a huge variety of ways throughout all history, and (b) the divine impulse felt by a small number of persons at a particular time and place to express and set down in writing some (foundational) experiences of the divine self-communication. Thus inspiration is one special case of the divine-human interaction in the whole complex plan of events initiated by God's will to call human beings to salvation.

We have described inspiration as an impulse to write. This is to distinguish it from other kinds of "inspired," or even specially inspired, impulses which human beings genuinely receive from God. People may experience a special inspiration to speak or to act in certain ways. Thus Luke's Gospel portrays Zechariah as being filled with the Holy Spirit and impelled to proclaim the canticle we know as the Benedictus (1:67ff.). A little later the same Gospel represents Simeon as being inspired by the Holy Spirit to enter the temple when Mary and Joseph brought the child Jesus there (2:27). Such divine impulses can prompt people not only to speak and act but also to think in this or that way. However, we are concerned here with *the biblical inspiration to write* and its specific character.

That said, it would be as well to note that the (prophetic) inspiration to *speak* is closely and clearly connected with the biblical or scriptural inspiration to *write*. As I noted in Chapter III, the Old Testament prophets were speakers rather than writers. It was left to others to collect, write down, expand, interpret and publish their prophetic utterances. These writers, as the immediate authors of the prophetic books of the Bible, enjoyed the charism of scriptural inspiration. Nevertheless, their charism obviously presupposed that Isaiah, Amos and others had the prophetic inspiration to speak. It was then natural for the Second Letter of Peter to describe the written texts of the prophetic writings as if they were the *spoken words* of prophets: "No prophecy of Scripture is a matter of one's own interpretation, because no prophecy ever came by the impulse of man, but men moved by the Holy Spirit spoke from God" (1:20f.). The author of the Book of Revelation likewise blurred any distinction between the spoken (prophetic) word and the written word when he called his book "words of prophecy" to be listened to (22:18). Hence it was more or less inevitable both that the early Church would understand the sacred writers to have the role of prophets and that later theologians like Thomas Aquinas would interpret biblical inspiration as prophetic. However, precisely as such biblical inspiration is the God-given impulse to write rather than to speak. Therefore, from this point on, unless otherwise noted, "inspiration" will be taken in that sense of biblical inspiration.

A summary statement of what such inspiration entails would run as follows. Biblical inspiration means that (a) certain books have been written under the special impulse and guidance of the Holy Spirit, *so that* (b) we can call God the "author" of these books and the Bible "the word of God."[2] Thus the effect of inspiration is to make the human word into the word of God and allow us to call the Scriptures "sacred." God stands at their origin.

Such a statement bristles with issues that need to be faced. Ordinary usage suggests that any kind of inspiration involved a special impulse. But in the case of biblical inspiration what form did this *special* guidance take? Then in what sense may we call God "author"? Can we specify that a bit more? These questions will be faced later in the chapter.

(2) Among the other notions concerning the writing of the Bible which should be quickly recalled here is its *truth*[3] or, as it has sometimes been called, its inerrancy. Despite the popular confusion of the two ideas, biblical truth is *not* synonymous with inspiration, but is rather one of its major consequences. Because the Holy Spirit specially guided the writing of the Scriptures, they convey truth and are free from error. Obvious questions instantly emerge here. What kind of truth do these books communicate? What errors are they immune from? For the moment let us bracket these questions and simply observe that the truth (or inerrancy) of the Scriptures should be examined as being a corollary of—and not identical with—inspiration.

(3) On the side of those who read and hear the Scriptures, two terms alert us to major themes and issues: the canon and hermeneutics.

The *canon*[4] is that list of inspired books which the Church has recognized as inspired and hence as authoritative. The formation of the canon *presupposes* the inspired writings. It is a subsequent act of recognition. Certain books are reckoned canonical because their writing was inspired and they have been recognized as such. Here the key questions clearly are: What principles guided and guide the Church in making such an act of recognition? How should we understand biblical authority?

Finally, we reach *hermeneutics* or the interpretation of the Scriptures.[5] Questions here would range across the object, criteria and presuppositions of interpretation. What is the reader primarily trying to understand and interpret—the mind of the inspired writer or the text itself? What criteria should guide the interpreter and what role do presuppositions play in acceptable hermeneutics? The next chapter will discuss the issues of the canon and hermeneutics. Let us turn now to the question of inspiration.

II
INSPIRATION

If asked to give an account of biblical inspiration, one might once again feel like parodying Augustine's remarks on time: "What then is inspiration? I know well enough what it is, provided nobody asks me. But if I am asked what it is and try to explain, I am baffled." Nevertheless, it would be intolerable and unnecessary to hold *that* the Scriptures are inspired and yet refuse to describe and explain even minimally *how* they are inspired. Something can be said, both positively and negatively, about biblical inspiration. First, let us exclude one untenable pattern.

(1) Various Fathers of the Church and later theologians adopted the model of *verbal dictation* or its equivalent to explain inspiration. In this view the inspired writers experienced a heavenly voice dictating the words which they were to set down. They then obediently reproduced the text which was revealed to them.

Christian art sometimes reflects this reduction of the inspired writers to the status of mere copyists. In the Pazzi chapel of the Basilica of Santa Croce in Florence, for instance, Luca della Robbia beautifully represents the evangelists in terra-cotta. An eagle has arrived from heaven to hold the text for John to copy down. A lion performs the same service for Mark.

Likewise some Fathers of the Church used images which radically minimalized the role of the biblical writers. In the second century Athenagoras described the Old Testament prophets as a flute played upon by the divine flute-player. Gregory the Great believed that the human authors enjoyed no more significance in the production of the Bible than a pen in the hand of an author.

Such approaches interpret inspiration in a mechanical way which drastically reduces the human role in the writing of the Scriptures. The hagiographers cease to be authors and become at best mere secretaries who faithfully take down the divine dictation. A set of tape-recorders could have served God's purposes just as well. In the verbal dictation view the divine causality counts for everything, the human causality for nothing. To experience the gift of inspiration is then to suffer the loss of one's own spontaneity and creativity.

This interpretation of inspiration resembles all those accounts of the incarnation which maximize the divinity of Christ at the expense of his humanity. Thus many classical Christologies presented schemes in which a credible human life got edged out for the sake of insisting that Jesus was consubstantial with the Father. When reading such Christologies I sometimes felt like taking a cue from St. Paul and crying out: "Humanity is swallowed up in divinity. O humanity, where is thy victory? O humanity, where is they sting?" To sum up: As the divine and the human meet in the person of Christ and the writing of Scriptures, Christology and the doctrine of inspiration can both go astray by one-sidedly stressing the divine component.

However, just as the humanity of Jesus with its historical characteristics and limitations has come back into its own in Christology, so also the true role of those human beings who wrote the Bible has been increasingly respected.[6] Just as the "being divine" in Christ has been interpreted so as not to prevail at the expense of the "being human," so God's special guidance in the process of inspiration has been seen to rule out neither genuine human activity nor the individual characteristics of particular authors. (To put it mildly, inspiration does not eliminate the striking personalities of Qoheleth and Paul!) In both cases we face a "both/and," not an "either/or." Jesus Christ is both true God and true man. The Holy Spirit and human beings work together to produce the inspired Scriptures. In neither case do we have to deny humanity in order to make room for divinity.

At bottom, every verbal dictation theory mistakenly believes that affirming the Sacred Scriptures to be the inspired word of God entails denying that they are also a genuinely human word. It wrongly portrays God and the human writers as competing rather than collaborating.

Apart from this basic *theological* flaw, the verbal dictation approach always faces a major difficulty at the level of the inspired product, the text itself. It cannot properly explain the many differences of form and style among the inspired writers. Did the Holy Spirit's style change from the decades when Paul's letters were written to the later period when the Gospels were composed? If the human authors played no real part in the literary process, such differences could only be due to a mysterious or even arbitrary divine choice to vary the style and alter the form.

All in all, there is little point in pursuing further the first negative. The naive model of verbal dictation may linger on in the fantasy of unreflecting fundamentalists. But most Christian circles have made their peace with the genuinely and fully human activity in the literary process that produced the inspired Scriptures.

(2) The hagiographers or inspired writers composed in various genres *but not* in all possible forms of literature. They wrote psalms, proverbs, letters, Gospels, apocalypses and so forth. But the Bible contains, for example, no epic poetry, no novels (in the proper sense) and no "scientific" history (in the modern sense).

The last point may be the most important in this second, negative thesis. Christians, including Christian scholars, have not always been easily and sufficiently educated out of the error of reading biblical history through modern spectacles. Beyond question, the historical books of the

Old and New Testaments convey much reliable information, but a sense of this general reliability should not be pushed to the point of interpreting the Gospels as if they were modern biographies or glossing over the fact that biblical history is "at best" folk history of an ancient kind.

In short, the Bible neither exemplified all the forms of literature present in the ancient world, nor did it miraculously anticipate future genres like modern scientific history.

(3) Some biblical authors deployed unusual resources as writers and produced works of literary beauty and greatness. It is understandable that the Bible has proved a great source of imagery and has profoundly molded English and other languages.

But the charism of inspiration did not mean that *the literary level* reached by sacred writers was necessarily higher than that of other writers. In fact, this special divine impulse to write respected rather than miraculously raised the artistic talents (and shortcomings) of those who received it. The first nine chapters of 1 Chronicles belong to the canon of inspired writings, but even if those dreary genealogies may once have excited some readers, they have not defended their charms against the ravages of time. Inspiration could co-exist with real dullness. *As such,* the presence of this gift did not automatically indicate anything about the literary standard of the product.

(4) We should likewise pull back from claiming that inspiration necessarily entailed a high *religious quality and effect* which lifted the books of the Bible above all non-inspired writings for all time. Of course, the Gospels, the psalms, the letters of St. Paul and many other books of the Bible continue to fire readers with their unique spiritual power. But experience shows how Augustine's *Confessions,* the *Imitation of Christ* and the works of Teresa of Avila enjoy a much deeper religious impact than the Letter of Jude, 2 Maccabees and all those sexual regulations from Leviticus. A striking spiritual effect is no necessary and inevitable index that some book has been written under the guidance of biblical inspiration.

The limits that we find in the literary quality and even in the religious power of inspired writings stem from the fact that these books resulted from genuine human activity, albeit activity carried on under a special divine impulse. Inasmuch as they were human products, they inevitably reflected the limitations of their community's culture and the writers' individual capacities.

(5) Like the charisms of prophecy and apostleship, the gift of inspiration *was not strictly uniform.* Just as there were major and minor prophets and just as Peter and Paul clearly acted as more significant apos-

tles than Andronicus and Junias (Rom 16:7), so it seems reasonable to hold that the writers of the Gospels, for example, enjoyed a higher degree of inspiration than was the case for books like the Letter of Jude.

All inspired authors received a special divine guidance to express and record something in writing. But there could obviously be different degrees of the Holy Spirit's presence and activity on their behalf. The divine impulse to write could prove stronger or weaker. Moreover, one would expect the nature of the theme—for instance, the life, passion and resurrection of Jesus in the case of the Gospels—to have affected the degree of inspiration. In general, as God's revealing and saving self-communication reached its absolute, definitive climax with Christ's coming, we might plausibly suppose that a higher degree of inspiration was associated with the human experience of that climax. Finally, since divine gifts are generally proportionate to the human qualities of the recipients, a higher charism of inspiration would match a dramatic personality like Paul of Tarsus.

(6) A further variation concerns the *consciousness* of the inspired writers. Some like Paul (Gal 1:1ff.) and the author of the Book of Revelation (1:3; 22:7, 9f., 18f.) knew themselves to be specially guided by the Holy Spirit or at least to be writing with particular divine authority. But other biblical authors like Luke (1:1–4) and the author of 2 Maccabees (15:38) acknowledged the struggle involved in composing their works, claimed to have done their best with the sources available to them, but showed no clear awareness that they were writing under a special divine guidance. This was all the more striking in the case of Luke. In his Gospel and the Book of Acts he included a fairly wide range of episodes in which the Holy Spirit intervened strikingly in the lives of individuals or groups, but Luke never clearly claimed that some such extraordinary impulse prompted and guided him in his writing.

Of course, it would be odd if *none* of the sacred authors ever showed themselves consciously aware of being inspired. But neither the notion of biblical inspiration as such nor the data from the Old and the New Testament support the conclusion that a special impulse to write inevitably meant that all the sacred writers were fully aware of that divine guidance and authority coming to them. The Holy Spirit could (and can) be at work in many ways without the beneficiaries necessarily being conscious of this influence at the time.

(7) Often it would be more accurate to speak of "special impulses to write," as *many books of the Bible emerged from a long process* of oral and written traditions. They did not come from a solo author. Frequently the cast of those sharing in the charism of inspiration was splen-

didly varied. Inasmuch as they really helped to form some part of the Bible, a special impulse of the Holy Spirit moved all of them to bring about the final text.

In these terms the charism of inspiration guided all those who contributed to the historical books of the Old Testament and was not restricted to the final editor. Likewise the same charism touched all those Christians who fashioned the collections of stories and sayings taken into the four Gospels. In the same way we should acknowledge the inspiration of the author(s) who created the hymn incorporated by Paul in his Letter to the Philippians (2:6–11).

(8) Further, our sense of contemporary literature will inevitably hover over our reflections on the inspired Scriptures. But *we should not compare the books of the Bible too closely with the writings of great modern authors*. For one thing, the biblical authors generally worked over oral or written material which had already taken some shape, and they did not fashion their books in a great blaze of creativity. Further, even if they remained unaware of their charism of inspiration, their aim was consistently religious—to communicate a religious message and not to win success for their literary prowess. Some of them did show a remarkable grasp of language and a deep intensity of human feeling. But they did not wish to be judged either by the art of their expression or by their capacity to articulate and enter into deep personal experiences.

The essential difference could be put this way: Modern poets, dramatists and novelists normally write for themselves, at times reflect greatly their own individual background, and are very much persons in their own right. The biblical authors, however, often wrote anonymously (or pseudonymously), drew on the general experience of believers, and produced their works to serve the community. Even if they were more, often much more, than mere mouthpieces of their communities, we would ignore at our peril the social setting, responsibility and function of their activity.

(9) I hope that the eight points so far made about scriptural inspiration have helped to clarify somewhat the special guidance of the Holy Spirit that it involved. That impulse of the Spirit worked through the historical conditions of the Biblical authors. Once we recognize the real human role of those writers (point 1), we are in a position to acknowledge the various limitations in their activity (points 2 to 8). Admittedly what has been so far said about inspiration in this chapter has tended to highlight what the special guidance of the Spirit did *not* involve. The biblical authors did not write in all available styles, their works did not always enjoy a religious effect superior to that of all non-inspired writings, they were not necessarily conscious of being inspired, etc. In a sense it would

be unreasonable to expect a direct, positive and full description of inspiration and its workings—let alone a totally clear explanation of it. Such a yield should not be looked for, once we recognize how this charism (which makes the biblical text both the word of God and the word of human beings) shared in the mystery of Christ, who was and is truly divine and truly human.

Nevertheless, *Karl Rahner's interpretation of inspiration* points the way toward a positive, if limited, account which offers the chance to weld matters into some kind of convincing and satisfying whole.[6a] I do not wish to adopt and describe his approach in every detail. But the following propositions based on his work illustrate how inspiration makes God the author of the Scriptures and allows us to call the Bible the word of God.

(a) The charism of inspiration belonged to the divine activity in the *special* history of revelation/salvation which led to the *foundation* of the Church with all the elements (including the Scriptures) that constitute its total reality. Where the Old Testament literature recorded the various events and experiences which prepared the way for Christ and his Church, the New Testament recorded events and experiences which were immediately concerned with the Church's foundation.

(b) Hence God can be called the "author" of the Scriptures, inasmuch as special divine activity formed and fashioned the Church. Creating the Church entailed "authoring" the Bible.

(c) Third, the charism of inspiration was communicated primarily to the community, and to individuals in that they belonged to the community. This social dimension of biblical inspiration has already been noted under points 7 and 8 above.

(d) Since God communicated the charism of inspiration precisely as part of the divine activity *in bringing the Church into being,* we can appreciate why that charism did not continue beyond the apostolic age. It resembled and overlapped with the unique, non-transferable role of the apostles and the apostolic community in witnessing to Christ's resurrection and founding the Church. Back in Chapter III we saw how the apostles in that double role as resurrection-witnesses and Church-founders shared in the once-and-for-all quality of the Christ-event itself. The biblical authors and, specifically, the New Testament writers likewise had a once-and-for-all function, whether they were apostles like Paul or simply members of the apostolic (or sub-apostolic) community. In short, since the charism of inspiration belonged to the divine activity of establishing the Church, it ceased once the Church was fully founded. Along with the apostolic charism it ended with the apostolic age. The disappearance of the charism of inspiration was part of the qualitative difference between the periods of foundational and dependent revelation.

Later generations of Christians bear the responsibility of proclaiming the resurrection, keeping the Church in existence and living by the Bible. But they neither directly witness to the risen Christ (as did those who met him gloriously alive after his death), nor found the Church nor write inspired Scriptures.

(e) Through the inspired record of their foundational and constitutive experience, preaching and activity, the members of the apostolic Church remain uniquely authoritative for all subsequent generations of Christians. Thus the priority of that apostolic Church was and is much more than a merely temporal one. In the next chapter we shall come back to this theme of authority. Let me now move to one of the major consequences of inspiration, the saving truth of the Bible.

III
SAVING TRUTH

Inspiration carries many results and consequences which one could usefully study: for instance, the use of inspired Scriptures in the liturgical and prayer life of the Church. However, I want to single out one question which has often held and sometimes horrified Christians: Does the inspired record of their experiences left by those men and women who, under God's special guidance, brought the Church into existence necessarily communicate truth and exclude error?[7] To put the question bluntly: Is the Bible necessarily true and inerrant?

Errors and inconsistencies have been seen to abound in the Scriptures—to the distress of the believers and the delight of the unbelievers. The account of the creation within a week looked incompatible with the findings of astronomy and the theory of evolution. If the origins of the universe posed problems, so too did its structure. The psalms and other Old Testament books, it was noted, reflected in places the view that the earth was a flat disc and the sky above was a solid vault supported by two columns at the ends of the earth. Particular books had their special puzzles. How could Jonah have survived three days in the belly of the whale—not to mention his passage into and out of the great fish?

Add too the fact that the Bible could give us conflicting accounts of the same episode. How did the Israelites elude their Egyptian pursuers? In describing the escape through the Reed Sea, Exodus 14–15 has three versions to offer. Moses stretched out his hand and—as in the Cecil B. De Mille scenario—the waters piled up like walls to let the Israelites through. Then the waters flooded back over the Egyptians (14:16, 21a, 22, 27a, 28). In a second version, an East wind proved decisive. It dried up the sea for the Israelites, while the Egyptian chariots got stuck. Then Yahweh stopped the Egyptians with a glance and threw them into the sea (14:21b, 25–26). Finally, an angel of the Lord and the column of cloud no longer went in front of the Israelites but behind. The result? The pursuing Egyptians could no longer see their quarry who thus happily escaped (14:19–20).

Then who killed Goliath—David or Elhanan (1 Sam 17; 2 Sam 21:19)? Did the site of the Jerusalem temple cost David fifty shekels of silver or six hundred shekels of gold (2 Sam 24:24; 1 Chr 21:25)? In the New Testament Matthew (1:1–17) and Luke (3:23–38) give us notoriously irreconcilable genealogies of Jesus. Repeatedly it proves impossible to harmonize into a single, coherent whole the different accounts which the Gospels provide of incidents concerned with his ministry, passion and resurrection. Were there one (Mk 10:46) or two (Mt 20:30) blind men outside Jericho? Did the risen Christ appear in Galilee (Mk 16:7; Mt 28:16–20) or only in and around Jerusalem (Lk 24)? In short, factual inconsistencies and errors of an historical, geographical and scientific nature turn up frequently in the Bible.

Worse than that, various moral and religious errors appear with daunting frequency. Job denied life after death. Could God really have given Saul and his people the command to kill every human being and animal in the city of Amalek: "Go and smite Amalek, and . . . do not spare them, but kill both men and woman, infant and suckling, ox and sheep, camel and ass" (1 Sam 15:3)? St. Paul and other early Christians apparently expected the world and its history to be terminated speedily by the parousia of the Lord (1 Thess 4:15ff.).

Faced with such evident factual, moral and religious errors, those who put the cause for biblical truth have frequently recalled three interconnected points: the *intentions* of the sacred writers, their *presuppositions* and their *modes of expression*. Thus the authors of Genesis could be defended. They intended to teach a number of religious truths about the goodness and power of the Creator, the sinfulness of human beings and so forth, but *not* to teach some ancient piece of cosmogony and cosmology. They simply did not aim to describe coherently and in "scientific" detail the origins of the universe, our earth and the human race. In recalling the parousia of the Lord, Paul did not intend to communicate a timetable of its arrival but to encourage a full and urgent commitment to Christian life. In brief, it is unfair to accuse biblical or any other writers of making various errors if one fails to acknowledge the difference between the points they really wished to communicate and affirm and those that lay outside such an intention.

Second, some biblical authors betrayed the way they shared with their contemporaries certain false notions about cosmology and astronomy. But their acceptance of a flat earth, for instance, remained at the level of their *presuppositions*. It was not the theme of their direct teaching. The Bible was not artificially protected against geographical, cosmological and astronomical errors to be found in the presuppositions of the authors. Similarly the view that real life ceases at death formed a presupposition for the drama of Job and no more. In a world where death was believed to end all, how could an innocent man interpret and cope with massive and undeserved suffering? Job was not debating with his friends "Is there life after death?" but, rather, "Since a good and powerful God exists, how can we explain evil" (Si Deus, unde malum)?

Third, Pius XII among others pointed out how alleged errors are often simply legitimate *modes of expression* used by the biblical writers:

> Not infrequently ... when some people reproachfully charge the sacred writers with some historical error or inaccuracy in the recording of facts, on closer examination it turns out to be nothing else than those customary modes of expression and narration peculiar to the ancients which used to be employed in the mutual dealings of social life and which in fact were sanctioned by common use.[8]

Modern historians would be expected to scrutinize the evidence and settle the issues. Just how did the Israelites escape their pursuers? Who really killed Goliath? How much did David pay for the temple site? But the kind of religious history represented by the Books of Exodus, Samuel, Kings and Chronicles could take final shape without any need to tidy up inconsistencies and settle disputed details. Admittedly, the honesty of Hebrew historiography put it in a class by itself in the Middle Eastern world. It recorded King David's shameful sin of adultery and murder, along with many other failures on the part of leaders and people. It showed itself clearly superior to the stereotyped and empty glorification of monarchs found in the records of other nations. Nevertheless, the religious significance of events for the story of salvation mattered more to the Hebrew historians than a material exactitude. They felt no overwhelming curiosity that would have pushed them into clarifying the record when various traditions reported conflicting details.

In the case of the Book of Jonah it is only by massively overlooking its literary genre that one could ask about the prophet's survival inside the fish. The book is a piece of fiction, an extended parable which keeps its religious punch for the last few verses. Any question about its truth or error will be decided only by agreeing or disagreeing with that religious message. To read Jonah as if it were an historical work lands one in absurd puzzles about the story-teller's details. Was Nineveh, for instance, really such a huge city that it took three days to cross (3:3)?

Likewise we save ourselves from all kinds of silliness by acknowledging the kind of literature we deal with in Genesis. The early chapters of that book reflect on the nature of God and the nature of human beings, and in no sense do they attempt to give even an incomplete account of the pre-historical "origins" of the human race. If we ignore that fact, hopeless puzzles turn up. When, for instance, Cain murdered Abel and was about to be sent away as "a fugitive and a wanderer on the earth," God "put a mark on Cain, lest any who came upon him should kill him." So Cain left Eden for the land of Nod, "knew his wife, and she conceived Enoch" (Gen 4:15–17). We would mistreat this story if we started asking: Where did these others come from who might have threatened Cain's life? For that matter where did his wife come from, if Adam and Eve were the parents of all the living? Genesis is not such a book about human origins.

Doubtless, respect for the intentions, presuppositions and modes of expression used by the sacred authors goes a long way towards mitigating the force of many difficulties and doubts, both serious and silly, about biblical truth. All of this concerns the *human* side of things. Augustine makes a similar point apropos of the divine intention. The inspiration from the Holy Spirit had a religious purpose and did not as such aim to further "secular" truth: "We do not read in the Gospel that the Lord said: 'I shall send you the Paraclete who will teach you about the movements of the sun and the moon.' He wished to make Christians, not mathematicians."[9] Nevertheless, more needs to be said—not for the sake of mounting a fully successful rescue operation but simply to elucidate further the truth of the Scriptures. What has been said so far concerns the intentions, presuppositions and literary styles found in one individual book after another. What if we stand back and view the Bible as a whole? In that case we cannot slide around the broad question: What is the truth of the Bible in general?

Many, if not most, people are set like a piece of machinery to reproduce—perhaps not in technical terms but nonetheless clearly—a Scholastic answer to Pilate's question: What is truth? Truth is a function of judgment. If what the intellect judges about reality (and hence causes us to say and write) conforms to reality (*adequatio intellectus et rei*), then we have the truth. This common way of understanding truth highlights the individual person's intellect. It emphasizes the mind and judgment of the thinking subject. In the public sphere it will assess the truth of propositions by their correspondence with the "facts," as well as by their inner coherence. How does this version of truth fit the Bible?

We would grievously mistreat the scriptural texts if we tried to reduce them to a mere set of informative propositions whose sole function was to make factual claims and state true judgments, religious or otherwise. The Bible forms no catalogue of propositions which are to be tested for such logical truth or error. The Scriptures, if they do contain such true statements as "Christ died for our sins" (1 Cor 15:3), also include many moral exhortations, laws, prayers of praise, poetic images, cries of joy, questions and other items about which it is quite inappropriate to ask (as least in a Scholastic sense): Is this true or false?

The joyful cry "Alleluia" as such is neither true nor false. Questions asked in the biblical story—like questions elsewhere—may be "correct," "helpful," "right," and "meaningful," but as such they do not inform or describe and hence elude classification under the usual headings of truth and falsity. To ask a question does not result in saying anything true or false. Furthermore, exhortations abound in the Bible. Such affective language can arouse, evoke and change attitudes, but in themselves exhortations cannot be true or false. Likewise with laws. Whether recorded in the Bible or in other texts, laws may be just or unjust, cruel or compassionate. Yet precisely as such they are neither true nor false. Finally, poetic images in the Scriptures or elsewhere can be vivid and evocative or trite and dead. But we cannot call them as such true or false judgments.

In brief, believers do violence to the Scriptures whenever they seek to reduce them simply to a set of (infallibly) true propositions. All the verses of the Bible are inspired and written under the special guidance of the Holy Spirit. But that does not mean that all the verses of the Bible are in the business of claiming facts or communicating Scholastic-style truth. In *that* sense of truth, inerrancy is not co-extensive with inspiration. We cannot take the whole Bible and deal with it as if it offered a series of propositions to be checked for their conformity with the facts and declared true.

Here we might construct some more tenable patterns of argument if we recall what biblical truth (*'emet* in Hebrew and *alētheia* in Greek) claims to be. The biblical versions of truth, if not utterly different from that common understanding of truth just described, have their own special accents. They tend to be interpersonal, less one-sidedly intellectual, oriented toward transformation and action, and progressive and essentially Christocentric. In both Old and New Testaments the language of truth, whether writers use *'emet, alētheia* or equivalent terms, locks into the people's experience of God. In the Old Testament God is shown through word and deed to be true—that is to say, constantly trustworthy and sincerely reliable. "The Lord your God is God, the faithful God; with those who love him and keep his commandments he keeps covenant and faith forever" (Deut 7:9). By their fidelity to the covenant, the people should prove themselves to be loyally conformed to the divine reality and hence persons of "truth" (Ex 18:21). In the New Testament the God who remains faithful and reliable (Rom 3:1–7) is fully revealed[10] through the person of his Son. "The truth is in Jesus" (Eph 4:21). "Grace and truth have come to us through Jesus Christ" (Jn 1:17). In a sense only *one* thing is revealed, the mysterious truth of salvation in Christ. The powerful presence of Christ and his Holy Spirit strengthens believers to "do the truth" (Jn 3:21) and "be of the truth" (Jn 18:37). The truth which will set them free (Jn 8:32) does much more than conform their minds to reality. It transforms their entire persons.

This rapid account of truth in the Old and New Testaments leaves aside various fine shades of meaning but it helps us to reach certain biblically-based conclusions.

No theories about biblical truth will justify the weight placed upon them if they fail to take account of five interrelated considerations.

(a) Biblical truth is progressive. Hence the assertion of biblical truth not only tolerates but also implies the kind of unsatisfactory views of God and humanity which we saw above in the case of the divine command to Saul to utterly destroy the city of Amalek. Here the Bible faithfully records the need for growth toward the full truth.

(b) Biblical truth should be looked for in the context of the complete Bible. The truth is in the whole. In *this* sense the truth of the Bible is co-extensive with inspiration. The whole Bible is both inspired and true.

(c) Biblical truth is primarily found in a person, Jesus Christ. He is the truth attested prophetically in the Old Testament and apostolically in the New Testament. Ultimately the Bible does not convey a set of distinct truths but has only one truth to state, the personal disclosure of God in Jesus. "Other" biblical truths or "mysteries" with their distinct contents do nothing else than articulate that one primordial Mystery which the apostolic generation of Christians experienced in their (partly) unique and unrepeatable way.

(d) The biblical writings which record the preparation for Christ's coming and the coming itself participate in the truth which he himself is. Through testifying to the divine self-communication which reaches its climax in him and the various human responses to that divine self-giving, these writings help to communicate truly that saving and revealing event.

(e) The Scriptures set up conditions in which God so speaks to us that we are enabled to see and practice the truth. Here if anywhere the truth will be known by living in it. Biblical truth is to be experienced and expressed in action as much as it is to be seen or affirmed in judgment. Hence what William Reiser writes about "truth and life" bears very much on the Bible: "Spiritual experience is critical, since to understand what truth is we need to know what truth does."[11]

X. "CANONIZING" AND INTERPRETING THE SCRIPTURES

> *In Christum enim velut centrum omnes utriusque Testamenti paginae vergunt.*
>
> Benedict XV

> *The Scriptures spring out of God, and flow into Christ, and were given to lead us to Christ. Thou must therefore go along by the Scriptures as by a line, until thou come at Christ, which is the way's end and resting place.*
>
> William Tyndale

> *The Fathers are convinced that all Scripture refers not only to Christ, but also to the Church.*
>
> Yves Congar

Where the previous chapter focused more on the *writing* of the Jewish-Christian Scriptures, this chapter reflects on what *readers* in the post-apostolic Church have done with that inspired record of human experience and activity which came from the period of foundational revelation. Those later readers essentially did two things. They both anchored themselves to their past by recognizing an authoritative list or canon of inspired books, and by their constant use and interpretation of these books they sought to relive something of those experiences which lay behind the making of the Bible. Thus the two themes for this chapter can take shape: the canon and the interpretation of the Bible.

I
"CANONIZING" THE SCRIPTURES

1. The Canon[1]

In a provisional way one could describe the canon as a closed collection of inspired books which provides an authoritative standard for Christian belief and practice. In these terms "canonization" presupposed and went beyond inspiration or the special guidance of the Holy Spirit for the actual composition of the Sacred Scriptures. In the Old Testament period inspired writings came into existence centuries before there was any question of a canon, be it a Jewish or a Christian one. The exercise of the charism of inspiration preceded in time the later process of "canonization." In that process inspired books were recognized as such by the post-apostolic Church. Roman Catholics acknowledge in a decree from the Council of Trent (DS 1501–04) a definitive act of recognition which finally established a clear canon of inspired writings. In making its solemn definition of the canon, Trent confirmed the decision of the Council of Florence (DS 1334–35), which in its turn drew on various decisions of local Christian communities about the canon.

What were the criteria which guided Christian churches, bishops, theologians, councils and believers over the centuries as they fashioned a canon which was to exclude such works as the Epistle of Barnabas, the First Epistle of Clement and "The Shepherd" of Hermas, and to include the deuterocanonical books of Jewish origin (Tobit, Judith, the Wisdom of Solomon, 1 and 2 Maccabees, etc.)? As Albert Sundberg has insisted, inspiration itself did not function as a criterion for early Christians when they selected or rejected sacred books. They understood the inspiration of the Holy Spirit to be widely and constantly present in the Church both during the apostolic era and later. Granted such a broad recognition of inspiration, an appeal to inspiration could not serve to establish the canon of sacred books. Moreover, both at the time of their writing and even more after the death of the writers such a claim, simply taken in itself, was and is uncontrollable. How could other Christians tell that *this* author had been specially guided by the Holy Spirit unless they were willing to introduce other criteria? In fact three such criteria governed the community's recognition of the inspired writings: *apostolic origin*, *orthodoxy* and *liturgical use*.

First, there was the historical criterion of apostolic origin. The canonical writings belonged to the period of foundational revelation which climaxed with the coming of Christ and the activity of his apostles in witnessing to the resurrection and founding of the Church. Of course, apostolic origin was often taken strictly, so that the books which came to constitute the New Testament were all represented either as the writings of apostles in person or as their teachings which two close associates set down in writing (Mark for the Second Gospel and Luke for the Third Gospel and Acts). In such terms the apostles gave their authority both to the Jewish Scriptures (which they inherited) and to the new works which they or those two associates (of Peter and Paul, respectively) composed for the Christian communities. Nowadays such a strict version of apostolic origin no longer works. Very few scholars, for example, would agree that Paul wrote Hebrews or that Peter was the author of 2 Peter.

Nevertheless, in a broader sense the criterion still carries weight in sorting out canonical from non-canonical writings. Only those works which witnessed to Christ prophetically (the Jewish Scriptures) or apostolically (the Christian Scriptures) could enter and remain in the canon. Those works formed an inspired record of believers who experienced the foundational revelation which ended with the apostolic age. Only persons who shared in the events which climaxed in the crucifixion, resurrection, sending of the Holy Spirit and foundation of the Church were in a position to express through inspired Scriptures their written testimony to those experiences. Later writings like the Chalcedonian Definition, the works of Thomas Aquinas, the Augsburg Confession or the documents of the Second Vatican Council all belonged to the period of dependent revelation, could not as such directly witness to the experience of foundational revelation, and emerged at a time when the charism of inspiration had ceased. Seen in this way, the criterion of apostolic origin still works as a way of accrediting canonical writings. Canonicity rests on apostolicity.

Second, there was the theological criterion of conformity to the essential message, "the purity of the Gospel," "the Catholic faith that comes to us from the apostles," or call it what you will. Because they failed to match the test of orthodoxy, writings like "The Shepherd" of Hermas, which belonged perhaps to the sub-apostolic age and hence might have made the grade in terms of time, were excluded from the canon. Other writings like the Book of Revelation eventually got included when their orthodox content was sufficiently recognized.

Of course, there was and is a certain circularity involved in this criterion. Since they fitted their interpretation of Christianity, the faithful judged certain writings to be orthodox, accepted them into their canon and then proceeded to use them to test orthodoxy. At the same time, these ancient Scriptures which were genuinely written under the special guidance of the Holy Spirit never simply mirrored what the Church community was but in fact challenged Christians by picturing what they should be. In calling them and actually leading them to a full, transformed life, the Scriptures established orthodoxy by vindicating themselves in practice.

Third, constant usage, particularly in the context of the liturgy, also secured for the inspired writings their place in the final canon of the Christian Bible. This process resembled but was not identical with the "canonization" of such classical authors as Cervantes, Dante, Goethe, Homer, Plato and Shakespeare. In both cases gradually or more quickly readers came to recognize the permanent value of given writings. Yet the two processes were not quite on a par. Classics could and can occur not just as the beginning of a particular literature (for example, Homer) but also in the later history of that literature (for example, Plato and Shakespeare). And this feature sets such classics apart from the inspired books of the Bible which belong to the *origins* of Christianity. The charism of biblical inspiration ceased with the age of foundational revelation, while classics can appear at any period in the story of a particular literature.

This third criterion of liturgical usage has occasionally been challenged. Congar, for instance, maintains that it did not serve as an original criterion for "canonizing" inspired writings:

> Liturgical use . . . would actually presuppose canonicity. Once established, it could serve as a guide in practice, since canonicity and liturgical use coincided. But at the level of the earliest institution, the recognition of canonicity preceded adoption for liturgical use.[2]

I wonder how fully effective this objection is. At "the level of the earliest institution," the Christians at Corinth or Rome received, let us say, a letter from Paul and adopted it for liturgical use because this written document obviously shared the authority of the apostle's oral witness and teaching. In that sense Congar is right. Even if there was still no question at that point of a collection of sacred Christian books, churches could have more or less instantly accepted the normative, canonical value of Paul's writings. However, what of cases like that of 1 Clement which around 170 was still being read in liturgical assemblies at Corinth? Did such liturgical use necessarily presuppose canonicity? If the Corinthian Christians correctly recognized its canonicity before adopting the letter for such liturgical use, was it right that such an early Christian writing of orthodox content never finally got lodged in the canon? Surely the fact that this letter failed to win long and widespread liturgical acceptance counted against its canonical status?

2. A Closed Canon?

Earlier in this chapter the canon was called a "closed collection." Now it is relatively easy to organize reasons for justifying the closed nature of the canon which the Council of Trent finally proclaimed. Since the charism of inspiration ended with the apostolic and sub-apostolic age, there could be no later instances of inspired writings. The canon was closed in the way that a particular epoch of history—in this case the foundational, constitutive period of the special history of revelation and salvation—ends.

In the second place, unless the canon is essentially closed and thus not open to substantial modification, it cannot function as a canon—that is, as a truly normative standard for Christian belief and practice. Precisely as constituting a canon, these books, despite the fact that they were mostly written to meet particular needs and serve particular occasions, were and are acknowledged as an adequate version of Christianity. If they do not sufficiently reveal the basic Christian experience and identity in the face of the divine self-communication, they cease to be an authoritative norm for Christian faith and life.

Third, the closed nature of the canon clearly ties in with the closed and normative nature of the apostolic age and charism. Just as the apostolic Church shared in the unique, once-and-for-all character of the Christ-event, so too did their sacred writings—both those which they produced and those which they took over from Jewish sources. The inspired books shared thus in the unrepeatable role of the apostles and their associates.

The consequences of this argument are clear. On the one hand, to exclude some writings and thus *reduce* the canon (as Marcion and others have done) would be to tamper with the richness of the Church's foundational experience of the divine self-communication, to minimize the diversity in the apostolic experience and witness, and ultimately to challenge the divine fullness of Christ's person and work (Col 1:19f.). On the other hand, increasing the canon by adding later writings like conciliar documents or works by Fathers of the Church would be tantamount to challenging the absolute and definitive quality of what Christ did and revealed with and through his apostles.

Granted the essentially closed nature of the canon, is it still feasible, however, to entertain the possibility of adding to the collection, for example, some Jewish prayers discovered in a Qumran cave or a missing letter of St. Paul recovered by archeologists in Asia Minor? Such writings could satisfy the historical and theological criteria, and inasmuch as they would not substantially modify the total message expressed through the existing canon of inspired Scriptures, they could win a place in the canon—under one condition, however. Such newly recovered works from the period of foundational revelation would have to vindicate themselves through liturgical usage, a process that could take at least a little time.

3. The Authority of the Canon

In the provisional account given at the beginning of this chapter, the canon was said to provide "an authoritative standard for Christian belief and practice." Can we clarify and systematize somewhat the nature of the authority involved?

(a) To begin with, we would wrongly construe the authority of the biblical canon if we glossed over the fact that here, as elsewhere, authority is primarily vested in persons. *The authority of Scriptures as such is secondary;* it is derived from that ultimate and absolute authority which belongs to the God revealed definitively in Jesus Christ. In this way the normative quality of the Scriptures goes back through the authority of the apostolic tradition to Christ himself. These inspired writings, in recording and interpreting for all subsequent generations the experiences of the Jewish people, the apostles and all those who shared directly in the events of foundational revelation, expressed all that authentically, adequately and authoritatively because they shared in the normative, regulative value of the prophetic and apostolic witness which was ultimately legitimized by the person of Christ.

Sometimes the authority of the Scriptures is presented in a self-authenticating fashion. One can point to the unquestionable fact that over the centuries Christians have experienced the Scriptures as a source of faith and life. The Bible has thus proved itself to be religiously effective and hence authoritative. Clearly there is much truth in this way of expressing the authority of the Scriptures. Nevertheless, one must also be ready to point beyond the human experience of the text to the Holy Spirit, the personal authority which has made that experience possible.

(b) The divine authority guaranteed the Scriptures in a way and to a degree that was not to be the case with creeds, conciliar statements or any other documents of the post-apostolic Church, even the most solemn definitions. No such later documents, despite their truth and binding quality, would ever be written under that special guidance of the Holy Spirit which constituted the charism of inspiration and allows us to call the canonical Scriptures "the word of God" in written form. No writings of the post-apostolic Church were ever to enjoy precisely that kind of status.

Hence Schubert Ogden proves misleading when he writes: "There is no difference in principle, but only in fact, between the authority of Scripture, on the one hand, and that of the Church's tradition and *magisterium* on the other."[3] This statement obliterates the difference between the apostolic Church and the later Church or, to put it in equivalent terms, between the periods of foundational and dependent revelation. Ogden passes over the fact that the charism of inspiration guided and guaranteed the Scriptures to a degree that no writings from the post-apostolic tradition in general or from the magisterium in particular could ever claim. In a way that recalls what was maintained about "the Acts of God" in Chapter III, the divine guidance normatively guaranteed the inspired Scriptures to a special extent which went beyond the backing of even the most authoritative statements of faith coming from the present, interpretative phase of the Church's existence. Here, as elsewhere, the divine guarantee and authority can be engaged and revealed in various degrees. Any claim that a text enjoys God's authority calls for a measure of explanation to indicate something about the degree and quality of divine authority involved.

(c) As in the case of other "authorities," the divine authority that stands behind the Bible must not be isolated from the faith of those who hear and read the Scriptures. We saw in Chapter IV how genuine authority is never despotically imposed but always accepted through a free personal decision. Here it is a matter of the scriptural witness gently commending itself, questioning its hearers, pointing their way to the truth and making it possible for them to live in fidelity to the foundational self-communication of God in Christ.

(d) To clarify further the nature of biblical authority, it seems helpful to point to some things which such authority does *not* entail. First of all, as I observed when dealing with the *sola Scriptura* principle in Chapter VII, the Bible does not clearly provide authoritative answers to new questions which arise in the life of the Church, or at least does not always do so. The Bible is not that kind of "norm for every problem and every situation."[4]

Second, biblical authority cannot be simply equated with truth, or at least with truth in all the senses of that word. In the last chapter we saw some kinds of errors which the Bible contains and which do not conflict with a careful and correct approach to biblical truth.

Third, just as there are differing degrees of inspiration, so the canonicity and authority of the Bible are not flatly uniform. Some books, for example, are more valuable and authoritative inasmuch as they treat more directly of formal religious questions than others. The Second Vatican Council pointed toward this kind of variation in *Dei Verbum:* "Among the inspired writings, even among those of the New Testament, the Gospels have a special place, and rightly so, because they are our principal source for the life and teaching of the Incarnate Word, our Savior" (n. 17).

We could speak here of an analogy of biblical authority which corresponds to the analogy of biblical inspiration. Certain books and passages of the Bible enjoy more weight and open up more truth than others. The authority of the Scriptures is not equally distributed throughout all the sections of the Bible.

(e) Lastly, like the truth of the Bible the question of authority must be raised within the context of the whole Bible. Admittedly historical criticism has brought out the diversity between the biblical witnesses who wrote in and out of their specific situations. Nevertheless, unless the Scriptures enjoy a certain wholeness and unity as they focus prophetically (the Old Testament) and apostolically (the New Testament) on the one Truth which is Jesus Christ, they cannot really be authoritative. Their diversity would collapse into irreconcilable differences, and their normative function would be lost.

Having said that, however, I must acknowledge that we do not receive the scriptural message simply as a kind of undifferentiated whole but seek to understand verses, chapters and entire books of the Bible. Here we once again run up against the problem of divergent interpretations. All Christians have taken the Bible as a common point of reference. In it they find a basis for faith and a rule of conduct by which to test and verify their preaching, teaching and other activities. And yet the Bible has constantly been used to justify divergent and even irreconcilable positions. How can the Bible function then to decide authoritatively specific issues if the exegetes and/or other members of different churches do not agree on *the* correct interpretation of given passages and texts from the Bible? What would be the use of a scriptural authority which attached to the Bible as a whole but could never vindicate itself in terms of particular texts? With this let us move on to the question of interpretation.

II
INTERPRETING THE SCRIPTURES

1. The Interpreter

Before tackling the question of *what* is understood and interpreted in biblical interpretation, it looks wise to say something about the person *who* seeks to establish and express the meaning of the Scriptures.[5]

(a) Right from the outset, belief or non-belief in inspiration will affect the understanding and interpretation of the Bible. Where interpreters do not read the Bible as a religious text written under the special impulse of the Holy Spirit, they will not see their activity as a religious act and they will not be conscious of a special affinity to the text through sharing in the experience of faith which found expression in it, nor can they expect that the Spirit who guided the writing of the Bible will in some way also direct their interpretation of it. Such interpreters can only evaluate the New Testament texts as examples of post-classical Greek, as expressions of new currents in the story of the human spirit, or as sources of historical knowledge about the life of Jesus, the birth of Christianity and conditions of life in the first-century Middle East.

To put matters positively: It must clearly make a massive difference to their understanding of the Bible if the interpreters believe that as part of the special history of the divine self-communication the Holy Spirit stood behind the composition of the Scriptures and endowed them with a revealing and saving function. This is to admit that what was written in the Spirit must be read in the Spirit (*Dei Verbum,* n. 12), and that although biblical inspiration ended with the constitutive, normative phase of foundational revelation, this charism would remain incomplete without subsequent divine guidance in the interpretation of the Scriptures. Thus the doctrine of inspiration implies that the inspired text will prove inspiring, that the Holy Spirit who was once at work in forming the Scriptures will continue to work in arousing faith through them, and that those texts which expressed various religious experiences "then" will generate similar religious experiences "now."

In effect, belief in inspiration here entails two convictions. Since the Bible like other religious works aims to bring its readers into a living contact with God, it asks them to approach the text with a readiness to accept that experience as part of their continuing conversion. Further, unlike other Christian books the Bible presents itself as the normative record of what happened at the time of God's special self-communication which climaxed with Christ.

Hence without a lived faith in Christ, or at least the openness to such a faith, the conditions will not be present for the full meaning and truth of the Bible to disclose itself. Only the active cooperation of such faith will lead to a proper understanding of the basic biblical message of revelation and salvation. One can appreciate then why the Church Fathers of the second and third centuries repeatedly insisted that heretics could not really understand the meaning of the Bible. In a way these Fathers were doing nothing more than re-expressing the Lukan theme that only docility to the risen Christ brings a true appreciation of the Scriptures (Lk 24:27, 32, 45). Back in Chapter I of this book we touched what was essentially the same problem in asking if non-believers can "do theology." Whether it is a question of doing theology or studying the Scriptures, nothing less than the sympathetic faith of an insider will guide one to a full understanding of the matter.

To sum up: In a genuine sense the Bible gains its true existence only when it is read, heard or proclaimed with faith. Its effect on its audience is no optional extra but part of its nature as inspired Scripture. The God who once guided its composition now by new acts of grace allows the text to come alive, communicate meaning and stir faith.

(b) Further, a full doctrine of inspiration respects also its ecclesial quality. Since the Bible was written in and for the community, it will be properly understood and interpreted when read in the Church under the guidance of the Holy Spirit. In a paper on "The Role of Tradition" Frank Sullivan puts this point well:

> Even on purely natural grounds, one would expect that the written documents on which the life of a community is based would be best interpreted by the community which lives according to those writings. . . . If this is true of *any* community, how much more is it true in the case of the Church where we have the promise of Christ to send his Holy Spirit . . . to abide with his Church and lead it into all truth.[5a]

Within the total Church community we can distinguish scholars, worshipers, preachers and teachers. Each group will use the Bible somewhat differently and will tell us somewhat different things when we ask them what the Scriptures mean. Faced with the same biblical texts on poverty, a saint like Francis of Assisi will speak and act in ways that will not be precisely matched by the response of contemporary scholars in biblical departments. Nevertheless, such saints, scholars, teachers and others all approach the Bible within the Church, expecting to understand and interpret it as members of that community. They know that without sharing in the group identity they may interpret the letter but miss the spirit of the Scriptures.

2. Three Levels of Interpretation

What then are interpreters trying to understand when they approach the Bible? Manifestly the object of their interpretation will vary according to the different questions and focuses which they bring to their task. But what is that object? In general one can distinguish three possibilities which admittedly are no more than formal divisions that inevitably and properly overlap each other. Let me adopt here the terminology of *intentio auctoris* (what the author meant), *intentio legentis* (what the Scripture means to the present reader) and *intentio textus ipsius* (what the text communicates). This is a scheme which Emilio Rasco very kindly passed on to me.

(a) Stated sharply, the *intentio auctoris* is the literal sense—that is to say, the meaning that the biblical author intended to transmit. "Literal" here, incidentally, does not involve falling into that basic error of fundamentalism by taking texts "literalistically" or *au pied de la lettre.* Rather the focus on the *intentio auctoris* respects the limits indicated by the author's choice of literary forms and (otherwise ascertainable) intentions. Where biblical authors, for example, wrote parables, legends or apocalypses, they should be expounded accordingly and not literalistically interpreted as if they were offering us a straight historical account or prediction of events.

Biblical exegetes are professionally in the game of establishing the *intentio auctoris.* Their historical scholarship investigates the oral and/or written sources of given books, the literary forms used by the authors, the date and occasion of their writing, the motives and interests which led them to write, the identity of their addressees, and other historical circumstances which any attempt to recreate the composition of these works must take into account. For such exegesis the original intention of the author writing to and for a particular audience constitutes the meaning of the work. In his encyclical letter *Divino Afflante Spiritu* Pius XII summed up this approach: "Everyone knows that the supreme rule of interpretation is to discover and define what the writer intended to express" (n. 34). Ultimately such a concern with the *intentio auctoris* does nothing less than attempt to relive the situation and action in which and by which the author first brought the work into existence. To quote a medieval adage: "The reader becomes the author" (*Lector fit auctor*).

Obviously many difficulties attend this enterprise. First there is the large cultural and historical gap between the biblical times and the late twentieth century. Working in the context of our modern experiences, how can scholars hope to recapture the intentions of authors who wrote thousands of years ago in a very different kind of world? To deal with this difficulty we might reasonably recall both the basic *human* affinity between the biblical authors and modern interpreters and that sense of mutual understanding brought by sharing in the same *faith.* Contemporary believers can rightly expect this common faith to help them into the world and mind-set of the original writers.

A second difficulty concerns the fact that in investigating the *intentio auctoris* there is more than merely something to be studied philologically, understood historically and expressed propositionally. The biblical authors constantly used metaphorical and symbolic language which cannot be simply transposed to the level of rational, technical concepts. The language of scientific exegesis will always fall short of the original images when it seeks to expound the meaning and content of the Scriptures. However, provided that historical exegesis refuses to deal with the Scriptures as if they could be reduced to a long series of abstract concepts and rational propositions, such exegesis can at least partly expound and translate the biblical witness. Even if they are not doing everything, exegetes are doing something true and useful when they study the scriptural texts philologically, understand them historically and re-express them propositionally.

Before leaving the kind of interpretation characteristic of historical exegesis, it would be as well to emphasize the tentative quality of many of its conclusions. Here "scientific" scholarship cannot be construed to mean "assured results." In fact the conclusions range from the highly probable through the possible to the highly unlikely. Perhaps no attempt to reconstruct the genesis of ancient texts and the intention of their historical authors can hope for a higher or more certain yield. Over this issue no other critic has been more devastating and amusing than C. S. Lewis in his essay "Fern-Seed and Elephants," which provided the title for a posthumous collection of his papers.[6]

Finally, scientific exegetes ignore at their peril the confessional traditions and other predispositions which—as was pointed out in Chapter II—will influence all interpretative activity. This is the challenge which the 1963 meeting of the Faith and Order Commission raised and which I reported in Chapter VII. No less than other interpreters and perhaps more subtly than others, professional exegetes *create* as well as discover meaning when they pore over the Scriptures and offer to tell us exactly what the authors meant to say.

(b) Where the *intentio auctoris* highlights what the biblical writers *meant,* an "existential" interpretation focuses on the present reader and what the Bible now means to me or to us. This *intentio legentis* approach reminds us that just as every piece of art remains incomplete without a viewer, so every piece of literature and especially the Scriptures are of their very nature incomplete without their readers. Further, this interpretation at the existential level can even seek to understand and interpret the mind of the reader rather more than the mind of the ancient writer. Thus the meanings that such an interpretative process reaches are ones to be shared and acted on from the inside and not merely judged from the outside as we look back at some remote past.

The *intentio legentis* approach begins from the interests and questions that in general fuel the human search for meaning and values and in particular drive me now to read this biblical text. In answering my questions the Bible invites me to accept freely the total claim of God whose Scriptures have become a living word to me. Hence interpreting the Bible amounts to understanding myself and deciding to let God's word change my life. In essence, such biblical interpretation becomes self-interpretation.

If the *intentio auctoris* approach presumes that meaning was objectively there in the minds of the biblical writers and should be rediscovered, the interpretation at the level of the *intentio legentis* makes the subjectivity of the reader dominant and looks for meaning to happen now. Of course, it recognizes that not every passage in the Bible will have that effect. Doubtless the ancient writers intended to convey something through their work, but that is no guarantee that each section of the Bible will have some contemporary meaning.

Both methods of interpretation have their own particular dangers. The *intentio auctoris* method is peculiarly open to the temptation to treat the Scriptures like any other (religious) texts from the ancient world and forget that exegesis is an activity of ecclesial faith. The *intentio legentis* method, by neglecting the objective control of the author's intention, can arbitrarily fashion its own meanings and turn the Scriptures into a mechanism for satisfying felt needs. Both methods, however, converge in tending to see *the text as such* to be no more than a kind of bridge between the "inner" history of the biblical writers and that of the contemporary readers. And yet we would play false to the Bible and written texts in general if we failed to respect a certain independence of any written texts over against both their writers and their readers.

(c) To focus on the *intentio textus ipsius* is to accept the text itself (with its structure and meaning) as the primary object of interpretation. Once any text is written and published, it begins to have its own history as people in different situations read and interpret it. Whether it is a novel, a poem, a psalm, a political constitution or a letter by St. Paul, it sets up on its own, maintains its own identity, and can mean and communicate to its readers more than its author ever consciously knew or meant. The meanings of such texts go beyond the literal sense intended by the original authors when they wrote in particular situations for specific audiences.

Gadamer makes this a universally valid principle: "Not only occasionally, but always the meaning of a text goes beyond the author."[7] In a later passage Gadamer makes the same point and asserts as well the independence of any given text from its original addressees: "The horizon of understanding cannot be limited either by what the writer originally had in mind, or by the horizon of the person to whom the text was originally addressed."[8] In short, "what is fixed in writing has detached itself from the contingency of its origin and its author and made itself free for new relationships."[9]

From the standpoint of literary criticism rather than philosophy W. K. Wimsatt joins many others in propounding what amounts essentially to the same position: "The poem is not the critic's own and not the author's; it is detached from the author at birth and goes about the world beyond his power to intend it or control it."[10] The poem "Lorca" by D. M. Thomas embodies a similar conviction about the freedom which literary and artistic compositions enjoy.

Lorca
walking
in a red-light
district at night

heard one of his own songs
being sung
by a whore

he was moved
as if the stars
and the lanterns
changed places

neither the song
to himself
belonged
nor the girl
to her humiliation
nothing
belonged to anyone

when she stopped singing
it went on

death must be a poor thing
a poor thing[11]

Changes of context strikingly show how texts can express further ranges of meaning. We will make something different of Matthew 26:52 ("All who take the sword will perish by the sword") if we proclaim it in a cemetery at Verdun than when we study it at the Biblical Institute in Rome. What such verses say and convey in one setting will differ at least somewhat from what they communicate in another. An incident involving a friend of mine exemplifies this point well. One Saturday in 1968 a number of trade union leaders in his parish found themselves arrested for holding an illegal meeting. At the time the country was still under a very right-wing government. The following day my friend used no words of his own in his sermon but simply quoted such appropriate passages as these from the Old Testament:

Then the Lord said, "I have seen the affliction of my people who are in Egypt, and have heard their cry because of their taskmasters; I know their sufferings, and I have come down to deliver them out of the hand of the Egyptians" (Ex 3:7f.).

Then the Lord said to Moses, "Go in to Pharaoh and say to him, 'Thus says the Lord, "Let my people go, that they may serve me"'" (Ex 8:1).

Woe to him who builds a town with blood and founds a city on iniquity (Hab 2:12).

On the following Monday morning a police official arrived with an order for the priest to present himself before a judge. After the preliminary hearing my friend was charged with the tendentious use of the Scriptures, but eventually the case was dropped. One thing came through loud and clear. The government appreciated the message of powerful protest which those texts carried in that particular context—the days following the arrest of union leaders in a working-class suburb. And obviously the meaning conveyed there in 1968 went beyond anything envisaged by those who composed the Books of Exodus and Habakkuk more than two thousand years ago.

This brief discussion of the *intentio textus ipsius* presents an opportunity to comment on the *sensus plenior* of the Bible.[12] I want to suggest that the Roman Catholic scholars who have championed the need to recognize this meaning of the Scriptures have in fact attributed solely to the special influence of the Holy Spirit what is in fact a general phenomenon of the *intentio textus ipsius*.

Under the *sensus plenior* those scholars understood meanings which the Sacred Scriptures, especially the Old Testament, truly carried and conveyed, which were intended by the principal author (God), but which went beyond the literal sense which the human authors were aware of communicating. In the light of later events in the divinely guided history of salvation the *sensus plenior* became clear. Thus, for example, Christian writers like St. Paul or the author of the First Gospel were inspired to detect in the Jewish Scriptures a "fuller" meaning which the original writers did not consciously intend to communicate.

This *sensus plenior* theory, however, seems to me to overlook the universal fact that all texts become detached from their authors and—especially in new and later contexts—can express ranges of meaning which the authors of those texts never intended. If other texts and their meanings move beyond the control of their authors, we would expect this to be all the more true of the Scriptures where God who controls history and its ever new contexts once guided the inspired writers. In sum, the protagonists of the *sensus plenior* saw something which was really there but treated it as if it were a phenomenon peculiar to the Bible.

When we compare and contrast the three approaches (*intentio auctoris, intentio legentis* and *intentio textus ipsius*), their temporal focus can be seen to differ. Those who investigate the *intentio auctoris* concern themselves with the *past*—with the historical intentions and mind-set of ancient Jewish and Christian authors and their audiences ("what it meant to them"). The *intentio legentis* takes us to the present—to the existential interests and questions which the contemporary reader brings to the biblical texts ("what it means to me/us"). Lastly, the *intentio textus ipsius* hints at that mysterious openness which all texts, and especially the Scriptures, have for *future* meanings. As the history of the world, the Church and individual believers unfolds, the new and unexpected situations which fresh experiences bring can suggest richer ranges of meaning. In its future depth the *intentio textus ipsius* corresponds to the mysterious God who comes to us out of the future.

3. An Integral Approach

After this summary account of three ways of interpreting the Scriptures, I want to end this chapter by sketching an integral approach which can incorporate and go beyond the values that they embody. There is in fact no need to lock ourselves resolutely into one or other system.

(a) An increasing number of writers have expressed dissatisfaction with the pursuit of historical exactitudes practiced by the critical exegesis which seeks to establish the *intentio auctoris*. Gadamer, for instance, describes the "reconstruction of what the author really had in mind" as at best "a limited undertaking."[13] It was interesting to see the Vatican's Congregation for the Doctrine of the Faith in their 1977 "Declaration on the Question of the Admission of Women to the Ministerial Priesthood" refusing to line up with those who wish to erect the literal sense into *the* meaning of the Bible: "In order to reach the ultimate meaning of the mission of Jesus and the ultimate meaning of Scripture, a purely historical exegesis of the texts cannot suffice" (n. 2).

Nevertheless, a proper attention to the *intentio auctoris* can rule out bizarre interpretations (like literalistic explanations of the Jonah story) and—even more importantly—restrict any falsely "spiritual" versions of the Scriptures which could forget their historical origins. The Bible emerged through a history which can be scientifically studied. Even if the meaning of the texts grows and changes as they are read in new contexts, their independence from their historical authors and origins can never become total. As a philosopher Gadamer may be inevitably inclined to show less interest in the *concrete* data and flow of history, but he does after all agree that the "reconstruction" of what the original author had in mind is a legitimate undertaking, even if a "limited" one.

All in all, an interpreter's attention to the *intentio auctoris* belongs to a proper respect for the historical nature of the Jewish-Christian experience of the divine self-communication. Just as faith cannot exist without some historical knowledge even if it is not simply reducible to such knowledge (excursus to Chapter V), so an integral approach to biblical interpretation cannot afford to dispense with the help of historical exegesis even if it refuses to identify the interpretative process with such exegesis.

(b) The *intentio legentis* likewise has its place inasmuch as it clarifies what in fact constantly takes place. Christians are always reading the Scriptures in the light of their questions and experiences. They instinctively push beyond what the author meant to ask what it "means to me/us."

A respect for the *intentio legentis* is well and good, provided that we truly listen to the Scriptures and do not allow the element of subjective pre-conditioning to so predominate that we cannot hear what they are saying to us. Our mind-set, concern with our needs, horizon of settled expectations or call it what you will may be so strong that we cannot appreciate the message of the Scriptures and their drastic claim on us to live in new ways. In short, if I read the Bible in the light of my questions and experiences, I must also let the Bible "read" me.

(c) There should be little need to insist that to be rightly interpreted the Scriptures should be read *as a whole*. The meaning(s) and truth of the Bible should be looked for in the context of the entire text. The *intentio textus ipsius* comes fully into its own when the *intentio textus totius* is allowed to speak for itself. One can agree that the biblical text is its own meaning, provided that it is a matter of the whole text.

(d) As has been said earlier, Gadamer among others underscores the mistake involved in attempts to ignore tradition in the interpretation of texts. In particular the Bible does not drop into our hands here and now, but comes to us through centuries of use and interpretation in the life of the Church. If Scripture serves to interpret and at times challenge particular traditions, the whole traditionary process helps us to understand and interpret the Scriptures. Here under "the whole traditionary process" I wish to include elements as various as the liturgical use of the Bible, the interpretation of the Scriptures by the Fathers and Doctors of the Church, scientific exegesis, the appeal to the Bible in documents of the magisterium, and the expression of the Scriptures in the lives of holy men and women. In a word, the community and its tradition have their proper place in the interpretation of the Bible. Like theology itself biblical interpretation is no private, solitary affair which ignores the past.

(e) Finally, in one way or another our interpretation of the Bible should have a Christological character. From the beginning Christians have witnessed to this conviction. Back in the third century Origen declared: "We who belong to the Catholic Church do not despise the Law of Moses, but accept it, so long as it is Jesus who interprets it for us. Only thus shall we understand it aright."[14] The twelfth-century Augustinian canon, Hugh of Saint Victor, shared a similar Christological vision: "All divine Scripture speaks of Christ and finds its fulfillment in Christ, because it forms only one book, the book of life which is Christ."[15] From the sixteenth century William Tyndale among others took this approach:

> The Scriptures spring out of God, and flow into Christ, and were given to lead us to Christ. Thou must therefore go along by the Scriptures as by a line, until thou come at Christ, which is the way's end and resting place.[16]

In the twentieth century Pope Benedict XV had this to say in *Spiritus Paraclitus:* "All the pages of both the Old and New Testament lead toward Christ as the center."[17]

Such a Christological interpretation of the Scriptures is one that springs from and leads to an experience of Christ. If it is "Jesus who interprets" the Bible for us, there can ultimately be no divorce of critical exegesis from spiritual practice.

A PERSONAL EPILOGUE

> *We all [the Pope and the bishops] need your work,*
> *your dedication and the fruits of your reflection. We*
> *desire to listen to you and are eager to receive the valued*
> *assistance of your responsible scholarship.*
>
> Pope John Paul II to Theologians,
> October 7, 1979

On rereading this book, I was struck by two things: the topics I might have dealt with but did not, and the key role of three themes in my work. Let me take up those two points in turn.

(1) The discussion of *revelation* should be supplemented by attention to the issues of verification and credibility. To state matters starkly, what came up in Chapter III (on authentic or inauthentic prophecy and Israel's notion of God) and in Chapter V (on the reasonableness of faith) barely touched those issues. A comprehensive fundamental theology would need to attend to the verification and credibility of at least two items: the absolute climax of the divine self-communication in the life, death and resurrection of Jesus Christ, and the identification of the Christian-Catholic community as the people specially guided by the Holy Spirit.[1]

The question of *tradition* could have been developed even more theologically. The ultimate ground for an understanding of tradition lies also in the doctrines of the Trinity, creation and incarnation and not simply in the sending of the Holy Spirit. Those first three doctrines involve, in one form or another, the self-communication of God. This divine self-giving or "handing over" calls for a loyal "handing on" which human believers carry through in the light of the transcendent pattern. Just as, for instance, the Father lovingly "transmitted" the Son into this world, so Christians are called to transmit with loving fidelity the good news about that Son. In this way such a vision of the ultimate ground of tradition in God can yield a fuller theological approach to the subject.

As regards *inspiration,* the status of non-Christian Scriptures calls for attention. One cannot argue, as I did in Chapter IV, that within the general history of revelation and salvation non-Christian religions, despite any errors and depravity, historically objectify and socially institutionalize the transcendental experience of God's self-communication, *without also* acknowledging the role of Sacred Scripture in those religions. In some sense God was positively present in the making and use of their sacred writings. To the extent that their Scripture served as a vehicle for revelation and salvation, the active divine role must be recognized in the formation and lived interpretation of that Scripture. One could call this divine influence "inspiration," or else contrast such inspiration (lower case) in the general history of revelation and salvation with Inspiration (upper case) in the special history of revelation and salvation.

So much for *some* of the things which I might have treated when dealing with inspiration, tradition and revelation. What does a retrospective look bring to light about the actual content of this book?

(2) The structure of my approach to fundamental theology largely stands or falls with the validity of the analysis of *experience* given in Chapter II. If that analysis helps to clarify somewhat the way human beings experience divine revelation, the process of tradition and the functioning of the inspired Scriptures, well and good. I presented an earlier form of that analysis in 1977.[2] Since then E. Schillebeeckx and B. van Iersel edited an issue of *Concilium* on the topic of "Revelation and Experience" which first appeared in 1978.[3] That particular issue encouraged me to think that I was on the right track, as did an earlier work which I read only at the beginning of 1980. In his *Jesus and the Spirit*[4] James Dunn throws much light on the origins of Christianity by focusing precisely on the religious experience of Jesus and the first Christians.

A second key theme of my fundamental theology is undoubtedly *the break* between the period of foundational revelation (which climaxed with the apostolic age) and the period of dependent revelation. In that first period there was something distinctive and different about the divine self-communication which established the status of Israel, the contrast between the special and general histories of revelation and salvation, the unique identity of Jesus as true God and true man, the unrepeatable role of the apostles (as resurrection witnesses and founders of the Church), the Scriptures as witnessing prophetically (the Old Testament) and apostolically (the New Testament) to Christ, and the cessation of biblical inspiration with the coming-into-being of the Church.

We can only accept these items if we acknowledge that, so far from being equally related to all times and places, God's active presence enjoys different degrees of engagement. To allege that there are no such variations in the dynamic divine presence logically means denying the distinctive status of Israel, the existence of a special history of revelation and salvation, the (partially) non-transferable role of the apostles, the temporal limits to the occurrence of biblical inspiration and, ultimately, the unique identity of Jesus Christ. The acceptance or rejection of all these beliefs hangs together. In his *The Bible in the Modern World* James Barr, for instance, makes the following observations about inspiration:

> Today I think we believe, or have to believe, that God's communication with the men of the biblical period was not on any different terms from the mode of his communication with his people today. "Inspiration" would then mean that the God whom we worship was also likewise in contact with his people in ancient times, and that ... he was present in the formation of their tradition and in the crystallization of that tradition as a Scripture; but that the mode of this contact was not different from the mode in which God has continued to make himself known to men.[5]

The logic of this position would alter one's stance to much more than biblical inspiration. If "God's communication with the men [and women] of the biblical period was *not on any different terms* from the mode of his communication with his people today" (italics mine), we simply cannot maintain, for example, the once-and-for-all nature of the apostolic experience and the unique identity of Jesus.

A third key theme which has repeatedly emerged in this book is the link between *practice and theory*. Thus theologians do their work as committed, if "critical," members of the Church; real experience of the Christian faith, or of anything else for that matter, can never be secondhand; revelation is essentially a personal encounter with the Triune God; faith calls for commitment and confidence alongside the confession of truth; contact with the risen, eucharistic Lord is the ultimate guide for Christians searching for the Tradition within the traditions; scientific exegesis is required but insufficient for an integral interpretation of the Scriptures; and so forth. Over and over again and from different points of view, this book has put the case for a proper union between critical, scientific understanding and committed, spiritual practice as the right way into fundamental theology.

Here I may be permitted to quote my sister, Dr. Maev O'Collins, who knows far better than I do how to combine practice and theory. In October 1979 she concluded her inaugural lecture as professor and head of the department of anthropology and sociology at the University of Papua New Guinea with these words:

> We cannot remain detached and aloof from the society in which we live and work. We must share in the work of sifting through the

debris and deposits of colonization and in the examination of Papua New Guinean ways. But we must leave to Papua New Guineans the final task of selecting what they want from these two elements and reshaping their own society. Today more and more questions are being asked as to the relevance of much that was accepted from the colonial past. We are also part of this assessment process, as the University is not only a critic of society but also must accept criticism and evaluation from society.

When I read these words, it struck me how closely they could be applied to the role which a fundamental theologian is called on to play. Let me close by making such a professional and personal application.

We fundamental theologians cannot remain detached and aloof from the Church in which we live and work. We must share in the work of sifting through the debris and (indispensably precious) deposits of the past and in the examination of present ways in which the Holy Spirit is guiding the Church: for instance, toward both a greater Christ-centeredness and a deeper desire to work for human rights, economic justice and international peace.

But we must leave to the members of the Church at large and their leaders the final task of selecting, under the rule of the risen Lord's Spirit, what they need to reshape their future. Today more and more questions are being asked as to the relevance of much that was accepted from the Church's past. We theologians are also part of this assessment process, as any theological faculty is not only a critic of the Church but also must accept criticism and evaluation from the Church in general.

NOTES

ABBREVIATIONS

CD   K. Barth, *Church Dogmatics* (ET: Edinburgh, 1936–69).

DBTH   *Dictionary of Biblical Theology*, ed. X. Léon-Dufour (2nd ed.: ET, London, 1973).

DS   *Enchiridion Symbolorum, definitionum et declarationum de rebus fidei et morum,* ed. H. Denzinger, rev. A. Schönmetzer, (25th ed.: Freiburg, 1973).

EncBrit   *The New Encyclopaedia Britannica* (Chicago, 1974–77).

EncTh   *Encyclopedia of Theology. A Concise Sacramentum Mundi,* ed. K. Rahner (ET: London, 1975).

ET   English translation.

Flann   *Vatican Council II. The Conciliar and Post-Conciliar Documents,* ed. A. Flannery (Tenbury Wells, 1975).

IDB   *The Interpreter's Dictionary of the Bible,* ed. G. A. Buttrick, 4 vols. (New York & Nashville, 1962); supplementary volume, ed. K. Crim (Nashville, 1976).

JBC   *The Jerome Biblical Commentary,* ed. R. E. Brown *et al.* (Englewood Cliffs, 1968).

LThK   *Lexikon für Theologie und Kirche* (Freiburg, 1957–68).

NCE   *New Catholic Encyclopedia* (New York, 1967).

Princ   J. Macquarrie, *Principles of Christian Theology* (rev. ed.: London, 1977).

RahR   *A Rahner Reader,* ed. G. A. McCool (London: 1975).

RGG   *Religion in Geschichte und Gegenwart* (3rd ed.: Tübingen, 1957–65).

SM   *Sacramentum Mundi* (ET: New York & London, 1968–70).

SystTh   Paul Tillich, *Systematic Theology* (London, 1978).

ThInv   K. Rahner, *Theological Investigations* (ET: London, 1961–).

Note: In this book the translation of documents from the Second Vatican Council is taken from Flannery's edition. The scriptural texts are taken from the Revised Standard Version of the Bible.

PREFACE

1. Cork & South Bend, 1968.
2. Chicago, 1971.
3. London & New York, 1975. In England the book appeared under the title *Has Dogma a Future?*

CHAPTER I

1. See K. Barth, CD I/1, pp. 3–11; G. Ebeling, "Theologie," RGG 6, col. 754–69; *The Study of Theology* (ET: London, 1979); J. Macquarrie, Princ, pp. 1–40; J.-B. Metz, "Theologie," LThK 10, col. 62–71; G. O'Collins, *Foundations of Theology* (Chicago, 1971) pp. 1–20; K. Rahner, "Theology," SM 6, pp. 233–46 (= EncTh, pp. 1686–1701); "Theology and Anthropology," ThInv 9, pp. 28–45 (partly in RahR, pp. 66–74); P. Tillich, SystTh 1, pp. 3–68; Vatican II, *Gaudium et Spes*, no. 62 (= Flann, pp. 966–68); *Optatam totius*, nos. 13–18 (= Flann, pp. 717–21); H. Thielicke, "Theology," EncBrit 18, pp. 274–76; G. F. Van Ackeren, "Theology," NCE 14, pp. 39–49.
2. G. Hallett, "Light Dawns Gradually Over the Whole," *Heythrop Journal* 18 (1977) pp. 316–19.
3. To an extent W. Pannenberg (*Theology and the Philosophy of Science* [ET: London, 1976] pp. 225ff.) interprets theology as "understanding seeking faith."
4. "Theses on the Relationship between the Ecclesiastical Magisterium and Theology," issued June 6, 1976 (ET: Washington, 1977) thesis 6, no. 2; hereafter *Theses*. See Pope John Paul II, *Redemptor Hominis*, no. 19; W. Reiser, "The Primacy of Spiritual Experience in Theological Reflection," paper at Lonergan Workshop, Boston College, June 15, 1978.
5. *Truth and Method* (ET: London, 1975) pp. 238ff.
6. B. Lonergan has stressed the role of a many-layered conversion, which will radically reorient the theologian and produce a truly authentic horizon of understanding; see his *Method in Theology* (London, 1972) pp. 237ff., 267ff.
7. Pope John Paul II, *Redemptor Hominis*, no. 13; K. Rahner, "Anonymous Christians," ThInv 6, pp. 390–98, at pp. 390–91 and 393–95 (= RahR, pp. 211–14); "Concerning the Relationship between Nature and Grace," ThInv 1, pp. 297–317, at pp. 300–02 and 310–5 (= RahR, pp. 185–190); "Existential, Supernatural," SM 2, pp. 306–07; *Foundations of Christian Faith* (ET: New York, 1978) pp. 116–33; Vatican II, *Gaudium et Spes*, no. 22 (= Flann, pp. 922–24).
8. London, 1939, p. 185.
9. *Über die Christlichkeit unserer heutigen Theologie* (2nd ed.: Leipzig, 1903) p. 25; cf. p. 147; *Christentum und Kultur* (Basle, 1919) p. 20.
10. See Ebeling, "Theologie und Philosophie," RGG 6, col. 782–830; C.-F. Geyer, "Philosophie und Theologie," *Neue Zeitschrift für system. Theol.* 18 (1976) pp. 1–21; Rahner, "Philosophy and Philosophizing in Theology," ThInv 9, pp. 46–63 (partly in RahR, pp. 80–89); "Philosophy and Theology," SM 5, pp. 20–24 (= EncTh, pp. 1228–33).

11. On Hume, Keats and others see A. R. Manser, "Imagination," P. Edwards (ed.), *Encyclopedia of Philosophy* 4 (New York & London, 1967), pp. 136–39.

12. See *Truth and Meaning*, ed. G. Evans & J. McDowell (Oxford, 1976); *Truth*, ed. G. Pitcher (Englewood Cliffs, 1964); P. F. Strawson, *Meaning and Truth* (Oxford, 1970); C. J. F. Williams, *What Is Truth?* (Cambridge, 1976).

13. See W. Kasper, "History, Theology of," SM 3, pp. 43–47 (= EncTh, pp. 632–35).

14. "Theology," SM 6, p. 234 (= EncTh, p. 1687).

15. *Theses* 7, no. 2.

16. *Ibid.* 8, no. 2. See Y. Congar, "Bref historique des formes du 'magistère' et de ses relations avec les docteurs," *Revue des sciences phil. et théol.* 60 (1976) pp. 99–112; A. Dulles, "The Theologian and the Magisterium," *Catholic Mind* 75 (1977) pp. 6–16; *Chicago Studies* for summer 1978 dealt with "The Magisterium, the Theologian and the Educator."

17. *Gaudium et Spes*, no. 62 (= Flann, p. 966).

18. *An Essay on Man* (New Haven & London, 1944) p. 53.

19. Here one might ask: To what extent is theology intrinsically denominational, so that as such it calls for dialogue between Christian denominations? Vatican II's Decree on Ecumenism, *Unitatis Redintegratio* (= Flann 452–70), heavily stressed the need for interchurch dialogue. See also part two of *Directory Concerning Ecumenical Matters: Ecumenism in Higher Education* (= Flann, pp. 515–32). Ultimately, however, as all Christian theologians like Christian believers are united in confessing Jesus as Lord, the differences between denominational theologies can only be secondary and hence interdenominational dialogue cannot be primary.

20. See Moltmann, *The Crucified God* (ET: London, 1974).

21. Clement of Alexandria, *Stromata* 5, 71.

22. On fundamental theology see P. J. Cahill, "Fundamental Theology," NCE 6, pp. 222–23; H. Fries, "Fundamental Theology," SM 2, pp. 368–72 (= EncTh, pp. 546–51); P. Knauer, *Der Glaube kommt vom Hören* (Vienna & Cologne, 1978); *Problemi e Prospettive di teologia fondamentale*, ed. R. Latourelle and G. O'Collins (Brescia, 1980); J.-B. Metz, *Faith in History and Society* (ET: New York, 1979); D. Tracy, "The Task of Fundamental Theology," *Journal of Religion* 54 (1974) pp. 13–34. *Concilium* vol. 6, no. 5 (June, 1969) was devoted to the theme of "Fundamental Theology." See also D. Tracy, *Blessed Rage for Order* (New York, 1975) and reviews of the book: A. Dulles, *Theological Studies* 37 (1976) pp. 304–16; G. O'Collins, *Gregorianum* 57 (1976) pp. 778–81; W. M. Shea, *Heythrop Journal* 17 (1976) pp. 273–92 and *Thomist* 40 (1976) pp. 665–83.

23. P. J. Cahill, "Apologetics," NCE 1, pp. 669–74; H. Lais, "Apologetik," LThK 1, col. 723–28; J.-B. Metz, "Apologetics," SM 1, pp. 66–70 (= EncTh, pp. 20–24); H.-H. Schrey, "Apologetik. III Systematisch-theologisch," RGG 1, col. 485–89.

24. See above, no 10. See also L. B. Geiger, "Christian Philosophy," NCE 3, pp. 640–44; C. F. Geyer, "Philosophie und Theologie," *Neue Zeitschrift für systematische Theologie* 18 (1976) pp. 1–21; L. Malevez, "Le Croyant et le philosophe," *Nouvelle Revue Théologique* 82 (1960) pp. 897–917; "Théologie et philosophie: leur inclusion réciproque," *ibid.* 93 (1971) pp. 113–44; J. Macquarrie,

Princ, pp. 21–25, 43ff.; K. Rahner, "The Current Relationship between Philosophy and Theology," ThInv 13, pp. 61–79; "Philosophy and Theology," *ibid.* 6, pp. 71–81; P. Tillich, SystTh 1, pp. 18–28; *The Protestant Era* (Chicago, 1948) pp. 83–93.

25. On the regulation of theological speech see St. Augustine, *De Civ. Dei,* X, 23.

CHAPTER II

1. See P. L. Heath, "Experience," *Encyclopedia of Philosophy* 3, pp. 156–59; K. Lehmann, "Experience," SM 2, pp. 307–09; A. S. Kessler et al., "Erfahrung," *Handbuch philosophischer Grundbegriffe,* ed. H. Krings et al., (Munich, 1973) 2, pp. 373–86; L. Richter, "Erfahrung," RGG 2, col. 550–52; P. Tillich, SystTh 1, pp. 40ff.

2. *Truth and Method,* pp. 55ff.
3. *Reconstruction in Philosophy* (Boston, 1966) p. 86.
4. *Genesis* (ET: Philadelphia, 1961) pp. 14f.
5. Oxford, 1975, pp. 24–40.
6. Lonergan, *Method in Theology,* pp. 130–32.
7. *Paul among Jews and Gentiles* (Philadelphia, 1976) pp. 7–23.
8. This phraseology turns up repeatedly in J. L. Houlden's otherwise helpful *Patterns of Faith* (London, 1977); see pp. 46, 56, 69, 75f., 77, 82.
9. *The Mystery of Being* (ET: Chicago, 1960) p. 102.
10. *Foundations of Christian Faith,* pp. 19ff., 31ff., 51ff.
11. See Ch. I, fn. 7.
12. See W. J. Hill, "Experience, Religious," NCE 5, p 751–53; J. Mouroux, "Religious Experience," SM 5, pp. 292–93; J. E. Smith, *Experience and God* (New York, 1968); "Religious Experience," EncBrit 15, pp. 647–52; P. Tillich, SystTh 3, pp. 221ff.
13. Hence I wish to withdraw the distinction I introduced in *Foundations of Theology* between "human experience which is *simply* human experience" and "human experience which is *also* the experience of receiving revelation" (p. 62).

CHAPTER III

1. On revelation see K. Barth, CD I/1, pp. 295ff.; I/2, pp. 1ff.; R. Bultmann, "The Concept of Revelation in the New Testament," *Existence and Faith* (ET: London, 1961) pp. 58–91; A. Dulles, *Revelation and the Quest for Unity* (Washington, 1968); *Revelation Theology* (New York, 1969); "Revelation, Theology of," NCE 12, pp. 440–44; P. Eicher, *Offenbarung. Prinzip neuzeitlicher Theologie* (Munich, 1977); H. Fries, *Revelation* (ET: New York, 1969); R. Latourelle, *The Theology of Revelation* (ET: New York, 1966); J. Macquarrie, Princ, pp. 84–103; G. Moran, *Theology of Revelation* (New York, 1966); C. F. D. Moule, "Revelation," IDB 4, pp. 54–58; H. R. Niebuhr, *The Meaning of Revelation* (New York, 1962); W. Pannenberg, *Revelation as History* (ET: London, 1969); K. Rahner, "Observations on the Concept of Revelation," *Revelation and Tradition, Quaestiones Dis-*

putatae 17 (ET: London, 1966) pp. 9–25; "Wort Gottes," LThK 10, col. 1235–38; P. Ricoeur et al., *La revelation* (Brussels, 1977); "Toward a Hermeneutic of the Idea of Revelation," *Harvard Theol. Review* 70 (1977) pp. 1–37; B. Rigaux and P. Grelot, "Revelation," DBTh, pp. 499–505; N. Schiffers et al., "Revelation," SM 5, pp. 342–59 (= EncTh, pp. 1453–73); P. Tillich, SystTh 1, pp. 71–159. All commentaries on the Second Vatican Council's *Dei Verbum* provide further material on revelation, as well as on tradition and the Scriptures.

2. On grace see E. M. Burke, "Grace," NCE 6, pp. 658–72; P. Fransen, *The New Life of Grace* (ET: London, 1969); J. Haspecker et al., "Gnade," LThK 4, col. 977–1000; K. Rahner, *Foundations of Christian Faith,* pp. 116ff.; "Grace II. Theological," SM 2, pp. 415–24 (= EncTh, pp. 587–95); H. Rondet, *The Grace of Christ* (ET: Westminster, 1967).

3. The Second Vatican Council uses "mystery" in the singular 106 times, and in the plural only 21 times. Pope John Paul II's *Redemptor Hominis* exhibits the same tendency: around 50 times this encyclical speaks of "the mystery of God," "the mystery of Christ," "the mystery of the redemption," "the paschal mystery" etc. The Pope's Apostolic Exhortation *Catechesi Tradendae* (16 October 1979) likewise prefers to speak of "mystery" rather than "mysteries."

4. *Has Christianity a Revelation?* (London, 1964) pp. 291–93; see pp. 16f.

5. "The Problem of the Infallibility of the Church's Office," *Concilium* vol. 3, no. 9 (March, 1973) p. 77; italics mine. I presume that Schillebeeckx does not imply here that "expression" is an extra step *beyond* experience, as if one could have an experience without necessarily expressing it in some way or another. As we saw in Chapter II, expression is a necessary part of any experience.

6. See my *Foundations of Theology,* pp. 132–49.

7. H. W. Wolff, *The Old Testament: A Guide to Its Writings* (ET: Philadelphia, 1973) p. 30.

8. *Ibid.,* p. 62.

9. On this theme of the past, present and future see W. Pannenberg, *Revelation as History,* pp. 125ff.

10. See G. Ahlström, "Prophecy," EncBrit 15, pp. 62–68; P. Beauchamp, "Prophet," DBTh, pp. 468–74; M. J. Buss, "Prophecy in Ancient Israel," IDB supplementary vol., pp. 694–97; J. L. Crenshaw, *Prophetic Conflict* (Berlin, 1971); D. J. McCarthy, "Prophetism (in the Bible)," NCE 11, pp. 867–72; J. L. McKenzie, *A Theology of the Old Testament* (New York, 1974) pp. 102–26; R. Meyer, "Propheten II. In Israel," RGG 5, col. 613–18; B. D. Napier, "Prophet, Prophetism," IDB 3, pp. 896–919; K. Rahner, "Prophetism," SM 5, pp. 110–13 (= EncTh, pp. 1286–89); B. Vawter, "Introduction to Prophetic Literature," JBC 1, pp. 223–37.

10a. See G. von Rad, *Old Testament Theology,* vol. 2 (ET: Edinburgh, 1965) pp. 80ff.

11. *Catholic Biblical Quarterly* 30 (1968) p. 608.

12. *The Interpretation of the New Testament 1861–1961* (London, 1964) pp. 267f.

13. *Prophecy and Tradition,* pp. 33ff.

14. *Quodl.* 12, q. 17, a. 26.

15. *The Varieties of Religious Experience* (Fontana: London, 1974) p. 41.

16. See R. Clements, *Prophecy and Tradition,* pp. 53f.

17. See J. J. Castelot, "Religious Institutions of Israel," JBC 2, pp. 710–14; O. Wintermute, "Sites, Sacred," IDB supplementary vol., pp. 827–29.

17a. On female imagery for God see P. Trible, "God, nature of, in the Old Testament," IDB supplementary vol., pp. 368–69.

18. See J. A. Fitzmyer, "Pauline Theology," JBC 2, pp. 800–27; A. C. Purdy, "Paul the Apostle," IDB 3, pp. 681–704; D. E. H. Whiteley, *The Theology of St. Paul* (Oxford, 1964).

19. See W. Baird, "Knowledge in the New Testament," IDB supplementary vol., pp. 524–25; J. Corbon and A. Vanhoye, "Know," DBTh, pp. 296–99; O. A. Piper, "Knowledge," IDB 3, pp. 42–48.

20. See X. Léon-Dufour, "Apostles," DBTh, pp. 24–26; K. H. Schelkle and H. Bacht, "Apostel," LThK 1, col. 734–38; M. H. Shepherd, "Apostle," IDB 1, pp. 170–72; D.M. Stanley and R. E. Brown, "Aspects of New Testament Thought," JBC 2, pp. 797–99.

21. See C. F. D. Moule, *The Phenomenon of the New Testament* (London, 1967) pp. 21–42; *The Origin of Christology* (Cambridge, 1977) pp. 47ff.

22. Here I accept W. Kümmel's arguments for considering 2 Corinthians one letter rather than a collection of several letters or fragments of letters. See his *Introduction to the New Testament* (ET: Nashville, 1975) pp. 287–93.

23. See D. E. H. Whiteley, *The Theology of St. Paul,* pp. 127–29.

24. See my "Power Made Perfect in Weakness: 2 Cor 12: 9–10," *Catholic Biblical Quarterly* 33 (1971) pp. 528–37.

25. On Jesus' "Abba-experience" see E. Schillebeeckx, *Jesus* (ET: London & New York, 1979) pp. 256–71.

26. See my *What Are They Saying About Jesus?* (New York, 1977) pp. 25–29, 36–43.

27. For further material see I. de la Potterie, *La Vérité dans Saint Jean,* 2 vols (Rome, 1977).

27a. It is interesting that the *Oxford Annotated Bible* (which, of course, uses the RSV translation) may decline to adopt "experience" when it translates Jn 4:39–42, but adds the note: "Faith based on the testimony of another (the woman) is vindicated in personal experience."

28. P. 13.

29. Pp. 45–47, 49f.

30. SystTh 1, pp. 126–28; Tillich speaks of "Original and Dependent Revelation" rather than "Foundational and Dependent Revelation," and uses this language with the nuances of his own system.

31. 1 Clem. 42; Ignatius of Antioch, *Romans* 4, 3; *Didache* 4, 13; Barnabas 19, 11.

31a. For some cautionary remarks on the "signs of the times" see J. Moltmann, *The Church in the Power of the Spirit* (ET: London, 1977) pp. 38–50.

32. See, for instance, M. Nicolau, *Sacrae Theologiae Summa* 1 (Madrid, 1952) pp. 94–95; P. de Letter, "Revelations, Private," NCE 12, pp. 446–48.

33. *Letters and Papers from Prison* (ET: London, 1971); hereafter LPP.

34. *Christology* (ET: London, 1966) p. 39.

35. G. B. Kelly calls this question "the theological turning point" in Bonhoeffer's correspondence from prison. He remarks that in this and subsequent letters "Bonhoeffer struggled to discern the specific way Christ was manifesting

himself in a world torn apart by war and hatred. In prison he called for an even more practical search into the concrete form Christ was assuming in the critical time during and beyond the war" ("Revelation in Christ, A Study of Bonhoeffer's Theology of Revelation," *Ephemerides Theolog. Lovanienses* 50 [1974] p. 54). However, the question was more than a *theological* turning point; it was a personal turning point for Bonhoeffer. It was a matter of discerning the specific way Christ manifested himself to Bonhoeffer. Besides calling for such a practical search, Bonhoeffer engaged himself in intense reflection on the concrete form Christ was assuming right then for Bonhoeffer himself in that closing year of the war.

36. *Christology,* p. 43.

37. See further on Bonhoeffer my "A Neglected Source for the Theology of Revelation," *Gregorianum* 57 (1976) pp. 757–68, and *The Second Journey* (New York, 1978) pp. 40–42.

CHAPTER IV

1. *History and Hermaneutics* (Philadelphia, 1966) p. 15.

2. See K. Rahner, "The Eternal Significance of the Humanity of Jesus for Our Relationship with God," ThInv 3, pp. 35–46; J. Alfaro, *Cristologia y Antropologia* (Madrid, 1973) pp. 170–82.

3. K. Rahner, "History of the World and Salvation-History," ThInv 5, pp. 97–114; *Foundations of Christian Faith,* pp. 138–61.

4. K. Rahner, "The One Christ and the Universality of Salvation," ThInv 16, pp. 199–224; *Foundations of Christian Faith,* pp. 311–21.

5. See K. Rahner, "Anima naturaliter christiana," LThK 1, col. 564f. Tertullian (*Apol.* 17, 6) attributes to the human soul—right from its very beginning— a knowledge of God which can never be fully lost. In this notion there is more than a suggestion of that transcendental experience of God analyzed by Rahner and others.

6. K. Rahner, "Current Problems in Christology," ThInv 1, p. 149. See my *Has Dogma a Future?,* pp. 18ff., 33ff., 47ff.

CHAPTER V

1. See K. Hecker and others, "Society," SM 6, pp. 123–32 (= EncTh, pp. 1610–13); J. Moltmann, *Man* (ET: Philadelphia, 1974); W. Pannenberg, *What Is Man?* (ET: Philadelphia, 1970); J. Splett et al., "Man (Anthropology)," SM 3, pp. 358–70 (= EncTh, pp. 880–93).

2. See *Gaudium et Spes,* pp. 4ff.

2a. Undoubtedly the "understanding and knowledge" intended here refer directly to the exalted Christ who is *now* head of the Church. However, Christians also know Christ's *past* death and its benefits (1: 20; 2: 14f.).

3. "On the Meaning of 'Act of God'," cf. *Harvard Theological Review* 61 (1968) pp. 171f.

3a. On faith see E. C. Blackman, "Faith, faithfulness," IDB 2, pp. 222–34; J. Duplacy, "Faith," DBTh, pp. 158–63; H. Fries, "Faith and Knowledge,"

SM 2, pp. 329–34 (= EncTh, pp. 518–24); C. H. Pickart et al., "Faith," NCE 5, pp. 792–804; K. Rahner and J. Alfaro, "Faith," SM 2, pp. 310–26 (= EncTh, pp. 496–514); C. H. Ratschow et al., "Glaube," RGG 2, col. 1586–1611; J. Ratzinger, *Introduction to Christianity* (ET: New York, 1969) pp. 15–49; J. Reumann, "Faith, Faithfulness in the NT," IDB supplementary vol., pp. 332–35; R. Schnackenburg et al., "Glaube," LThK 4, col. 913–931; P. Tillich, SystTh 3, pp. 129ff.; J. M. Ward, "Faith, Faithfulness in the OT," IDB supplementary vol., pp. 329–32.

4. *The Epistle to the Romans* (ET: London, 1933) pp. 143f.

5. See my *The Easter Jesus* (London, 1973) pp. 65–69, where I discuss the limited nature of the evidence for the resurrection.

6. In its *Dignitatis Humanae* the Second Vatican Council pointed to the example of Jesus; in his ministry he called for faith but left people thoroughly free to believe or not (n. 11).

7. Apropos of Christ's resurrection, Thomas Aquinas held that certain visible signs revealed its reality but denied that the truth of the resurrection was "demonstrated by proofs" (*Summa theol.* 3, q. 55, a. 5).

8. Cited in F. Herzog (ed.), *The Future of Hope* (New York, 1970) p. 130.

9. *Hearers of the Word;* ET in RahR, p. 44.

10. *Ibid.,* p. 45.

11. III *Sent.* 35, 1, 2.

12. See *Revelation as History*, pp. 138f.

13. See J. Alfaro, *Cristologia y Antropologia,* pp. 413–76.

14. See A. Darlap, "Faith and History," SM 2, pp. 326–29 (= EncTh, pp. 514–18); V. Harvey, *The Historian and the Believer* (New York, 1966); A. Richardson, *History Sacred and Profane* (London, 1964).

15. *Theology of the New Testament,* vol. 1 (ET: London, 1965) p. 26.

CHAPTER VI

1. P.-T. Camelot, "Creeds," SM 2, pp. 37–40; J. R. Durham, "Credo, Ancient Israelite," IDB supplementary vol., pp. 197–98; F. X. Murphy, "Creed," NCE 4, pp. 432–38; W. A. Quanbeck, "Confession," IDB 1, pp. 667–68; K. Rahner, *Foundations of Christian Faith,* pp. 448–60; J. Ratzinger, *Introduction to Christianity,* pp. 50–64.

2. A. Flew, *New Essays in Philosophical Theology* (London, 1969) p. 98.

3. ET from *Documents of the Christian Church,* ed. H. Bettenson (2nd ed.: London, 1967) p. 210.

4. *Truth,* ed. G. Pitcher, p. 45.

5. The sermon of Pope John Paul II at the opening of the last academic year (16 October 1979) stressed "the fathomless mystery of the infinite God" which means, as Augustine, Aquinas and a long line of Christian writers in the tradition of the *via negativa* have insisted, that rather than succeeding in positive descriptions it is easier for us to say what the God revealed in Jesus Christ is *not.*

6. On meaning see W. P. Alston, "Meaning," *Encyclopedia of Philosophy* 5, pp. 233–40; J. Splett, "Meaning," SM 4, pp. 3–9 (= EncTh, pp. 945–52); P.

F. Strawson, *Meaning and Truth;* Z. Vendler, "Semantics," EncBrit 16, pp. 506–12.

7. *Meaning and Truth,* p. 5.

8. D. J. Keefe, review of my *The Case against Dogma* (= *Has Dogma a Future?*), *Review for Religious* 36 (1977) p. 322.

9. *The Archaeology of Knowledge* (ET: London, 1972) pp. 109–10.

10. *Acta Apostolicae Sedis* 56 (1964) p. 646; italics mine.

11. *Gaudium et Spes,* no. 16 (= Flann, p. 916).

12. On truth see J. Möller, "Truth," SM 6, pp. 308–13 (= EncTh, pp. 1771–76); F. P. O'Farrell et al., "Truth," NCE 14, pp. 327–35; also articles on "Coherence Theory of Truth," "Correspondence Theory of Truth," "Performative Theory of Truth," and "Pragmatic Theory of Truth" in *Encyclopedia of Philosophy,* ed. P. Edwards.

13. "Questions on Christian Salvation on and for Man," *Towards Vatican III,* ed. D. Tracy et al., (Dublin, 1978) p. 37.

14. On authority see S. J. Benn, "Authority," *Encyclopedia of Philosophy 1,* pp. 215–18; G. J. McMorrow, "Authority," NCE 1, pp. 1111–13; W. Molinski, "Authority," SM 1, pp. 129–33 (= EncTh, pp. 60–65).

15. *The Theory of Social and Economic Organization* (ET: New York, 1964) p. 152.

16. *Ibid.,* p. 328.

17. No. 4.

18. See Chapter III, note 10 for material on the personal truthfulness and authority of prophets.

19. J. R. Lerch, "Teaching Authority of the Church (Magisterium)," NCE 13, pp. 959–65; K. Rahner, "Magisterium," SM 3, pp. 351–58 (= EncTh, pp. 871–80); *Foundations of Christian Faith,* pp. 378ff.; see also Chapter I, note 16, and commentaries on the Second Vatican Council's *Dei Verbum* (n. 10) and *Lumen Gentium* (nn. 24–25).

20. See K. Rahner and C. Pozo, "Dogma," SM 2, pp. 95–111 (= EncTh, pp. 352–70); and the bibliography in my *Has Dogma a Future?,* p. 107.

21. B. C. Butler, *Downside Review* 93 (1975) pp. 226–31; A. Dulles, *Theological Studies* 37 (1976) pp. 147–49; D. Keefe, *Review for Religious* 36 (1977) pp. 321–22; N. Lash, *Tablet* for 10 May 1975, pp. 433–34; M. Williams, *Heythrop Journal* 17 (1976) pp. 461–63.

22. See the First Vatican Council (DS 3011).

23. The Second Vatican Council was the first ecumenical council of the Church to teach explicitly something about theology and its relationship to the magisterium (*Dei Verbum,* nn. 12, 23 and 24; *Gaudium et Spes,* n. 62). See also J. Alfaro, "La Teologia di fronte al Magistero," *Problemi e Prospettive di Teologia Fondamentale,* ed. R. Latourelle & G. O'Collins. Chapter I, notes 8 and 16, of this present work contains further items.

CHAPTER VII

1. P. Berger and T. Luckmann, *The Social Construction of Reality* (New York, 1967); G. W. Coats, "Tradition Criticism, OT," IDB supplementary vol.,

pp. 912–14; R. D. Coote, "Tradition, Oral, OT," *ibid.,* pp. 914–16; H. G. Gadamer et al., "Tradition," RGG 6, col. 966–84; J. Hasenfuss et al., "Tradition," LThK 10, col. 290–99; J. Jensen and J. A. Fichtner, "Tradition," NCE 14, pp. 223–28; S. Mowinckel, "Tradition, Oral," IDB 4, pp. 683–85. K.-H. Weger, "Tradition," SM 6, pp. 269–74 (= EncTh, pp. 1728–34). Commentaries on the Second Vatican Council's *Dei Verbum* contain useful material: for example, J. Ratzinger, *Commentary on the Documents of Vatican II,* ed. H. Vorgrimler 3 (ET: London, 1969) pp. 181–98.

2. "Tradition at the Beginning of the Reformation," *Perspectives on Scripture and Tradition,* ed. J. F. Kelly (Notre Dame, 1976) pp. 65f.

3. Y. Congar, *Tradition and Traditions* (ET: London, 1966) pp. 139ff.; hereafter *Tradition.*

4. *The Fourth World Conference on Faith and Order, Montreal 1963,* ed. P. C. Rodger and L. Vischer (New York & London, 1964) p. 51; hereafter *Montreal.* See A. Dulles, "Reflections on 'Sola Scriptura'," *Revelation and the Quest for Unity,* pp. 65–81.

5. "Scripture and Tradition," SM 6, pp. 54–57 at p. 54 (= EncTh, pp. 1549–54).

6. H. de Lubac, *Exégèse médiévale. Les quatre sens de l'Écriture* 2 vols. (Paris, 1959).

7. W. Pannenberg, "The Crisis of the Scripture Principle," *Basic Questions in Theology* 1 (ET: London, 1970) pp. 1–14.

8. Y. Congar, *Tradition,* pp. 411f.; J. Ratzinger, *Revelation and Tradition,* pp. 50–68.

9. *Theology and Proclamation* (ET: Philadelphia, 1966) pp. 22f. But see also his *Dogmatik des christlichen Glaubens* 1 (Tübingen, 1979). W. Pannenberg shows himself open and even favorable to the principle of tradition (*Theology and the Philosophy of Science* [ET: London, 1976] p. 198), as did P. Tillich (SystTh 3, p. 184). On the issue of tradition in recent Protestant theology see Congar, *Tradition,* pp. 459ff.

10. *Truth and Method,* pp. 142ff., 351ff. etc.

11. Paris, 1960 and 1963.

12. *Dei Verbum* reflects here and there the older model of revelation when it slips into phrases about "the divinely revealed realities" which are "contained" in the Scriptures (n. 11), and speaks about the Scriptures which "contain the word of God" (n. 24). This second phrase, incidentally, does not appear in the Flannery translation. The Montreal report also goes back to the older language when it speaks of "the Christian Tradition" whose "content is God's revelation" (p. 52).

13. Flann, p. 754; italics mine.

14. *Montreal,* p. 50.

15. *Ibid.,* p. 50.

16. *Ibid.,* p. 52.

17. *Ibid.,* p. 54.

18. *Ibid.,* p. 52.

19. *Tradition,* pp. 338–46.

20. Flann, p. 755.

21. *Montreal,* p. 52.

22. *Ibid.,* p. 52.
23. Flann, pp. 466–67.
24. *Montreal,* p. 52.
25. *Acta Synodalia Conc. Vat. II,* vol. III, pars III, pp. 150–51.
26. Flann, p. 763.
27. *Ibid.,* p. 755.
28. *Montreal,* pp. 53f.

CHAPTER VIII

1. *Dei Verbum,* 8.
2. *Unitatis Redintegratio,* 5.
3. CD II/2, pp. 482ff.
4. *Montreal,* p. 52.
5. *Lumen Gentium,* 25.
6. *Dei Verbum,* 10.
7. *Commonitorium* II, 2.
8. *Contra Epist. Parmeniani* III, 3.
9. "Omnium consensus naturae vox est" (*Tuscul. Disput.* I, 26, 35). "Vetus opinio est iam usque ab heroicis ducta temporibus eaque et populi Romani et omnium gentium firmata consensu versari quandam inter homines divinationem . . . id est praesensionem et scientiam rerum futurarum" (*De Divin.* I, 1).
10. *An Essay on the Development of Christian Doctrine* (Penguin, 1974) p. 94; hereafter *Development.* What Newman called "early or recurring intimations" (*ibid.,* p. 134) can correspond to the presence of truly prophetic minorities. The difficulty remains the same. How can we determine here and now what will be later accepted as genuine intimations and prophetic minorities?
11. DS 271, 370, 396, 399, 485, 501, 520, 548, 550, 575 etc.
12. *Development,* p. 76.
13. *Commonitorium,* IV, 6.
14. *Ibid.,* IV, 2.
15. *Development,* p. 88.
16. *Ibid.,* p. 84.
17. H. Küng, *On Being a Christian* (ET: London, 1976) p. 20.
18. *Development,* p. 104.
19. *Dei Verbum,* 8; see J. M. R. Tillard, "Sensus Fidelium," *One in Christ* 11 (1975) pp. 2–29.
20. I. de la Potterie, *La Vérité dans Saint Jean* 1, p. 471.
21. *Lumen Gentium,* n. 12; the constitution here cites Augustine.
22. *Tradition,* p. 416.
23. "Sacred Tradition and Sacred Scripture, then, are bound closely together, and communicate one with the other. For both of them, flowing out from the same divine wellspring, come together in some fashion to form one thing, and move toward the same goal" (*Dei Verbum,* n. 9). "This Sacred Tradition, then, and the Sacred Scripture of both Testaments are like a mirror, in which the Church . . . contemplates God" (*Ibid.,* n. 7).
24. *Dei Verbum,* nn. 25ff.

25. *Ibid.,* 9 and 24.
26. *De Arca Noe Morali,* II, 8–9.
27. See H. Wagenhammer, *Das Wesen des Christentums* (Mainz, 1973).

CHAPTER IX

1. L. Alonso-Schökel, "Inspiration," SM 3, pp. 145–51 (= EncTh, pp. 719–26); *The Inspired Word* (ET: New York, 1966); K. Barth, CD I/2, pp. 457ff.; A. Bea, "Inspiration," LThK 5, col. 703–11; J. T. Forestell, "Bible, II (Inspiration)," NCE 2, pp. 381–86; G. Lanczkowski et al., "Inspiration," RGG 3, col. 773–82; J. J. Scullion, *The Theology of Inspiration* (Cork, 1970); R. F. Smith, "Inspiration and Inerrancy," JBC 2, pp. 499–514.

2. "Holy Mother Church . . . holds that the books of both the Old and New Testament . . . are sacred and canonical because [a] having been written under the inspiration of the Holy Spirit . . . [b] they have God as their author" (*Dei Verbum,* n. 11).

3. O. A. Piper, "Truth," IBD 4, pp. 713–17; I. de la Potterie, "Storia e Verità," *Problemi e Prospettive di Teologia Fondamentale,* ed. R. Latourelle and G. O'Collins; "Truth," DBTh, pp. 618–21; "La vérité de la Sainte Écriture e l'Histoire du salut d'après la Constitution dogmatique 'Dei Verbum'," *Nouvelle Revue Théologique* 98 (1966) pp. 149–69.

4. F. W. Beare, "Canon of the NT," IDB 1, pp. 520–32; H. F. von Campenhausen, *The Formation of the Christian Bible* (ET: Philadelphia, 1972); J. D. G. Dunn, "Has the Canon a Continuing Function?," *Unity and Diversity in the New Testament* (London, 1977) pp. 374–88; W. G. Kümmel, *Introduction to the New Testament,* pp. 475–510; W. G. Most et al., "Bible, III (Canon)," NCE 2, pp. 386–414; P. Neuenzeit, "Canon of Scripture," SM 2, pp. 252–57 (= EncTh, pp. 168–73); R. H. Pfeiffer, "Canon of the OT," IDB 1, pp. 498–520; J. Schildenberger et al., "Kanon, biblischer," LThK 5, col. 1277–84; E. Schott et al., "Kanon," RGG 3, col. 1116–22; J. C. Truro and R. E. Brown, "Canonicity," JBC 2, pp. 515–34.

5. R. E. Brown, "Hermeneutics," JBC 2, pp. 605–23; F. F. Bruce, "Exegesis and Hermeneutics, Biblical," EncBrit 7, pp. 60–68; G. Ebeling, "Hermeneutik," RGG 3, col. 242–62; K. Lehmann "Hermeneutics," SM 3, pp. 23–27 (= EncTh, pp. 611–15); R. Marlé, "Ermeneutica e Scrittura," *Problemi e Prospettive di Teologia Fondamentale,* ed. R. Latourelle and G. O'Collins; W. Pannenberg, "Hermeneutic," *Theology and the Philosophy of Science,* pp. 156–224.

6. In official Catholic documents there is a development in the respect for the human role of the biblical writers from Leo XIII (DS 3293) down to the Second Vatican Council's recognition of their being "true authors" (*Dei Verbum,* n. 11).

6a. K. Rahner, *Foundations of Christian Faith,* pp. 369ff.; *Inspiration in the Bible* (ET: London, 1965; this translation in *Studies in Modern Theology* is superior to the one provided in the *Quaestiones Disputatae* series).

7. See *Dei Verbum,* n. 11.

8. *Divino Afflante Spiritu,* in *Enchiridion Biblicum* (3rd ed: Rome, 1956) p. 219.

9. *Contra Felicem Manichaeum,* I, 10.

10. Here the New Testament comes close to that philosophical notion of truth according to which something is true when it ceases to be hidden (*a-lēthes* = not hidden) and discloses itself. In this sense truth is the unveiling and throwing open of being.

11. "Truth and Life," *The Way* 19 (1979) p. 258.

CHAPTER X

1. J. Barr, *The Bible in the Modern World* (London, 1973) pp. 150–56; D. L. Dungan, "The New Testament Canon in Recent Study," *Interpretation* 29 (1975) pp. 339–51; D. N. Freedman, "Canon of the OT," IDB supplementary vol., pp. 130–36; A. C. Sundberg, "The Bible Canon and the Christian Doctrine of Inspiration," *Interpretation* 29 (1975) pp. 352–71; "Canon of the NT," IDB supplementary vol., pp. 136–40; "The Making of the NT Canon," *The Interpreter's One Volume Commentary,* ed. C. M. Laymon (Nashville, 1971) pp. 1216–24. See also Chapter IX, note 4.

2. *Tradition,* p. 418.

3. "The Authority of Scripture for Theology," *Interpretation* 30 (1976) pp. 242–61, at p. 252. Since the New Testament expresses in written form the apostolic preaching and tradition, we could accept Ogden's statement if it read: "There is no difference in principle, but only in fact, between the authority of the New Testament, on the one hand, and that of the apostolic tradition, on the other."

4. "Interpreting the Sources of Our Faith," *Faith and Order. Louvain 1971* (Geneva, 1971) p. 21. On biblical authority see further J. Barr, *The Bible in the Modern World,* pp. 23–30, and "Scripture, Authority of," IDB supplementary vol., pp. 794–97.

5. On biblical interpretation see L. F. Hartman et al., "Bible, VI (Exegesis)," NCE 2, pp. 496–512; L. E. Keck and G. M. Tucker, "Exegesis," IDB supplementary vol., pp. 296–303; D. Robertson, "Literature, the Bible as," *ibid.,* pp. 547–51; J. A. Sanders, "Hermeneutics," *ibid.,* pp. 402–07. See also Chapter VI, note 6 and Chapter IX, note 5.

5a. *Theological Reflections on the Charismatic Renewal,* ed. J. C. Haughey (Ann Arbor, 1978) p. 82.

6. *Fern-Seed and Elephants* (London, 1975) pp. 104–25, esp. pp. 113ff.

7. *Truth and Method,* p. 264.

8. *Ibid.,* p. 356.

9. *Ibid.,* p. 357.

10. *The Verbal Icon* (New York, 1954) p. 5.

11. From the *Times Literary Supplement* for 3 September, 1976.

12. R. E. Brown, "The Sensus Plenior," JBC 2, pp. 615–18.

13. *Truth and Method,* p. 336.

14. *In Lib. Iesu Nave,* hom. 9, n. 8.

15. *De Arca Noe morali* II, 8–9.

16. *The Work of William Tyndale,* ed. G. E. Duffield (Philadelphia, 1965) p. 353.

17. *Enchiridion Biblicum,* p. 172.

A PERSONAL EPILOGUE

1. See, for example, R. Latourelle, *Christ and the Church; Signs of Salvation* (ET: New York, 1972) and *Finding Jesus Through the Gospels* (ET: New York, 1979).

2. "Theology and Experience," *Irish Theological Quarterly* 44 (1977) pp. 279–90.

3. ET: New York, 1979.

4. London, 1975.

5. Pp. 17f.

INDEX OF NAMES